"When you find yourself confron [...] fast. *The Biblical Counseling Refere[n]* [...] at your fingertips. From complica[...] mon problems like worry, this to[o] [...] questions from A to Z."

—Dr. David Jeremiah
Senior Pastor, Shadow Mountain Community Church
President and founder, *Turning Point*
Author, *What to Do When You Don't Know What to Do*

"Here we have a wealth of Scripture information packaged in a way that is helpful and accessible. It's not only a useful tool for counseling, but I intend to use it in preparing my sermons!"

—Dr. Erwin W. Lutzer
Senior Pastor, *The Moody Church*
Author, *Life-Changing Bible Verses You Should Know*

"Savoring June Hunt's *Biblical Counseling Reference Guide,* I felt like a kid in a candy store. Here is a book of 400-plus delectable spiritual topics richly filled with savory Bible references. Here's a book that every Bible lover will want, especially those in counseling and teaching."

—Dr. Bruce Waltke
Professor Emeritus of Biblical Studies, Regent College
Distinguished Professor Old Testament, Knox Theological Seminary
Editor, *An Old Testament Theology*

"What a gold mine representing years of biblical research and real-life application. I had the privilege of brainstorming with June Hunt and her team in the early days when they began this project. The end result, as you'll see, is an invaluable resource for us all."

——Dr. Gene A. Getz
Director, Center for Church Renewal
Host and teacher, Renewal Radio
Author, *Life Essentials Study Bible: Biblical Principles to Live By*

"How thrilled I am to see this proven, well-tested *Biblical Counseling Reference Guide*—the fruit of June's life-transforming ministry. Psalm 107:20 says God 'sent His word and healed them.' Now you can have the fruit of June's years of labor at your fingertips so that you can confidently direct others to God's healing Word. Because the Word of God has the answer to every situation, every need of life, this is a book every Christian should own."

—Kay Arthur
Co-CEO, Precept Ministries International
Author, *How to Study Your Bible:*
Discover the Life-Changing Approach to God's Word

"You never need to be without biblical answers again. Here's a ready reference to help you apply God's timeless truth to life's most vexing issues."

—Dr. Ron Cline
Global Ambassador, HCJB Global
Author, *Feel the Zeal*

"A very useful part of the biblical counselor's toolbox—or, indeed, for any kind of Bible teacher. What a helpful handbook!"

—Dr. Kirsten Birkett
Lecturer in Pastoral Care and Counseling
Oak Hill Theological College
Author, *The Essence of Psychology*

"June Hunt knows two things. First, the Bible says 'keep your heart with all diligence, for out of it spring the issues of life.' Consequently, her ministry is called Hope For The Heart. She also knows that the heart receives its guidance and healing from the Word of God because Jesus said, 'Man shall not live by bread alone but by every word that proceeds from the mouth of God.' This *Biblical Counseling Reference Guide* is the perfect reference book, providing quick direction to speak to the heart's deepest needs."

—Dr. Paige Patterson
President, Southwestern Baptist Theological Seminary
Managing Editor, *The Believer's Study Bible*

"Handy and holy. June Hunt's *Biblical Counseling Reference Guide* provides a ministry tool that is user friendly, travels anywhere, and speaks to anyone, with words fit for any occasion. But, one warning! Don't go here in search of human insight into human problems. You won't find any. As always, June's only interest is guiding us to God's wise answers preserved for us in the Bible."

—Dr. Jeffrey Bingham
Professor of Theology and Associate Dean of Biblical and
Theological Studies at Wheaton University
Author, *Pocket History of the Church*

"June Hunt's latest reference is a must-have for anyone providing biblical counsel. The information is accurate, accessible, and completely applicable for any ministry context. I highly recommend it!"

—Dr. John Ankerberg
Host, *The John Ankerberg Show*
Coauthor, *Ready with an Answer*

"*The Biblical Counseling Reference Guide* is a landmark to biblical counseling. With an easy-to-use concordance format, this ideal companion for the pastor-teacher, the counselor, students, and lay leaders involved in formal and nonformal counseling illuminates God's truth for the real needs of real people in today's complex world."

—Dr. Carlot D. Celestin
Administrator, Master of Arts in Counseling Program
Gordon-Conwell Theological Seminary, Boston Campus

"June Hunt is a proven, skilled listener…to the 'whole counsel of God' for divine truth, and to the deepest spiritual and psychological needs of fellow sons and daughters of Adam. This concordance is a remarkable integration of both. My prayer is that it will be used by many—pastors, counselors, chaplains, moms and dads, and ordinary godly friends—to bring hope and help to those in need."

—Dr. W. Daniel Blair
Assistant Professor of American Sign Language; Director,
Center for Deaf Education California Baptist University

"For those searching for biblical answers to life's most challenging questions, here's an instant classic. You'll love having God's truth at your fingertips as you seek God's help and give it to others."

—Chip Ingram
President and Teaching Pastor, Living on the Edge
Author, *Finding God When You Need Him Most*

"By providing this reference tool to find biblical texts bearing on very personal and very contemporary problems, June Hunt makes a most needed contribution to counseling. She shows us scriptural pathways for a relationship of love and trust, which can develop over time between the one helping and the one needing help. Perhaps best of all, this concordance makes clear that all problematic behaviors come ultimately from substituting something else for the love and grace of Christ."

— Dr. Joseph (Skip) Ryan
Chancellor, Redeemer Seminary

"What Dr. James Strong did for Bible students in his *Exhaustive Concordance*, June Hunt has now done for anyone involved in Christ-centered counseling! This volume will be a favorite for professional and lay counselors alike—and should be found in every household."

—Dr. Georg Huber
National Director, Precept Ministries International,
Germany, Austria, and Switzerland

"Today more than ever, people are in bondage to their negative, destructive emotions and are in deep need for the truth that will set them free. I am very thankful for June Hunt, who understands that it is the Word of God and the work of the Holy Spirit that changes people's lives. *The Biblical Counseling Reference Guide* will undoubtedly be a priceless resource for helping people break free from the lies that keep them captive and find the awesome freedom Christ created us to enjoy."

—Dr. Charles Stanley
Senior Pastor, First Baptist Church, Atlanta, GA
President and Founder, In Touch Ministries
Author, Emotions: Confront the Lies. Conquer with Truth.

The
BIBLICAL
COUNSELING
REFERENCE
GUIDE

HARVEST HOUSE PUBLISHERS
EUGENE, OREGON

Cover by Garborg Design Works, Savage, Minnesota

THE BIBLICAL COUNSELING REFERENCE GUIDE
Copyright © 2014 by Hope for the Heart, Inc.
Published by Harvest House Publishers
Eugene, Oregon 97402
www.harvesthousepublishers.com

ISBN 978-0-7369-2330-9 (pbk.)
ISBN 978-0-7369-4238-6 (eBook)

CIP (to come)

Printed in the United States of America

14 15 16 17 18 19 20 21 22 / VP-JH / 10 9 8 7 6 5 4 3 2 1

Dedication

In 1986 I founded Hope For The Heart, never imagining that it would one day reach 80-plus countries in 28 different languages. Throughout the years, the *Counseling Keys* have been the foundation for our every teaching, outreach, conference, and radio broadcast (we have two). The *Counseling Keys* represent biblical teaching on life's most pressing issues and also provide the backbone for this reference guide.

Today, our 100-topic *Biblical Counseling Library* is used worldwide in counseling offices, churches, universities, seminaries, and by people who simply have a heart to help others. Also, 21 Hope Centers span the globe providing *biblical hope and practical help* in at-risk communities that are being transformed...and dozens more of these counseling outposts will be launched to spread hope to the world.

With a mixture of genuine humility and heartfelt gratitude, I dedicate *The Biblical Counseling Reference Guide* to our international partners and to counselors who serve to provide biblical hope and relevant help to those in need around the world.

Acknowledgments

At times this project seemed insurmountable…yet because of the expert help and diligent collaboration between our Hope For The Heart team and those at Harvest House Publishers, *The Biblical Counseling Reference Guide* is now a reality…the culmination of a monumental cooperative effort dedicated to its completion!

With so many involved in the compilation of this concordance it would truly be impossible to recount the names of everyone involved. I offer my deepest gratitude to every hand and heart who worked on the project—the resourceful researchers and writers…those who searched and surveyed the Scriptures…those who compiled key verses, delineated the definitions, and partnered with us in prayer.

From the inception of this project, we have always had as our foundation...

"First seek the counsel of the LORD."

(1 KINGS 22:5)

Preface

Today, more than ever, we need *biblical hope and practical help* when the challenges of life threaten to overwhelm us. That is the reason for *The Biblical Counseling Reference Guide*. This resource connects our current concerns and contemporary questions with biblical wisdom.

After becoming a Christian, I was deeply drawn to biblical truth—especially to passages that pointed to the practical application of that truth. In 1989, I began teaching a topical Bible study called *Counseling Through the Bible*. Week by week, over the next three years, I taught on 96 topics—a daunting task that reminds me of the work that went into putting this reference guide together. God used these studies to bring real change to so many lives. Even now, they still provide *God's Truth for Today's Problems*...for those who need counsel and for those with a heart to counsel others.

Although much has changed since founding the ministry Hope For The Heart in 1986, the most important foundational truths remain the same—God's Word and God's ways have not changed, and I firmly believe the Bible provides the only reliable framework for dealing with all of life's issues.

Even though certain topics and modern terminology may not be found in the pages of Scripture, that does not mean the Bible is silent on those themes. For example, even though Scripture doesn't mention anorexia (the cause of untold suffering and many deaths every year), the Bible does address underlying struggles related to eating disorders, such as self-worth, perfectionism, anger, and loneliness. Therefore, we can be more successful when we learn how to mine the Scriptures for principles relevant to our real-life problems and develop steps to put those principles to work in our lives.

It is with this goal in mind that we designed *The Biblical Counseling Reference Guide*. My prayer is that it will help you—and help you help others—as you seek God's truth for today.

—June Hunt

Part 1:

Biblical Counseling
Reference Guide

Abandonment

Definition:
Leaving or deserting a person (often a spouse and children) and failing to provide necessary support for their well-being.

Key Verses:
Psalm 27:10
2 Corinthians 4:8-9

See Also:
Abuse
Betrayal
Child Abuse
Death
Desertion
Neglect

By God
Deuteronomy 31:17

Consequences of abandoning God
Joshua 24:20
Jeremiah 2:19

God will not abandon His people
1 Samuel 12:22
1 Kings 6:13
Nehemiah 9:17
2 Corinthians 4:8-9

Of a spouse
Proverbs 2:17

Of God
Deuteronomy 31:16
Joshua 24:16

Of the way of truth
2 Peter 2:15
Jude 11

Ability

Definition:
The capacity to accomplish an intended purpose or task.

Key Verses:
Zechariah 4:6
2 Corinthians 9:8

See Also:
Accomplishment
Adversity
Capability
Decision Making
Employment

Appraisal of
2 Corinthians 11:5-6

From God
Exodus 4:10-12
Exodus 28:3
Exodus 31:3
1 Samuel 17:32-37
John 14:12
Acts 6:8
Philippians 4:13
1 Peter 4:11

Human
Genesis 11:1-6
Genesis 47:6
1 Chronicles 26:6

Human strength inadequate
1 Samuel 2:9

Ecclesiastes 9:11
Amos 2:14-16

Lack of
Exodus 6:30

Trust God for
Nehemiah 4:1-10
2 Corinthians 9:8

Abomination

Definition:
A vile, detestable, or repulsive action or person.

Key Verses:
Proverbs 6:16-19
Proverbs 11:20

See Also:
Apostasy
Immorality
Judgment
Punishment
Shame
Sin

Abomination of desolation
Daniel 9:27
Daniel 12:11
Matthew 24:15
Mark 13:14

Of dishonesty
Deuteronomy 25:13-16
Proverbs 12:22
Proverbs 20:10
Proverbs 20:23

Of hypocrisy
Proverbs 21:27
Proverbs 28:9
Matthew 23:2-3
Matthew 23:13
Luke 16:15

Of idolatry
Deuteronomy 7:25
Deuteronomy 27:15
Hosea 9:10

Of practices
Leviticus 18:20-24
Deuteronomy
18:9-12
Deuteronomy 22:5
Proverbs 6:16-19

Abortion

Definition:
The termination of a pregnancy, resulting in death of the unborn.

Key Verses:
Psalm 139:13-16
Jeremiah 1:5

See Also:
Adoption
Forgiveness
Guilt
Mother
Pregnancy…
  Unplanned
Single Parenting

Abortion is not a loving choice
Romans 13:9

An unborn child is a living soul
Hosea 12:3

Child before birth
Jeremiah 1:5
Luke 1:41
Luke 1:44

Child wonderfully made
Psalm 139:13-16
Ecclesiastes 11:5

Choose life
Deuteronomy 30:19

Comfort in
Psalm 10:14

Condemned
Genesis 9:5-6
Exodus 20:13
Exodus 21:22-25
Deuteronomy 5:17
Proverbs 6:16-17

God forms the child
Deuteronomy 32:6
Isaiah 44:2
Isaiah 44:24
John 9:1-3

God's care for all those involved
Psalm 68:5

Importance of children
Luke 18:15-16

Indicates rebellion against God
Psalm 106:38

Physical bodies belong to God
1 Corinthians
6:19-20

Rescues the innocent
Proverbs 24:11-12

Reunion with lost child
2 Samuel 12:23

Abuse

Definition:
The wrong use of something or the insulting or cruel treatment of someone, usually resulting in harm.

Key Verses:
Psalm 28:4-7
Psalm 34:18

See Also:
Alcohol and Drug
  Abuse
Childhood Sexual
  Abuse
Emotional Abuse
Incest
Spiritual Abuse
Spouse Abuse
Verbal and Emotional
  Abuse

Condemned
Exodus 22:21
Leviticus 19:33
Ezekiel 22:29

Prayer for abusers
Luke 6:28

Reward for enduring
Matthew 5:11-12
Hebrews 11:37-39

Acceptance

Definition:
Receiving or approving of.

Key Verses:
Romans 15:7
1 John 3:18

See Also:
Friendship
Love

By God
Ezekiel 20:40
Acts 10:34-35
Ephesians 1:4-6

Of good and bad
Job 2:10

Of others
Romans 14:1
Romans 15:7
Galatians 2:9-10
1 Timothy 6:1

Of teaching
Proverbs 4:10
Proverbs 19:20

Accomplishment

Definition:
Completion or achievement of a purpose or goal.

Key Verses:
Psalm 127:1-2
John 15:5

See Also:
Ability
Humility
Pride
Success

Boast in God
2 Corinthians 10:17-18

Examine yourself
Galatians 6:4

Preparation for
1 Corinthians 9:24-27

Through Christ
John 15:1-8
Romans 15:18-19
1 Corinthians 3:7
Philippians 4:13

Accountability

Definition:
Being responsible for something or answerable to someone.

Key Verses:
Proverbs 27:17
Romans 14:12

See Also:
Employment
Friendship
Integrity

For one's actions
Ezekiel 18:20
Luke 12:48
Luke 19:15

To God
Matthew 12:36-37
Romans 3:19
Romans 14:12
1 Peter 4:4-5

Addiction

Definition:
Obsession involving a person, object, or behavior resulting in psychological or physical dependence.

Key Verses:
Romans 6:12-14
2 Peter 2:19

See Also:
Alcohol and Drug Abuse
Anorexia and Bulimia
Codependency
Gambling
Habits
Overeating
Sexual Addiction
Workaholism

Enslaved to desires
Romans 6:12
Romans 6:16
Titus 3:3

Enslaved to what defeats you
2 Peter 2:19

Freedom from sin
Romans 6:17-18

Overcome by alcohol
Proverbs 20:1
Ephesians 5:18

Admonition

Definition:
A mild or kind warning for the purpose of correction.

Key Verses:
Exodus 18:20
Colossians 3:16

See Also:
Communication
Confrontation
Counseling
Discipleship
Mentoring

Benefit of heeding
Jeremiah 18:8

By church leaders
1 Thessalonians 5:12

From the Lord
Isaiah 8:11

From the Scriptures
Psalm 19:9-11

In love
1 Corinthians 4:14
2 Thessalonians 3:15

Of leaders
1 Timothy 5:20

To serve the Lord
Psalm 2:10-11

With wisdom
Colossians 1:28
Colossians 3:16

Adolescence

Definition:
The transitional period of growth between childhood and adulthood characterized by dramatic emotional, social, and physical changes.

Key Verses:
Psalm 71:5,17
2 Timothy 2:22

See Also:
Parenting
Puberty
Teenagers

Child labor
1 Samuel 2:18
Lamentations 5:13

Instruction of
Joel 1:1-3

Spiritual service
Jeremiah 1:4-7
Joel 2:28

Adoption

Definition:
The legal process of receiving someone else's child and the responsibility to raise the child as one's own.

Key Verses:
Romans 8:15-18
Ephesians 1:5

See Also:
Barren
Childlessness
Infertility

Adoptive parenting
Exodus 2:10
Esther 2:7
Psalm 27:10
2 Corinthians 6:18

Father and mother are vital for a child
Proverbs 1:8

Spiritual
Deuteronomy 14:1-2
Psalm 68:5-6
John 1:12
Romans 8:14-15
Galatians 3:26
Galatians 4:3-7
Ephesians 1:5-6
Ephesians 2:19
Ephesians 3:6
1 John 3:1-2

Wisdom is needed in adoption process
Proverbs 24:3

Adultery

Definition:
Voluntary sexual

intercourse between a married person and someone other than their legal spouse.

Key Verses:
Matthew 5:27-28
1 Corinthians 6:18

See Also:
Cheating
Immorality
Lust
Marriage
Sexual Integrity
Temptation

Adultery brings God's judgment
2 Samuel 12:1-12

Adultery leads to more sinful choices
2 Samuel 11:15

Attributed to false teachers
2 Peter 2:14

Avoidance of
Genesis 39:7-20
Job 31:1
Proverbs 6:23-26
1 Corinthians 6:18

Comes from the heart
Matthew 15:19
Mark 7:21-23

Condemned
Exodus 20:14
Leviticus 18:20
Proverbs 5:15
Proverbs 5:17-19

1 Corinthians 5:9-11
1 Corinthians 10:8
Galatians 5:19
Ephesians 5:3
1 Thessalonians 4:3

Consequences of
Proverbs 6:27-29
Proverbs 6:32-34
Proverbs 14:12
Galatians 6:7-8

Deceitful and destructive
Proverbs 5:3-4
Proverbs 6:27
Proverbs 7:6-23

Immoral lusts can never be satisfied
Ephesians 4:19

Immorality has no place in the life of the believer
Colossians 3:5

Importance of faithfulness
Malachi 2:14-15
Ephesians 5:25

Punishment for
Leviticus 20:10
Colossians 3:5-6
Hebrews 13:4

Relationship to lust
Matthew 5:27-28

Repentance from
Psalm 51:1-19

Result of divorce
Matthew 19:8-9

Run from lusts
2 Timothy 2:22

Severity of punishment
Deuteronomy 22:22-29

Symbolizes unfaithfulness to God
Jeremiah 3:6-10
Ezekiel 16:26
Ezekiel 16:37-38

Warning against
Proverbs 7:25-27

Adversity

Definition:
A situation or event that causes distress, hardship, or affliction.

Key Verses:
Psalm 10:1, 17
Proverbs 17:17

See Also:
Affliction
Persecution
Suffering
Trials

As part of discipleship
Job 5:7
Job 14:1
Romans 8:17

Because of disobedience
Deuteronomy 28:45-48

Benefits of
Psalm 119:71

Causes of
Genesis 3:13-16
Leviticus 26:14-16

Encouragement in
Genesis 50:20
Psalm 55:22
Psalm 119:107
Romans 8:28
2 Corinthians 4:17
Hebrews 4:15
1 Peter 1:6-7
1 Peter 5:7
1 Peter 5:10

Endurance in
Romans 5:3-4
2 Corinthians 4:8
Hebrews 12:5
James 1:2-4
James 5:8

From God
Isaiah 1:25
John 15:2

From the devil
1 Peter 5:8

God's grace in
2 Corinthians 12:7
2 Corinthians 12:9
Hebrews 4:16

God's presence in
Psalm 147:3

Of Jesus
Hebrews 2:18

Purpose for
Deuteronomy 8:16
Ezekiel 14:11
John 9:1-3
1 Corinthians 11:32

Rescue from
Psalm 46:1
Psalm 50:15
Psalm 71:20
Psalm 138:7
Psalm 140:1
Isaiah 33:2
Isaiah 41:10
Isaiah 43:2
Jeremiah 17:17
Matthew 11:28

Results of
Philippians 1:12

Sharing in
2 Corinthians 1:7

Strength in
Isaiah 40:29

Advice

Definition:
Opinion or counsel regarding an appropriate course of action.

Key Verses:
Proverbs 19:20
Proverbs 27:9

See Also:
Counseling
Mentoring

Avoidance of wicked advice
Psalm 1:1

For leaders
Esther 1:13
Acts 20:25-28

From elders
Job 8:8-10

From family
Proverbs 1:8

From the wise
Proverbs 10:31

Importance of heeding
Exodus 18:13-27
Proverbs 7:2
Proverbs 11:14
Proverbs 13:10
Proverbs 20:18
Proverbs 24:5-6

Leads to wisdom
Proverbs 12:15
Proverbs 15:22
Proverbs 19:20

Pleasant
Proverbs 25:11

Seek
1 Chronicles 13:1

Affection

Definition:
A feeling of tenderness or fondness toward someone or something.

Key Verses:
Jeremiah 31:3
Philippians 1:8

See Also:
Friendship
Love

A time for
Ecclesiastes 3:5

Between friends
Ruth 1:14-18
1 Samuel 20:41

Commanded
John 13:34
John 15:12
1 Peter 4:8
1 Peter 5:14
2 Peter 1:7

Of God
Jeremiah 31:3

Toward fellow believers
2 Corinthians 2:4
2 Corinthians 12:15
Philippians 1:7
1 Thessalonians 2:7-12

Affliction

Definition:
A condition of pain, distress, or suffering.

Key Verses:
Psalm 10:17
Psalm 119:67, 71

See Also:
Adversity
Suffering
Trials

By God
Ruth 1:21
1 Samuel 5:9
2 Kings 15:5
2 Chronicles 21:18

By the wicked
Deuteronomy 26:6

Care for the afflicted
Deuteronomy 15:11
1 Timothy 5:10

God delivers the afflicted
2 Samuel 22:28

Suffering for righteousness
Hebrews 11:37

Aggressive

Definition:
Marked by forceful, dominating, or even belligerent attitudes and actions.

Key Verses:
1 Samuel 25:10-11
Ephesians 4:2-3

See Also:
Attitude
Conflict Resolution
Confrontation
Manipulation
Passive-Aggressive

Aging

Definition:
Increase or advancing in years.

Key Verses:
Isaiah 46:4
2 Corinthians 4:16;
5:10

See Also:
Maturity
Mentoring

A crown for the righteous
Proverbs 16:31

Age is to be respected
Leviticus 19:32

As a blessing
Deuteronomy 25:15
1 Kings 1:31
Psalm 119:17
Zechariah 8:4

Based on obedience to parents
Exodus 20:12
Ephesians 6:2-3

Because of prayer
Isaiah 38:5

Blessing for obedience to God
1 Kings 3:14
Psalm 91:16
Proverbs 10:27
1 Peter 3:10-11

**By guarding
your tongue**
Psalm 34:11-13

Care for elders
Ruth 4:15
1 Timothy 5:4
1 Timothy 5:8

Depression in old age
Job 17:1

For the wise
Proverbs 3:2
Proverbs 9:11

From God
Genesis 5:27
Genesis 6:3
Genesis 15:15
Psalm 21:4

**God has important
purposes for the aged**
Luke 2:25-39

**God supports
the elderly**
Isaiah 46:4

Honor in old age
Proverbs 20:29

Inevitability of death
1 Kings 2:2
Psalm 39:5
Psalm 90:10
Zechariah 1:5

**Let your life be an
example to others**
Titus 2:2-5

Of Aaron
Numbers 33:39

Of the wicked
Job 21:7

Pains associated with
Ecclesiastes 11:8

Thriving in old age
Psalm 92:12-14

Wisdom with
Job 12:12

Agnosticism

Definition:
A position of not
knowing if God exists
or a doctrine that the
existence of God can-
not be known.

Key Verses:
Acts 17:30
1 Corinthians 2:14

See Also:
Apologetics
Atheism and
  Agnosticism
Doubt

Agreeable

Definition:
A willingness to con-
sent or to be harmo-
nious.

Key Verses:
Matthew 5:9
Romans 12:18

See Also:
Conflict Resolution
Friendship

**Agree with one
another**
Amos 3:3
Romans 12:16
Romans 14:19
1 Corinthians 1:10

Agreement from God
Romans 15:5-6

Commanded
Colossians 3:12
2 Peter 1:5-7

Fruit of the Spirit
Galatians 5:22-23

**Good to be in
agreement**
Psalm 133:1
Philippians 2:2

Alcohol and
Drug Abuse

Definition:
The use of a substance,
legal or illegal, that
typically results in
emotional, mental,
and/or physical harm.

Key Verses:
Isaiah 5:22-24
1 Corinthians
  10:12-13

See Also:
Addiction

Drug Abuse
Intoxication

Abstinence from
  Jeremiah 35:1-16
  Luke 1:15

Abstinence in sensitivity to others
  Romans 14:21

Abuse condemned
  Proverbs 20:1
  Isaiah 22:13
  Isaiah 28:1
  Romans 6:12
  Romans 12:1-2
  1 Corinthians 11:21
  Ephesians 5:18
  1 Thessalonians 5:7
  Titus 1:7
  Titus 2:3

Avoidance of
  Proverbs 22:3
  Proverbs 23:20
  1 Corinthians 15:33

Cannot satisfy
  Habakkuk 2:5

Consequences of
  Proverbs 23:20-21
  Proverbs 23:29-33
  Galatians 6:7

Do not be weighed down with
  Luke 21:34

Drinking in moderation
  1 Timothy 5:23

Drunkenness is condemned
  Deuteronomy 21:20

Harmful effects of
  Psalm 38:4
  Psalm 44:15
  Proverbs 5:21-23
  Proverbs 14:12
  Proverbs 21:17
  Proverbs 23:33-35
  Proverbs 31:4-7
  Isaiah 5:11-12
  Isaiah 24:9, 11
  Isaiah 28:7
  Isaiah 56:10-12
  Jeremiah 13:12-14
  Jeremiah 51:39
  Hosea 4:11
  Hosea 4:18
  Luke 21:34

Harmful effects on family
  Genesis 9:18-27
  Genesis 19:30-38

Overcoming
  Psalm 25:15
  Psalm 62:5
  Psalm 119:11
  Psalm 119:28
  Proverbs 2:6
  Proverbs 15:22
  Proverbs 19:20
  Ecclesiastes 4:9-10
  Matthew 6:33
  Mark 10:27
  Luke 1:37
  1 Corinthians 10:13
  Galatians 6:2
  Philippians 2:13

  Philippians 4:13
  2 Timothy 2:24-26
  2 Peter 1:3-4

Priests forbidden to drink on duty
  Leviticus 10:9
  Ezekiel 44:21

Punishment for
  Isaiah 5:22-24
  Habakkuk 2:15

Punishment for abusing
  Isaiah 5:22
  Habakkuk 2:15

Recovery from
  James 5:19-20

Repentance from
  Lamentations 3:40

Restoration from
  Galatians 6:1

Substance abuse is condemned
  Proverbs 20:1
  Isaiah 28:1
  1 Corinthians 11:21
  Ephesians 5:18
  1 Thessalonians 5:6-7
  Titus 1:7
  Titus 2:3

Alienation

Definition:
Being separated or estranged from someone or something.

Key Verses:
Psalm 22:1-2
Psalm 88:8-9

See Also:
Conflict Resolution
Depression
Friendship
Prejudice
Rejection

Because of workaholism
Ecclesiastes 4:8

Benefit of friends
Ecclesiastes 4:11

Condemned
Romans 14:7

Deliverance from
Psalm 68:6

From Christ
Galatians 5:4

From family
Job 19:13

From God
Colossians 1:21

From the church
Galatians 4:17

In affliction
Psalm 102:7

In widowhood
1 Timothy 5:5

Of Jesus
Matthew 27:46-49
John 16:32

Prayer in
Psalm 25:16

Ambition

Definition:
A strong desire for success, achievement, or distinction.

Key Verses:
1 Thessalonians 4:11
1 Timothy 6:9

See Also:
Humility
Pride
Success
Work
Workaholism

Benefits of
Proverbs 10:5

Cannot satisfy
Habakkuk 2:5
Matthew 16:26

Condemned
Jeremiah 45:4-5
Matthew 23:12
Luke 9:46-48
Luke 22:26

Godly ambitions
Philippians 3:7-11
1 Thessalonians 4:11-12

Leads to disputes
Mark 9:33-37
Mark 10:35-45
Luke 22:24

May lead to noble work
1 Timothy 3:1

To follow God
Psalm 119:1-5

Warning against
Mark 12:38-40

Angels

Definition:
Beings superior to humanity, created to be messengers and servants of God, some of whom fell in Satan's rebellion.

Key Verses:
Job 38:4-7
Hebrews 1:14

See Also:
God
Heaven
Providence

Anger

Definition:
A strong emotion of irritation or agitation in response to an unmet need.

Key Verses:
Ephesians 4:26-27, 31
James 1:19-20

See Also:
Fear
Rage

The Biblical Counseling Reference Guide

Resentment
Wrath

Against God
Job 15:12-13
Isaiah 8:21

Against the righteous
Matthew 2:16
Luke 6:11
Acts 5:30-33
Acts 7:54

Anger because of perceived injustice
Job 23:2

Anger is cruel
Proverbs 27:4

Anger leads to complaining
Numbers 20:3

Anger leads to violence
Genesis 49:5-7

Anger of Jesus
Mark 10:14

Anger of Moses
Numbers 16:15

Backbiting produces anger
Proverbs 25:23

Be patient and control anger
Proverbs 16:32

Blaming God for personal mistakes
Proverbs 19:3

Condemned
Genesis 4:3-8
Proverbs 16:32
Proverbs 19:19
Proverbs 22:24-25
Ecclesiastes 7:9
Amos 1:11
Matthew 5:22
Romans 12:19
Galatians 5:19-20
Titus 1:7
James 1:19-20

Do not stir up anger in children
Ephesians 6:4

Even noble people deal with anger
Exodus 32:19

Fear the wrath of angry men
Judges 18:25

Fight Satan by being self-controlled
1 Peter 5:8

Folly of
Proverbs 14:17
Proverbs 14:29
Proverbs 25:28
Proverbs 29:11

Inappropriate anger
2 Kings 5:11-12
Jonah 4:4
Jonah 4:9

In response to sinful actions
1 Samuel 20:32-34

King's anger to disgraceful servant
Proverbs 14:35

Leads to conflict
Proverbs 15:18
Proverbs 29:22

Love not easily angered
1 Corinthians 13:5

Of God
Exodus 4:14
2 Samuel 24:1
1 Kings 22:53
2 Kings 13:3
2 Kings 17:11
2 Kings 22:13
1 Chronicles 13:10
Psalm 2:12
Psalm 30:5
Psalm 86:15
Psalm 145:8
Isaiah 13:9
Isaiah 48:9
Isaiah 57:17
Jeremiah 4:4
Jeremiah 10:10
Ezekiel 5:13
Hosea 12:14
Hosea 14:4
Joel 2:13
Hebrews 3:10-11

Of God against the wicked
Exodus 22:24
Numbers 11:1

Numbers 12:9
Job 40:11
Romans 1:18
Romans 2:8
Revelation 6:16-17

Of God at disobedience
Joshua 7:1
Ephesians 5:6

Of God at idolatry
Exodus 32:10
Numbers 25:4
Deuteronomy 9:20
Deuteronomy
  13:12-17
Joshua 23:16
Judges 2:11-13
1 Kings 14:15
2 Kings 23:19
2 Chronicles 28:25

Overcoming
Psalm 37:8
Proverbs 15:1
Proverbs 17:27
Proverbs 29:8
Ephesians 4:31
Colossians 3:8

Pride produces anger
1 Samuel 18:8

Produces strife
Proverbs 30:33

Righteous anger
Exodus 11:8
Psalm 4:4
Matthew 21:12-13
Mark 3:5

Stay away from angry people
Proverbs 22:24

Take care of anger quickly
Ephesians 4:26

Time for anger to subside
Genesis 27:44

Anorexia

Definition:
An eating disorder characterized by compulsive, chronic self-starvation, and an irrational fear of being grotesquely obese.

Key Verses:
Psalm 139:13-14, 17
Romans 12:12

See Also:
Anorexia and Bulimia
Bulimia
Compulsive Eating
Self-Worth

Anorexia and Bulimia

Definition:
Eating disorders characterized by an irrational fear of weight gain and compulsive, self-destructive behaviors.

Key Verses:
1 Corinthians 6:19-20
1 Corinthians 10:31

See Also:
Anorexia
Bulimia
Compulsive Eating
Gluttony
Health
Self-Control
Self-Worth

Body belongs to God
1 Corinthians
  6:19-20

Body is weak
Romans 7:24

Harmful effects of
Philippians 3:19

Overcoming
1 Corinthians 10:31

Seek divine healing
Jeremiah 17:14

Sinful choices may damage body
Psalm 31:10

Antisocial

Definition:
Avoiding connection to others; hostile to people, certain groups of people, or normative behavior.

Key Verses:
1 Samuel 18:10-12
1 John 4:11-12

See Also:
Behavior
Identity
Intimacy
Mental Illness

Anxiety

Definition:
Apprehension, worry, or fear over the anticipation of a threatening event whether real or imagined.

Key Verses:
Psalm 27:1
1 Peter 5:7

See Also:
Apprehension
Fear
Worry

Condemned
Matthew 6:31-33

Confidence in the Lord
Joshua 1:9

Dulls spiritual senses
Luke 21:34

God delivers from
Psalm 43:5
Philippians 4:7

God will provide relief
Genesis 21:17
Luke 12:22-34
Psalm 94:19

Judgment on the wicked
Deuteronomy 28:66-67

Overcoming
Philippians 4:6
1 Peter 5:7

Weighs down a person
Proverbs 12:25
2 Corinthians 1:8

Apathy

Definition:
Lack of feelings, desire, or concern for matters considered enjoyable or important.

Key Verses:
Amos 6:1
Revelation 3:16

See Also:
Attitude
Insensitive

Be careful how you live
Ephesians 5:15-16

Judgment on apathy
Isaiah 32:9
Zechariah 7:11-12

Matthew 22:1-14

Of the wicked
Proverbs 29:7
Micah 2:8
Luke 18:2

Take care to be blameless
Psalm 101:2

Take care to obey
Ezekiel 3:10
Ezekiel 11:20

Woe to those at ease
Amos 6:1
Zephaniah 2:15
Luke 12:16-21

Apologetics

Definition:
A systematic, logical argument or answer in defense of a doctrine against external criticism or attack.

Key Verses:
Acts 17:2-3
1 Peter 3:15

See Also:
Agnosticism
Atheism
Boldness

Be ready to give an answer
1 Peter 3:15

Contend for the faith
Matthew 5:13-14

Jude 3

Examine all things
1 Thessalonians 5:21

**Public proclamation
of Jesus**
Acts 18:24-28

**Purposing to enter
discussions**
Acts 18:19

**Reasoning from
the Scriptures**
Acts 17:2-3

**Use reason and
persuasion**
Acts 18:4

Apostasy

Definition:
Abandonment of a
person's religious faith,
cause, or principles.

Key Verses:
2 Timothy 3:1-5
2 Peter 3:17

See Also:
Abandonment
Betrayal
Carnality
Loyalty
Rebellion
Rejection

Danger of
Hebrews 6:4-6
Hebrews 10:26
1 John 2:19

**Failed to follow
leaders**
Judges 2:17

Friends turn away
2 Timothy 1:15

In the last days
Matthew 24:11
2 Thessalonians 2:3

In the wilderness
Exodus 32:1

Of leaders
Jeremiah 10:21
Jeremiah 23:10-14

Punishment for
Isaiah 1:5
Ezekiel 3:20
Ezekiel 33:12
Jude 5

Reason for
2 Timothy 4:10

Restoration from
Hosea 1:9-10

Warning against
1 Chronicles 28:9
Ezekiel 18:24-26
Colossians 2:8
1 Timothy 1:19
2 Timothy 4:4
Hebrews 3:12
2 Peter 3:17

Appetite

Definition:
A natural desire to
satisfy a craving, espe-

cially for food, drink,
or sexual pleasure.

Key Verses:
Psalm 107:9
Proverbs 16:26

See Also:
Anorexia and Bulimia
Compulsive Eating
Eating Disorders
Gluttony
Overeating

**Acceptable to
eat meat**
Deuteronomy 12:15
Deuteronomy 12:20

Avoid gluttony
Proverbs 23:2
Proverbs 23:20

Encourages work
Proverbs 16:26

Feed your enemy
Proverbs 25:21
Romans 12:20

**Food provides
strength**
Acts 27:33-36

Fools loathe food
Psalm 107:18

For evil
Ephesians 4:19

For righteousness
Matthew 5:6

For spiritual food
1 Peter 2:2-3

The Biblical Counseling Reference Guide

God provides food
Psalm 107:9
Luke 12:22-23
Luke 12:29

Inability to satisfy
Ecclesiastes 6:7

No desire to eat
1 Samuel 1:7
1 Samuel 20:34
Job 3:24
Psalm 102:4
Daniel 6:18

**Not eating for
a long time**
Luke 4:2

Plants good for food
Genesis 1:29-30

**Provision for
the hungry**
Isaiah 58:6-7
Matthew 25:34-46
Mark 8:1-9

**The hungry eat
anything**
Proverbs 27:7

The lazy go hungry
Proverbs 19:15
Proverbs 26:15

Definition:
Anxiety over what
might happen.

Key Verses:
Matthew 6:25-27
2 Timothy 1:7

See Also:
Anxiety
Fear
Trust
Worry

Ask God to test
Psalm 139:23

Condemned
Matthew 6:25-27
John 14:27
2 Timothy 1:7

Fear of God
1 Chronicles 13:12

Fearful of death
1 Kings 1:50-53

God calms
Psalm 23:4
Psalm 27:1
Psalm 112:7

Love drives out
1 John 4:18

Approval

Definition:
Actions, words, and
attitudes that com-
municate acceptance,
support, and commen-
dation.

Key Verses:
Ephesians 1:4-6
2 Timothy 2:15

See Also:
Acceptance
Love

Respect
Self-Worth
Significance

Argue

Definition:
To dispute by engag-
ing in a quarrel or to
debate by presenting
opposing points.

Key Verses:
Philippians 2:4
2 Timothy 2:23

See Also:
Anger
Communication

**Arguing about
Christian
liberty issues**
Romans 14:1

**Arguing against
the Messiah**
Mark 8:11

Arguing with God
Exodus 3:11-12
Exodus 4:10-12
Job 13:3
Isaiah 43:26

Condemned
Philippians 2:14

**Messiah does
not argue**
Matthew 12:19

Arrogance

Definition:
Overestimation of one's own importance, expressed in a presumptuous, haughty, and overbearing manner.

Key Verses:
Proverbs 8:13
Jeremiah 13:15

See Also:
Humility
Pride

Boast in God not self
Jeremiah 9:23-24

God hates
Proverbs 8:13

God judges
1 Samuel 2:3
Isaiah 2:17-18
Isaiah 13:11
Ezekiel 16:49-50
Hosea 5:5-6
Zephaniah 3:11
Revelation 18:7-8

Of the wicked
Isaiah 16:6
Jeremiah 48:29

Prayer for God to judge the arrogant
Psalm 12:3

Ashamed

Definition:
Overcome with shame, disgrace, or humiliation.

Key Verses:
Romans 6:20-22
2 Timothy 1:8

See Also:
Fear
Shame

Because of sin
Ezra 9:6
Psalm 44:15
Romans 6:21
2 Thessalonians 3:14

Because of treachery
Psalm 4:2

Came through sin
Genesis 3:7

Do not be ashamed of the Lord
Luke 22:53-62
2 Timothy 1:8
1 Peter 4:16

Fools put to shame
Proverbs 3:35

Lack of
Genesis 2:25

Not ashamed of the gospel
Romans 1:16
2 Timothy 1:12
1 Peter 4:16

Of Jesus
Mark 8:38
Luke 9:26

Protected from shame by God
Psalm 31:1

To ask for help
Ezra 8:22

Assault

Definition:
A violent verbal threat or physical attack.

Key Verses:
Matthew 5:38-39
Mark 14:65

See Also:
Abuse
Anger
Bullying
Spouse Abuse
Violence

Against the righteous
Psalm 35:15
Psalm 54:3
Matthew 5:39
Matthew 26:67
Mark 14:65
Acts 7:55-58
Acts 16:22

Between friends
Psalm 55:20

In the family
Genesis 4:8
Genesis 32:11

Penalties for
Exodus 21:15-20

Prayer for help
Psalm 59:4
Psalm 86:14-16

Protection by the Lord
Psalm 27:2
Psalm 121:7
Acts 18:10
2 Timothy 4:18

Assertive

Definition:
Characterized by bold insistence growing out of a deep and abiding confidence.

Key Verses:
Proverbs 28:1
2 Corinthians 3:12

See Also:
Communication
Conflict Resolution
Confrontation
Leadership

Assurance of Salvation

Definition:
The confidence that authentic believers possess eternal life and will one day live in the presence of God.

Key Verses:
Romans 8:1
1 John 5:13

See Also:
Eternal Security
Salvation

Based on belief in Jesus
John 5:24
Romans 8:1
Romans 10:9
Ephesians 2:8-9
Titus 3:4-7
1 John 5:10-13

Based on call of Jesus
John 10:27-28

Based on Christ's work
Hebrews 7:25
Hebrews 10:14

Based on God's faithfulness
John 10:29
Romans 8:38-39
Philippians 1:6
2 Timothy 1:12
1 John 2:25
Jude 24

Christ obtained our salvation
Hebrews 9:12

Christ's sacrifice cleanses us
Hebrews 10:22
1 John 1:7

Deeds as evidence of salvation
1 John 1:6

God accepts all those who receive Him
John 1:12

God conforms us to the image of Christ
Romans 8:29

God is greater than our feelings
1 John 3:19-22

God's Spirit lives in believers
Ezekiel 36:26-27
1 John 3:24

Loss of salvation is not possible
John 10:28-30
Romans 8:38-39

Nothing separates us from God's love
Romans 8:35-39

Perfection does not occur in this life
Philippians 3:12-14
1 John 3:2

Relationship to predestination
Ephesians 1:4-5

Role of Holy Spirit in
Romans 8:15-16
Ephesians 1:13-14
Ephesians 4:30

Salvation produces good works
 1 John 3:9-10
 1 John 5:18

Test yourself
 2 Corinthians 13:5

The gospel brings salvation
 1 Corinthians 15:1-2

Atheism

Definition:
The doctrine of the absolute denial of the existence of God.

Key Verses:
Psalm 14:1
Jeremiah 29:13

See Also:
Apologetics
Atheism and
 Agnosticism
God

Atheism and Agnosticism

Definition:
Denial or doubt of the existence of God.

Key Verses:
Psalm 14:1
1 Corinthians 1:18

See Also:
Apologetics
God

Holy Spirit
Jesus

Be humble before God
 Proverbs 3:7

Christians live by faith
 2 Corinthians 5:7

Creation is a witness to God
 Psalm 19:1-6
 Psalm 104:24
 Isaiah 40:26
 Isaiah 42:5
 Isaiah 45:18
 Acts 14:15-17
 Romans 1:18-20

Faith is essential for knowing God
 Hebrews 11:1-3

God is above all
 Isaiah 55:8-9

God is the Creator
 Genesis 1:1
 Job 38:4-7

God oversees and influences world affairs
 Isaiah 13:17-19
 Jeremiah 51:11
 Ezekiel 26:3-4
 Ezekiel 29:2-6
 Ezekiel 29:15

God sees all
 Jeremiah 23:24

God the Son became a man
 Matthew 1:21-23
 John 1:14

Jesus is God, the Creator
 John 1:1-3

Jesus is the truth and the life
 John 14:6

Message of the cross sounds foolish
 1 Corinthians 1:18

Morality is a witness to God
 Romans 2:14-15

Moses witnessed God's presence
 Exodus 34:6-8

Respond to skeptics with grace and reason
 Colossians 4:5-6
 1 Peter 3:15

Unbeliever rejects knowledge of God
 Psalm 10:4
 1 Corinthians 2:14
 Hebrews 3:12

Atonement

Definition:
The reconciliation of God and humanity through the sacrificial death of Jesus Christ on the cross.

Key Verses:
Romans 5:1
1 John 2:1-2

See Also:
Gospel
Salvation

By Jesus
Acts 20:28
1 Corinthians 15:3
1 Timothy 2:5-6
1 Timothy 4:10
Hebrews 2:9
Hebrews 7:27
Hebrews 9:28
1 Peter 3:18
1 John 2:1-2
Revelation 5:9

Day of
Leviticus 23:27-28

Effects of
2 Corinthians 5:19

For the world
John 1:29

Jesus' blood of the new covenant
Matthew 26:28

Means of attaining
Leviticus 4:15-21
Hebrews 9:11-12
1 John 4:10

Of the high priest
Exodus 30:10
Hebrews 9:7

Produces reconciliation
Romans 5:1-11
Colossians 1:19-20

Attention

Definition:
Narrowly focused concentration in order to complete a specific purpose.

Key Verses:
Deuteronomy 7:12
Psalm 130:2

See Also:
Time Management

Attitude

Definition:
The state of mind or disposition of a person.

Key Verses:
Philippians 2:5-7
1 Peter 4:1

See Also:
Humility
Pride

Anger
Genesis 4:3-7
Jonah 4:1-11

Be gentle and patient
2 Timothy 2:24

Bitter heart
Ruth 1:20-21

Broken spirit harms
Proverbs 18:14

Cheerful
Psalm 100:1-2
Psalm 118:24
Proverbs 15:13
Proverbs 15:15
Proverbs 15:30
Proverbs 17:22
Ecclesiastes 8:15
1 Thessalonians
5:16-18

Discouraged
Psalm 31:10
Ecclesiastes 2:17
Luke 24:17

Do not quarrel
Genesis 13:8-9
Proverbs 17:14
2 Timothy 2:24

Evil attitudes
Genesis 6:5

God gives laughter
Job 8:21

In affliction
James 1:2-6
1 Peter 4:12-16

Nonjudgmental
Matthew 7:1
Acts 17:11

Of forgiveness
Matthew 6:14
Ephesians 4:32

Of humility
1 Kings 3:7-9
Psalm 138:6
Philippians 2:5-8

Of mercy
Luke 6:36

Prideful
Proverbs 16:18
Jeremiah 48:29-30

Remove anxiety
Ecclesiastes 11:10
1 Peter 5:7

Authority

Definition:
The right or power to command, make decisions, or enforce obedience.

Key Verses:
Matthew 28:18
Titus 2:15

See Also:
Government
Obedience
Submission

Evil desire for
3 John 9-10

From wealth
Proverbs 22:7

Granted by God
Exodus 7:1-2
Deuteronomy 1:17
John 19:8-11
Revelation 13:5

Revelation 17:12

In decision-making
Acts 16:4

Lack of
Acts 19:13-16

Of Christ
Matthew 11:27
Matthew 28:18
John 3:35
1 Corinthians 15:27
Ephesians 1:18-22
Colossians 2:10
Hebrews 1:3-4
Revelation 1:5

Of God
Isaiah 44:24-28
Luke 12:5

Of husbands
Ephesians 5:22-23
1 Peter 3:1

Pray for those in authority
1 Timothy 2:1-2

Recognition of
Matthew 10:24

Submission to
Acts 23:4-5
1 Peter 2:13-17

Teaching with
Matthew 7:29
Mark 1:27
Luke 4:31-36
Titus 2:15

To bind and loose
Matthew 18:18

To build up
2 Corinthians 13:10

To cast out demons
Matthew 10:1
Mark 3:14-15

To do evil
Revelation 13:2

To forgive sins
Matthew 9:6
Mark 2:10
Luke 5:20-24

To judge
Revelation 20:4

To rule creation
Genesis 1:26

Avoidance

Definition:
Measures taken to evade, withdraw, or show someone something.

Key Verses:
Romans 16:17-18
1 Thessalonians 5:22

See Also:
Abandonment
Manipulation
Rejection

By friends and family
Psalm 38:11
Proverbs 19:7

Of evil
Proverbs 4:14-15

Proverbs 16:6
Proverbs 16:17
1 Thessalonians 5:22

Of immorality
1 Thessalonians
4:3-4

Of impurity
Deuteronomy 23:9
Colossians 3:5

**Of those who
cause dissension**
Romans 16:17

**Of those who
talk too much**
Proverbs 20:19

Backbiting

Definition:
Spitefully and
maliciously slandering
a person not present.

Key Verses:
Psalm 101:5
Proverbs 25:23

See Also:
Gossip
Hatred
Judgment
Lying
Slander

**Behavior of
the godless**
Psalm 50:20

Dangers of
Proverbs 11:13

Proverbs 16:28
Proverbs 26:20

Produces anger
Proverbs 25:23

Wicked behavior
Romans 1:29-31
2 Corinthians 12:20

Backsliding

Definition:
Reverting or returning
to sin or wrongdoing.

Key Verses:
Romans 8:5
Hebrews 2:1

See Also:
Apostasy
Betrayal
Carnality
Rebellion
Rejection

**Because of difficult
teaching**
John 6:64-66

Ceasing
Judges 10:16

Condemned
1 Kings 11:9
Ezekiel 18:24
Matthew 5:13-16
Luke 9:62
1 Peter 1:14
Revelation 3:15-16

Danger of
Galatians 1:6-9

1 Timothy 1:18-20
Hebrews 6:4-6

Discipline for
Isaiah 63:10
Jeremiah 2:19
Ezekiel 3:20-21
Hosea 9:7

Effects of
Joshua 22:18
Jeremiah 17:13

Implications of
1 John 2:18-19

Led by the wicked
1 Kings 11:4

Loss of first love
Revelation 2:4-5

Natural desire
Hosea 11:7
Matthew 15:19

Of leadership
Ezekiel 8:12

Of Peter
Mark 14:66-72

Repeated offenses
Judges 2:18-19

Repentance from
1 Kings 8:33-34
Jeremiah 3:22
Revelation 3:2-5

Restoration from
Galatians 6:1
James 5:19-20

Resulting from idolotry
Exodus 32:1-6

Role of greed in
1 Timothy 6:10

Running from God
Jonah 1:1-3

Warning against
Deuteronomy 4:9
Matthew 6:24
2 Corinthians 6:1
Galatians 4:9
1 Timothy 6:20
Hebrews 2:1
Hebrews 3:12
Hebrews 10:26-27
2 Peter 2:20-22
2 Peter 3:17

Baptism

Definition:
Ritual washing with water symbolizing identification with a group, spiritual realities and relationships, or pursuit of a unique role or calling.

Key Verses:
Matthew 3:13
Romans 6:4

See Also:
Discipleship
Obedience
Salvation

Bargaining

Definition:
Negotiating the terms of a sale, agreement, or contract.

Key Verses:
Proverbs 20:14
Matthew 16:26

See Also:
Business Ethics
Ethics
Finances
Greed
Money

Deceitful
Genesis 25:27-34
Proverbs 20:14

Godly
Genesis 18:20-33
Joshua 2:14
Isaiah 55:1-2
Matthew 16:26
John 4:10

Wicked
Matthew 14:6-10
Matthew 26:14-16

Barren

Definition:
Childless or incapable of bearing children.

Key Verses:
Psalm 113:9
Hebrews 11:11

See Also:
Adoption

Celibacy
Childlessness
Family

A cause of anguish
Genesis 30:1-24
1 Samuel 1:1-20

God closes the womb
Genesis 16:1-2

God opens the womb
Genesis 20:17-18
Genesis 29:31-35
Judges 13:2-8
Psalm 113:9
Luke 1:5-25

The barren will rejoice
Galatians 4:27

Beauty

Definition:
A quality that appeals to the mind or senses.

Key Verses:
Proverbs 31:30
Ecclesiastes 3:11

See Also:
Vanity
Women

An enticement to sin
Isaiah 3:16-17

Good character is true beauty
1 Peter 3:3-4

Lusting after leads to sin
Genesis 12:11-16
2 Samuel 11:2-3
Esther 1:11

Only temporary
Proverbs 31:30

Pleasing to men
Deuteronomy
21:10-11
1 Kings 1:3-4
Esther 2:1-18
Psalm 45:11

Worthless without good character
Proverbs 11:22

Behavior

Definition:
The way in which someone acts or something functions.

Key Verses:
Proverbs 5:22
1 Thessalonians 2:10

See Also:
Example
Golden Rule

Exhortation for godly behavior
Psalm 15:1-5
Ephesians 4:31
Philippians 2:14-15
1 Timothy 3:2
Titus 2:11-15
James 3:13

1 Peter 1:15
1 Peter 2:12
1 Peter 3:16
2 Peter 1:5-9
1 John 3:2-3

Godly behavior modeled
Romans 16:19
2 Corinthians 1:12
1 Thessalonians 2:10

Godly speech
Colossians 4:6

Love is most important
1 Corinthians
13:1-13

Love leads to godly behavior
Philippians 1:9-10

Responsible
2 Thessalonians
3:7-10

Ungodly
1 Corinthians 3:3
Colossians 3:5-8
1 Peter 2:1

Belief

Definition:
Trusting in or relying on someone or something, including a doctrine or conviction.

Key Verses:
Genesis 15:6
John 1:12

See Also:
Faith
Trust

Failure to believe God
Psalm 78:22
Psalm 106:24
John 12:37

God's power to believers
Ephesians 1:18-19

In Jesus for eternal life
John 11:26
John 20:31
Acts 16:31
1 John 5:13

Judgment on unbelievers
2 Thessalonians 2:12
Jude 5

Produces success
2 Chronicles 20:20

Through preaching
1 Corinthians 1:21

Bereavement

Definition:
Grieving over a profound loss, especially the death or departure of a loved one.

Key Verses:
2 Samuel 18:33
1 Thessalonians 4:13

See Also:
Death
Grief
Loneliness
Mourning
Sorrow
Sympathy
Widowhood

Comfort for those who mourn
Isaiah 61:1-2
Zechariah 1:16-17

Death of children by the wicked
Matthew 2:17-18

Death of children by warfare
Deuteronomy 32:25
Lamentations 2:11

Death of children by wild animals
Leviticus 26:22

Deprived of sons
Genesis 42:36
Genesis 43:13-14

Refusal to be comforted
Genesis 37:35

Betrayal

Definition:
An act of disloyalty, violation of confidence, or a breach of trust.

Key Verses:
Psalm 41:9
Psalm 89:33

See Also:
Abandonment
Desertion
Marriage

By a friend
Job 17:5
Psalm 41:9
Psalm 55:12-14
Matthew 26:47-50
Mark 14:43-46
Luke 22:3-6
Luke 22:47-48
John 13:21-27

By a prisoner
Judges 8:13-14

By family
Genesis 37:21-28
Micah 7:6
Matthew 10:21
Mark 13:12
Luke 21:16

Cause for judgment
Luke 22:22-23

Characteristic of evil people
2 Timothy 3:2-4

For money
Judges 16:15-19
Matthew 26:14-16
Mark 14:10-11

God uses for a good result
Genesis 50:20

Bible Reliability

Definition:
The truthfulness, consistency, and dependability of the Bible.

Key Verses:
Psalm 12:6
2 Timothy 3:16

See Also:
Atheism and Agnosticism
Cults
Salvation

God used human authors to write
Luke 1:1-4

God used prophets to proclaim
Jeremiah 1:4-9
Jonah 1:1-2
Hebrews 1:1

God's Word is a shield against sin
Psalm 119:11

God's Word judges the heart
Hebrews 4:12

God's Word remains forever
Isaiah 40:8

Importance of the Scriptures
Matthew 22:9

Paul wrote with authority
Romans 1:1
Ephesians 1:1

Paul's preaching was empowered by
1 Corinthians 2:4

The apostles were witnesses for Christ
John 15:27

The Bible heals broken lives
Psalm 107:20

The Bible is God's Word
2 Timothy 3:16

The Bible is perfect and reliable
Psalm 19:7

The Bible is pure, without deceit
Psalm 12:6

The Bible provides guidance
Proverbs 6:23

The Bible provides instruction and hope
Romans 15:4

The Bible reveals Christ
John 5:39

The Spirit instructed the apostles
John 14:26
John 16:15

The teaching of the apostles came from
1 Thessalonians 2:13

The Word is certain
Matthew 5:18
2 Peter 1:19

The Word is effective
Isaiah 55:10-11

The Word is eternal
Matthew 24:35
Mark 13:31
Luke 21:33
1 Peter 1:24-25

The Word is flawless
Proverbs 30:5

The Word is our guide for life
James 1:25

The Word is true
John 17:17

The Word leads to eternal life
1 John 5:13

The Word must be preached
Matthew 28:18-20
2 Timothy 2:2

The Word witnesses to Christ
John 20:31

The writings of Paul were considered Scripture
2 Peter 3:14-16

Bigamy

Definition:
Being married to one person while still legally married to another.

Key Verses:
Genesis 2:24
Deuteronomy 17:16-17

See Also:
Marriage
Monogamy
Polygamy

Condemned
Genesis 2:24
Malachi 2:15

Corruption from
1 Kings 11:3-4

Leads to favoritism
2 Chronicles 11:21

Produces rivalry
1 Samuel 1:6

Prohibited for church leaders
1 Timothy 3:2
1 Timothy 3:12
Titus 1:6

Prohibited for leaders
Deuteronomy 17:17

Bigotry

Definition:
Narrow-minded intolerance, especially of

other races and religions, with an elevated view of one's own opinions.

Key Verses:
Romans 15:7
James 2:9

See Also:
Discrimination
Injustice
Prejudice

Condemned
Matthew 7:1-2
Romans 2:1
Romans 14:1
Romans 15:7
James 2:3-4
James 4:11
1 John 2:9
1 John 3:15

**God does not
show favoritism**
Acts 10:34-35

God is the judge
1 Corinthians
5:12-13

**God looks at
the heart**
Acts 15:8

Love commanded
Matthew 5:44
Romans 12:10
Romans 13:8-10
1 Corinthians 16:14

Bipolar

Definition:
Characterized by antagonistic or opposing natures or perspectives; bipolar disorder labels extremes of behavior alternating between depression and mania.

Key Verses:
Psalm 143:7-8
Proverbs 29:11

See Also:
Counseling
Depression
Mood Disorders

Birth, Physical

Definition:
The point in time when someone is born or something comes into existence.

Key Verses:
Psalm 22:9
John 16:21

See Also:
Children
Pregnancy…
  Unplanned
Salvation

Barren give birth
Genesis 18:10-14
Judges 13:3
2 Kings 4:14-16

Chosen before
Psalm 139:16
Jeremiah 1:5
Galatians 1:15

Difficulty in
Genesis 3:16
Genesis 35:16-20

God's care from
Psalm 22:9-10

John the Baptist
Luke 1:57-66

Of first child
Genesis 4:1

Of Messiah
Isaiah 7:14
Isaiah 9:6
Luke 2:9-11
Revelation 12:5

Sinner from birth
Psalm 51:5

Birth, Spiritual

Definition:
The point in time when a person accepts Jesus Christ as Lord and Savior and becomes spiritually alive.

Key Verses:
John 1:12-13
1 Peter 1:23

See Also:
Child Evangelism
Evangelism

The Biblical Counseling Reference Guide

Gospel
Salvation

Chosen by God
Ephesians 1:4-7

Given by God
Ezekiel 36:26-27

Made a new creature
2 Corinthians 5:17

**To a living hope
and inheritance**
1 Peter 1:23

Bisexual

Definition:
A person who feels
sexually attracted to
and engages in sexual
activity with members
of both sexes.

Key Verses:
Leviticus 18:22
Romans 1:26-27

See Also:
Homosexuality
Transsexual
Transvestite

Avoidance of
1 Corinthians 6:18

Condemned
Genesis 19:5-13
Leviticus 18:22
1 Corinthians 6:9-11

Judgment on
Leviticus 20:13

Romans 1:24-27
2 Peter 2:6
Jude 7

Bitterness

Definition:
A feeling of intense
resentment and caustic
animosity.

Key Verses:
Ephesians 4:31
Hebrews 12:15

See Also:
Anger
Hatred
Resentment

**Characteristic
of the wicked**
Romans 3:14

Defiles many
Hebrews 12:15

Prayer in
1 Samuel 1:10

Removal of
Ephesians 4:31

Solitude in
Proverbs 14:10

Spiritual poison
Acts 8:23

Blame

Definition:
To find fault with,
accuse, or condemn.

Key Verses:
Nahum 1:3
John 11:21

See Also:
Responsibility
Slander

Attempt to
Mark 3:2

**Confession
commanded**
Leviticus 5:5

**Confession
encouraged**
Psalm 32:5
Proverbs 28:13
James 5:16
1 John 1:9

God keeps from
1 Thessalonians 5:23

Of God
Job 1:22

Out of fear
Matthew 27:24

Result of deception
Genesis 3:13
1 Timothy 2:14

**Result of running
from God**
Jonah 1:10-12

**Result of turning
from truth**
2 Peter 2:21

Take responsibility
Genesis 42:21-22

Genesis 43:8-9
2 Samuel 14:9

Taking personal responsibility
Genesis 43:9-10

Definition:
Offensive, irreverent acts aimed at violating spiritual laws, insulting God, or claiming to possess the attributes of God.

Key Verses:
Exodus 22:28
1 Timothy 1:13

See Also:
Abomination
Apostasy

Against God
Leviticus 22:32
2 Chronicles 32:16-17
Nehemiah 9:26
Isaiah 37:17
Isaiah 37:23
Ezekiel 35:13

Against Jesus
Matthew 9:32-34
Matthew 27:41-43
Luke 11:15
John 10:19-20

Against the Holy Spirit
Matthew 12:31

Mark 3:28-30
Luke 12:10

Because of suffering
Revelation 16:10-11

By angels
2 Peter 2:10

By the Antichrist
Daniel 7:25

By the beast
Revelation 13:1
Revelation 13:5-6

By the man of lawlessness
2 Thessalonians 2:4

By the wicked
Psalm 73:9-11
James 2:7

Falsely ascribed to Jesus
Mark 14:64
John 5:18

Jesus called a deceiver
Matthew 27:62-63

Judgment for
Exodus 20:7
Leviticus 24:11-16
Deuteronomy 5:11
Acts 12:22-23
1 Timothy 1:20

Result of swearing in God's name
Leviticus 19:12

Will cease
Ezekiel 20:39

Definition:
A family into which one or both of the spouses have brought children from a previous relationship.

Key Verses:
Romans 14:19
Colossians 3:12-15

See Also:
Dysfunctional Family
Parenting
Remarriage

Disciplining a loved one
Proverbs 3:12
Proverbs 29:15-17

Guiltless divorce
1 Corinthians 7:15

Honor for parents
Exodus 20:12
Ephesians 6:1-3

Husband and wife constitute one flesh
Genesis 2:24

Remarriage acceptable
Romans 7:2-3
1 Corinthians 7:7-9
1 Corinthians 7:39

Restrictions on remarriage
Deuteronomy 24:1-4

Matthew 19:9

Wisdom in
Proverbs 24:3

Blessing

Definition:
Being a source of happiness and well-being to someone especially by speaking well-chosen words of favor, affirmation, or praise.

Key Verses:
Genesis 12:2
1 Corinthians 4:12

See Also:
Celebration
Honor

Dangers of
Hosea 13:6

For financial stewardship
Malachi 3:8-10

For following Christ
Luke 18:29-30

For obedience
Leviticus 26:4
Deuteronomy 4:40
Deuteronomy 12:28
Isaiah 1:19-20
Jeremiah 11:1-5
Zechariah 3:7

For perseverance
Matthew 5:11-12

For repentance
Joel 2:26

From God
Genesis 8:22
Genesis 12:3
Genesis 24:35
Genesis 26:12
Genesis 26:24-27
Genesis 39:5
Exodus 15:26
Exodus 23:25
Numbers 6:24-26
Deuteronomy 28:8
Deuteronomy 29:5
1 Kings 3:13
2 Chronicles 1:12
Nehemiah 9:25
Psalm 23:2
Psalm 24:5
Psalm 29:11
Psalm 32:10
Psalm 34:10
Psalm 81:16
Psalm 145:16
Isaiah 30:23
Zechariah 10:1
James 1:16-17

From leadership
Joshua 14:13
Joshua 22:6

Leading to good works
2 Corinthians 9:8

Obtained by deceit
Genesis 27:21-40

Of a father
Genesis 28:1
Genesis 48:16

Of diligent work
Proverbs 28:20

Of others
1 Samuel 2:20
1 Kings 8:14

Peace with God
Romans 5:1

Restoration of
Zechariah 9:12

Revoked because of idolatry
1 Kings 9:1-9

Seek the kingdom of God
Matthew 6:33

Blindness

Definition:
The inability or unwillingness to see.

Key Verses:
Isaiah 42:16
Matthew 13:15

See Also:
Chronic Illness
Ignorance

Compassion for the blind
Leviticus 19:14
Deuteronomy 27:18

God removes sight
2 Kings 6:18
Acts 9:8
Acts 13:6-12

God restores sight
Isaiah 35:5-6

Jesus heals
Matthew 9:27-30
Matthew 12:22
Mark 8:22-25
Mark 10:46-52
Luke 7:21-22
John 9:1-12

Relief for the blind
Isaiah 42:16

Spiritual
Matthew 13:14-15
Matthew 15:14
Matthew 23:19
Acts 28:26
2 Corinthians 3:14
2 Corinthians 4:4
Ephesians 4:18
2 Peter 1:5-9
1 John 2:11

Boasting

Definition:
Bragging with excessive pride about oneself (negative), or expressing confident pride in the Lord (positive).

Key Verses:
Galatians 6:14
James 3:5

See Also:
Arrogance
Conceit
Pride
Self-Exaltation

Condemned
Romans 12:16

Empty
Proverbs 25:14

Evil of
James 4:16

Folly of
Isaiah 10:15

God will humble
Isaiah 13:11
Isaiah 14:12-15

In God
Psalm 34:2
Psalm 44:8
Jeremiah 9:23-24
1 Corinthians 1:31
2 Corinthians 3:4-5
2 Corinthians 10:13-18

In riches
Ezekiel 28:12-19

In sin
Amos 4:4-5

Leads to destruction
Proverbs 16:18
Proverbs 18:12

Love does not boast
1 Corinthians 13:4

Only in the cross of Christ
Galatians 6:14

Unwise boast
Proverbs 27:1
Matthew 26:33-35

John 13:37-38
Ephesians 2:8-9

Boldness

Definition:
Exhibiting courage and bravery.

Key Verses:
Psalm 138:3
Philippians 1:14

See Also:
Faith
Oppression
Prayer
Zeal

Based on God's presence
Joshua 1:9

Prayer for
Acts 4:29
Ephesians 6:19-20

Righteous are bold
Proverbs 28:1

To approach God
Hebrews 4:16
Hebrews 10:19
1 John 2:28

To refuse idolatry
Daniel 3:16-18

To speak about Jesus
Acts 4:13
Acts 4:31
Acts 7:55-56
Acts 28:31

The Biblical Counseling Reference Guide

Bondage

Definition:
Being subjected to the power, force, or control of someone or something; a sexual practice in which one partner is physically bound.

Key Verses:
Isaiah 49:8-9
2 Timothy 2:25-26

See Also:
Adversity
Sexual Integrity
Spiritual Warfare

Benefits of
Philippians 1:12-14

Escaping the devil's trap
1 Timothy 3:7
2 Timothy 2:26

Freedom from disability
Luke 13:12

Freedom from prison
Acts 12:7-11

Freedom from sin
John 8:32
Romans 6:22

Freedom from slavery
Jeremiah 30:8

Redemption from slavery
Leviticus 25:47-49

Satan bound
Revelation 20:1-3

Sold into slavery
Isaiah 50:1

To righteousness
Romans 6:18

To sin
Proverbs 5:22
John 8:34
Acts 8:23
Romans 6:16
2 Peter 2:19

To the elemental forces
Galatians 4:3-7

Borderline Personality

Definition:
Uncontrolled impulsive behavior and sudden extreme changes often developing out of an irrational fear of abandonment, rejection, or isolation.

Key Verses:
Psalm 27:9
Isaiah 41:13

See Also:
Mood Disorder
Mental Illness
Self-Worth

Born Again

Definition:
Action of the Holy Spirit made possible by the redemptive death and resurrection of Jesus Christ to bring life to a dead human spirit through establishing a relationship with God.

Key Verses:
John 3:3
1 Peter 1:23

See Also:
Birth, Spiritual
Evangelism
Gospel
Salvation

Borrowing

Definition:
Obtaining the temporary use of something on loan with the understanding that it will be returned.

Key Verses:
Proverbs 22:7
Matthew 5:42

See Also:
Honesty
Lending
Restitution
Stealing

Borrower a slave to the lender
Proverbs 22:7

Lend generously
Deuteronomy 15:8
Psalm 37:26
Psalm 112:5
Matthew 5:42
Luke 6:35

Responsible for borrowed item
Exodus 22:14
2 Kings 6:5-7

Wicked does not repay
Psalm 37:21

Definition:
Money or favor offered, promised, or given to influence the judgment or conduct of a person to gain an unfair or unlawful advantage.

Key Verses:
Exodus 23:8
Ecclesiastes 7:7

See Also:
Ethics and Integrity
Honesty
Injustice
Manipulation

Brings trouble
Proverbs 15:27

Condemned
Exodus 23:8
Deuteronomy 16:19
Job 36:18-19
Isaiah 33:15-16
Amos 5:12

Of God
Deuteronomy 10:17
Acts 8:9-24

Resisting
Acts 24:26

Softens hearts
Proverbs 18:16

Sways people
Proverbs 17:8
Proverbs 21:14

Wickedness of
Proverbs 17:23
Micah 7:3

Brokenhearted

Definition:
Sadness, misery, or despair stemming from unmet expectations or tragic loss.

Key Verses:
Psalm 34:18
Isaiah 61:1

See Also:
Cry
Grief
Hope
Hopelessness

Bulimia

Definition:
An eating disorder characterized by repeated episodes of uncontrolled eating followed by self-induced vomiting, exercise, and misuse of laxatives to avoid gaining weight.

Key Verses:
Matthew 10:29-31
1 Corinthians 6:20

See Also:
Anorexia
Anorexia and Bulimia
Compulsive Eating
Self-Worth

Bullying

Definition:
Hostile, demeaning, or threatening pattern of behavior directed toward a person or group due to specific unique qualities they exhibit or possess.

Key Verses:
Proverbs 29:25
Romans 12:18

See Also:
Parenting
Teenagers
Verbal and Emotional
    Abuse

As cruelty
Nehemiah 4:1-3
Matthew 26:68
Matthew 27:27-31

By the wicked
Isaiah 57:4

Endured by those who suffer
Psalm 22:7
Psalm 69:10-11
Ezekiel 36:3-4

Of children against the elderly
2 Kings 2:23

Result of misunderstanding
Matthew 9:23-24
Acts 2:13

Results in judgment
Proverbs 30:17

Burial

Definition:
The process of placing something in the ground or the ceremony associated with placing someone dead in a grave.

Key Verses:
Matthew 27:57-60
Luke 9:60

See Also:
Death
Eternal Life
Terminal Illness

By family
Judges 16:31

Denied by the ungodly
Psalm 79:2
Jeremiah 14:16

Disinterment and reburial
2 Samuel 21:11-14

Embalming practiced in Egypt
Genesis 50:26

In a cave
Joshua 10:26-27

In a tomb
Matthew 27:59-60
Mark 15:46

In common burial plot
Jeremiah 26:23
Matthew 27:7

In family burial plot
Genesis 47:28-31
Joshua 24:32

Kindness to the dead
2 Samuel 2:4-5

Mass grave
Jeremiah 41:9

Mourning accompanying
1 Samuel 31:13

Of Samuel
1 Samuel 25:1

Of Sarah
Genesis 23:19

On the same day as death
Deuteronomy 21:23

Place unknown
Deuteronomy 34:5-6

Preparation for
Mark 16:1

Respect for the dead
1 Chronicles 10:11-12

Burnout

Definition:
Physical, emotional, or spiritual exhaustion from long-term stress; becoming weary from overwork or worn out from overuse.

Key Verses:
Psalm 119:28
Matthew 11:28

See Also:
Discouragement
Stress
Workaholism

Exhaustion from grief
Luke 22:45

Leads to irrational behavior
Jeremiah 19:9

Leads to irrational thinking
1 Kings 19:9-10

Physical exhaustion
Jeremiah 51:30

Rest needed
Exodus 23:12

Take time for rest
Mark 6:31

Definition:
A code of conduct or morals associated with commerce.

Key Verses:
Proverbs 11:1
Malachi 3:5

See Also:
Character
Cheating
Ethics and Integrity
Honesty

Diligence brings results
Genesis 39:6-8
2 Kings 12:15
Proverbs 6:6-8
Proverbs 10:4-5
Proverbs 12:11
Proverbs 13:4
Proverbs 20:13
Proverbs 22:29
Daniel 6:4

Honesty in business
Proverbs 11:1

Proverbs 13:11
Proverbs 19:1
Proverbs 20:7
Proverbs 21:6
Ezekiel 45:10

Injustice condemned
Leviticus 19:35-36
Deuteronomy 25:13-15
Proverbs 16:8
Jeremiah 17:11
Ezekiel 22:12-13
Amos 5:11

Laziness is destructive
Proverbs 18:9
Proverbs 24:30-34
Ecclesiastes 10:18

Pay your workers promptly
Deuteronomy 24:15
James 5:4

Definition:
A disaster that results in great loss, distress, or hardship.

Key Verses:
Proverbs 24:16
Isaiah 45:7

See Also:
Affliction
Destruction
Disaster

God rescues from calamity
Psalm 18:18-19

God's judgment
Lamentations 2:21
Revelation 11:13
Revelation 16:18

Trust God during
Job 1:20-21

Under God's control
Isaiah 45:7

Definition:
A state of serenity, quiet, tranquility or peace.

Key Verses:
Psalm 4:8
Ecclesiastes 10:4

See Also:
Hope
Peace
Trust

A blessing from God
Jeremiah 30:10
Jeremiah 46:27

A quiet spirit
Psalm 131:2

Jesus calms the winds and sea
Matthew 8:26
Mark 4:39
Luke 8:24

The Biblical Counseling Reference Guide

Of an angry crowd
Acts 19:35-36

Overcomes offenses
Ecclesiastes 10:4

Relationship to anger
Proverbs 15:18

Trust in God
Isaiah 7:4

Capability

Definition:
Having traits or attributes suitable for accomplishing a task.

Key Verses:
2 Samuel 22:34
Ecclesiastes 5:19

See Also:
Ability
Confidence
Spiritual Gifts

For wickedness
Micah 2:1

Through God's power
Exodus 31:1-5
Nehemiah 4:1-20

To do every good work
Hebrews 13:20-21

To serve before the king
Daniel 1:3-5

To withstand Satan
Ephesians 6:10-18

Capital Punishment

Definition:
Infliction of the death penalty for a crime.

Key Verses:
Genesis 9:6
Romans 13:4

See Also:
Death
Government
Justice
Murder

For disobedience to God
Numbers 15:32-36
Joshua 7:25-26

For idolatry
Exodus 22:20
Deuteronomy 13:1-18

For kidnapping
Exodus 21:16

For lying to God
Acts 5:1-10

For murder
Genesis 9:6
Exodus 21:14
Leviticus 24:17
Leviticus 24:21
Numbers 35:16-18
Numbers 35:30-31

For sorcery
Exodus 22:18

For spiritists
Leviticus 20:27

For treason
Esther 7:4-10

For violating the Sabbath
Exodus 31:14
Exodus 35:2

Never for the innocent
Exodus 23:7

To remove evil
Deuteronomy 17:12
Deuteronomy 21:18-21
Psalm 101:8
Ecclesiastes 8:11-13

Caregiving

Definition:
A person who provides emotional or physical support to someone who is unable to live independently.

Key Verses:
Matthew 25:35-36, 40
Luke 10:34-35

See Also:
Aging
Chronic Illness
Compassion
Responsibility
Terminal Illness

By God
Deuteronomy 32:10
Psalm 62:8
Psalm 68:19

2 Corinthians 1:3-4
1 Peter 5:6-7

Care for Christ's sheep
John 21:16

For one another
Galatians 6:2
Galatians 6:7-10
Colossians 3:12-13
Hebrews 6:10
1 John 4:12

For parents and grandparents
1 Timothy 5:4
1 Timothy 5:8

For the injured
Luke 10:25-37

From God's strength
1 Peter 4:11

God cares for all
Hosea 13:5

God sees and understands your condition
Jeremiah 15:15

God will strengthen those who trust in Him
Isaiah 40:31

God will take care of you
1 Corinthians 1:8-9

Jesus provides rest
Matthew 11:28

With a good attitude
Ephesians 6:7

Women ministered to Jesus
Matthew 27:55

Carnality

Definition:
Sensual indulgence of bodily appetites; used especially of lust and greed.

Key Verses:
Romans 6:14
1 Corinthians 3:3

See Also:
Backsliding
Immorality
Sin
Worldly

Avoidance of
Hebrews 12:1

Condemned
Psalm 52:1-5
Matthew 11:20
Romans 12:2
1 Corinthians 5:1-2
Ephesians 4:17
1 Peter 4:3
2 Peter 1:4
2 Peter 2:13-16
1 John 2:16

Dangers of
James 3:13-16

Description of
2 Timothy 3:2-7

Effects of
Romans 6:21
Romans 8:13-14
Galatians 6:7-10
James 1:13-15

Evidence of carnal thinking
Romans 8:5

No care for others
Proverbs 21:10

Of unbelievers
Colossians 1:21

Punishment for
Amos 1:11

Relationship to freedom
Galatians 5:13

Relationship to jealousy
1 Corinthians 3:3

Repentance from
2 Corinthians 12:21

Source of
1 John 2:15-17

Warning against
2 Peter 2:4-10

Caution

Definition:
Careful forethought given to avoid danger, harm, or unwanted consequences.

The Biblical Counseling Reference Guide

Key Verses:
Ezekiel 11:20
1 Corinthians 10:12

See Also:
Danger
Fear

Key Verses:
2 Samuel 6:5
Psalm 145:7

See Also:
Joy
Thankfulness

Key Verses:
1 Corinthians 7:4-5
1 Corinthians 7:8

See Also:
Childlessness
Purity
Sexual Integrity
Singleness

Against boasting
James 1:10-11

In friendships
Proverbs 12:26

In living
Ephesians 5:15

In obeying God's Word
Exodus 19:5
Exodus 23:22
Deuteronomy 12:28
Deuteronomy 15:5
Deuteronomy 28:1
Hebrews 2:1

In remaining faithful to God
Joshua 23:11
1 Corinthians 10:12

In remembering God's works
Deuteronomy 4:9

Celebration

Definition:
A time of joy to commemorate a special event.

At reading God's Word
Nehemiah 8:9-12

Because of God's deliverance
Psalm 13:5
Zephaniah 3:14-15

Enjoyment of
Luke 5:27-35

For repentance
Luke 15:3-10
Luke 15:21-24

In God's honor
Exodus 15:1-18
Exodus 23:14-17
2 Chronicles 7:8
Isaiah 42:10-11

Sound the trumpets
Numbers 10:10

With family
Genesis 21:8
Deuteronomy 14:26

Celibacy

Definition:
Abstaining or refraining from sexual activity.

Acceptable state
1 Corinthians 7:7-8
1 Corinthians 7:26-27

Benefits to ministry
1 Corinthians 7:32-40

Marriage forbidden by the wicked
1 Timothy 4:1-5

Only for some people
Matthew 19:10-12

The 144,000
Revelation 14:3-4

Change

Definition:
To alter, modify, or transform one's thoughts, feelings, and behavior.

Key Verses:
Jeremiah 7:5-7
Romans 12:2

See Also:
Attitude
Character

Repentance
Transform

**Cannot change
God's decree**
Numbers 23:19-20

**God does not
change His mind**
1 Samuel 15:29
Hebrews 7:21

**In priesthood
and law**
Hebrews 7:11-12

**Of laughter to
mourning**
James 4:9

Of mind
Exodus 13:17

Of residence
Genesis 12:1
Deuteronomy 1:6-7

Of wicked ways
Psalm 55:19
Jeremiah 7:5-7
Jeremiah 13:23
Zechariah 1:4

Character

Definition:
Moral values, traits,
and features that dis-
tinguish one person
from another.

Key Verses:
Isaiah 29:13
1 Peter 2:12

See Also:
Ethics and Integrity
Identity
Morality

Actions show
Proverbs 20:11
Isaiah 32:8
Matthew 7:18-20

Based on the heart
Proverbs 27:19
Romans 2:28-29

Blessed are the gentle
Matthew 5:5

Desired by God
Psalm 51:6
Micah 6:8

Fruit of the Spirit
Galatians 5:22-23

God honoring
Genesis 6:9
Job 1:8
Psalm 7:8
Psalm 15:2
Psalm 26:1
Psalm 106:3
Ezekiel 18:5-9
John 1:47
Romans 12:17
Romans 16:19
2 Corinthians 1:12
Ephesians 5:1-2
Philippians 2:14-15

Of God
Jeremiah 17:10

Of the wicked
1 Samuel 24:13
Psalm 10:2-4
Jeremiah 5:1
2 Timothy 3:2-4

Of wisdom
Proverbs 31:10-31

**Relationship to
bad influences**
1 Corinthians 15:33

Relationship to faith
Habakkuk 2:4

**Relationship
to worship**
Psalm 5:5

Renewal of
Ephesians 4:22

Suffering produces
Romans 5:3-4

Charity

Definition:
Benevolence, good
will, or love expressed
through helping those
who are in need.

Key Verses:
1 Timothy 5:16
James 1:27

See Also:
Hospitality
Love
Poverty

Consistent practice
Acts 9:36
Acts 10:2

For the poor
Proverbs 28:27
Acts 11:27-30
Romans 15:26-27
Galatians 2:10

Pleasing to God
Proverbs 19:17
Isaiah 58:3-7
Acts 10:4

Practice of godly wife
Proverbs 31:20

Toward fellow believers
Acts 4:32-35

Chastening

Definition:
Training or discipline intended to develop a certain attitude or behavior.

Key Verses:
Psalm 118:18
Hebrews 12:5-7

See Also:
Discipline
Parenting
Reproof

Cheating

Definition:
Defrauding, tricking, or depriving through dishonest means; being sexually unfaithful.

Key Verses:
Proverbs 20:23
Luke 19:8

See Also:
Adultery
Dishonesty
Lying
Stealing

Condemned
Psalm 62:10
2 Corinthians 7:2
1 Thessalonians 4:6

Dishonest business practices
Leviticus 19:13
Leviticus 19:35
Proverbs 11:1
Proverbs 20:10
Proverbs 20:14
Proverbs 20:23
Jeremiah 22:13
Hosea 12:7
Malachi 3:5

God judges
Amos 8:5-7
Micah 6:10-11
James 5:4

Honesty commanded
Deuteronomy 25:13

Lying to God
Acts 5:2-4

Robbing God
Malachi 3:8-9

Child Abuse

Definition:
Intentional harm or maltreatment of a child.

Key Verses:
Matthew 18:6
Matthew 19:14

See Also:
Childhood Sexual
  Abuse
Children
Parenting
Victimization

Brother sold
Genesis 37:12-36

Children bought and sold
Joel 3:3

Death of children by the wicked
Matthew 2:13-18

During wartime
Isaiah 13:16

Willing to kill child
Genesis 22:9-12
1 Kings 3:16-27

Child Evangelism

Definition:
Sharing with a child the good news of forgiveness through a relationship with Jesus Christ.

Key Verses:
Psalm 78:4, 6-7
Matthew 18:3

See Also:
Evangelism
Gospel
Salvation

A child is known by his actions
Proverbs 20:11

Answer skeptics with reason and grace
1 Peter 3:15

Ask God for wisdom
James 1:5

Be filled with the Word of God
Colossians 3:16

Believe in Jesus for eternal life
Matthew 18:3
John 3:16-18
Romans 10:13

Christ died for sins
1 Corinthians 15:2-4
1 Peter 3:18

Christ is perfect and removes sin
1 John 3:5

Christ removes condemnation
Romans 8:1

Come near to God
James 4:8

Confess sins to God for forgiveness
1 John 1:9

Encouraged by Jesus
Mark 10:13-16

Eternal life is found in Christ
John 11:25-26

Everyone is sinful
Isaiah 53:6

Failure to do good is sin
James 4:17

Faith in Christ and His resurrection brings salvation
Romans 10:9

God is love
1 John 4:16

God will complete what He begins
Philippians 1:6

God's Word provides direction
Psalm 119:105

Importance of
Psalm 51:5
Psalm 78:2-7
Proverbs 22:6
2 Timothy 1:5
2 Timothy 3:14-15

Love for God
Deuteronomy 6:5

Love of God
1 John 4:19

Loving Christ brings joy
1 Peter 1:8

Power of the gospel
Romans 1:16
Romans 10:14

Role of Scripture in
2 Timothy 3:16

Sinful from birth
Psalm 58:3

Sin hides us from God
Isaiah 59:2

Teach children about God's commands
Deuteronomy 6:5-9

The elder should be an example for the younger
Titus 2:7-8

The elder should mentor the younger
Titus 2:4

The Lord's love is everlasting
Jeremiah 31:3

The Spirit is our guide to truth
John 16:13

The Biblical Counseling Reference Guide

To enter God's kingdom become like a child
Matthew 18:1-4

Trust in God
Proverbs 3:5-6

Child Training

Definition:
The process of developing and directing the attitudes, values, and behavior of a child.

Key Verses:
Proverbs 22:6
Colossians 3:21

See Also:
Children
Discipleship
Parenting
Responsibility

Need for corporal discipline
Proverbs 13:24
Proverbs 22:15
Proverbs 23:13-14
Proverbs 29:15

Teach God's Word to children
Genesis 18:19
Exodus 12:26-27
Exodus 13:14-15
Deuteronomy 6:7
Deuteronomy 11:18-19

Childhood Sexual Abuse

Definition:
Any physical, visual, or verbal interaction with a minor by an older person whose purpose is sexual stimulation or sexual satisfaction.

Key Verses:
Psalm 82:3
Isaiah 12:2

See Also:
Abuse
Incest
Molestation
Rape
Victimization

Anguish of the psalmist
Psalm 55:4-5

Deliverance for victims
Psalm 10:14

Do not take revenge
Romans 12:19

Do not trust the wicked
Proverbs 26:24-26

Evil actions come from an evil heart
Mark 7:21-22

Evil and good happen to the just and unjust
Matthew 5:45

Forgiveness of oppressors
Matthew 6:14-15
Mark 11:25
Luke 17:4-5

God can bring consolation
Psalm 94:19

God cares about each child
Psalm 27:10
Matthew 18:10-14

God has good plans for you
Jeremiah 29:11

God heals broken lives
Psalm 30:2

God is near the brokenhearted
Psalm 34:18

God's compassion never fails
Lamentations 3:22-23

God's love is everlasting
Jeremiah 31:3

God will execute justice
Psalm 55:1-23

God will take care of you
Jeremiah 30:17

Importance of forgiveness
Ephesians 4:32

Justice must be executed for all
Proverbs 14:12
Proverbs 18:15
Proverbs 21:15

Overcome effects of abuse through new creation
2 Corinthians 5:17

Perpetrators of crimes should be punished
Deuteronomy 22:25-26

Sexual relations are regulated by God
Leviticus 18:6-18

The Lord brings justice
Psalm 9:12
Psalm 9:18
Psalm 72:2

The Lord cares for victims
Psalm 10:17
Psalm 22:24

The Lord is salvation
Isaiah 12:2

The Lord will guide and protect you
Isaiah 58:11

Treat others with respect
Matthew 7:12

Trust in God
1 Peter 5:7

Childlessness

Definition:
The state of not having any children, either by choice or as a result of infertility.

Key Verses:
1 Samuel 1:8, 10
Galatians 4:27

See Also:
Adoption
Barren
Infertility

As a judgment
2 Samuel 6:20-23

Divine intervention in pregnancy and
Genesis 15:2-4
Genesis 16:1-4
Genesis 18:13-14
Genesis 20:17-18
Genesis 21:1-3
Genesis 29:31
Genesis 30:1-2
Genesis 30:22
1 Samuel 1:1-20
Luke 1:5-7
Luke 1:24-25

Leads to desperate action
Genesis 16:1-5
Genesis 30:1-4

No memory preserved without children
2 Samuel 18:18

Children

Definition:
Boys and girls who have not reached the age of adolescence.

Key Verses:
Psalm 127:3
Proverbs 17:6

See Also:
Blended Family
Dysfunctional Family
Parenting

Abuse of
Mark 9:42

Adoption of
Esther 2:7

A promise for
Acts 2:38-39

As a blessing
Genesis 18:10
Judges 13:3
Psalm 113:9
Psalm 127:3
Proverbs 17:6
Zechariah 8:5
Luke 1:13

Belong to the Lord
Numbers 3:11-13

Blessing on
Mark 10:13-16

Dedicated to the Lord
Luke 1:14-15

Formation of
Jeremiah 1:4-5

God's heart for
Psalm 27:10
Matthew 11:25
Matthew 18:10
Mark 10:14
Luke 18:15-17

Grief from
Proverbs 10:1
Proverbs 17:21

Honor for parents
Deuteronomy 5:16
Deuteronomy 27:16
Proverbs 1:8
Proverbs 6:20
Proverbs 23:22
Matthew 15:4
Ephesians 6:1-4
Colossians 3:20

Hostility toward parents
Mark 13:12

Importance of teaching
Exodus 12:26-27
Deuteronomy 4:10
Deuteronomy 6:6-7

Deuteronomy 11:18-19
Psalm 78:1-8
Proverbs 22:6
Ephesians 6:4
2 Timothy 3:15

In the kingdom of heaven
Matthew 19:13-15

Listen to wisdom
Proverbs 8:32

Spiritual children
Ephesians 5:1
3 John 4

To honor parents
Exodus 20:12

Choice

Definition:
The freedom or ability to make a decision or selection.

Key Verses:
Joshua 24:15
John 15:16

See Also:
Decision Making
Responsibility

By God
Deuteronomy 7:6
1 Corinthians 1:26
1 Thessalonians 1:4
James 2:5

Divine wisdom in
1 Kings 3:9

God is sovereign over
Proverbs 16:9

In giving
Exodus 35:20-29

Of life or death
Jeremiah 21:8-9

Responsibility for
Deuteronomy 11:26-28
Joshua 24:15
Isaiah 65:12
Amos 5:15
John 3:36
1 Corinthians 4:21

To believe in Christ
John 1:12

To follow God
Ruth 1:16
1 Kings 18:21
1 Kings 18:39

To follow truth
Psalm 119:30

To heal
Mark 1:41

Chronic Illness

Definition:
A disease or persistent, unhealthy condition of the body that lingers over a long period of time.

Key Verses:
Romans 8:18
2 Corinthians 12:9

See Also:
Caregiving
Evil and Suffering
Terminal Illness

Affliction glorifies God
John 9:1-3
2 Corinthians 12:9
James 1:2-4
1 Peter 1:6-7

Affliction teaches obedience to God
Psalm 119:28
Psalm 119:67
Psalm 119:71

Christ's strength is shown in weakness
2 Corinthians 12:7-10

Endurance of trials
James 1:12

Experiencing pain
Jeremiah 15:18
Luke 22:42-44

God gives comfort
2 Corinthians 1:3-4

God gives strength
Isaiah 40:29
Isaiah 40:31

God heals
Psalm 147:3

God hears our complaints
Psalm 56:8

God may allow suffering
Mark 14:36

Guard against bitterness
Hebrews 12:15

Hope in
Romans 8:18

Jesus performs miracles
Matthew 9:20-22

Prayer in
Psalm 22:24
2 Corinthians 12:7-9
1 John 5:14-15

Redemption in
2 Corinthians 4:16-18

Rejoice in suffering
1 Peter 4:13-14

Sin leads to affliction
1 Corinthians 11:27-30

Suffering expected
John 16:33

Suffering of Jesus
1 Peter 4:1-2

Thanksgiving in
1 Thessalonians 5:18

Church

Definition:
The local or global community of believers in Jesus Christ.

Key Verses:
Colossians 1:18
1 Timothy 3:15

See Also:
Discipleship
God
Worship

Based on the foundation of Jesus Christ
1 Corinthians 3:11

Body of Christ
Ephesians 5:23
Colossians 1:18

Cared for by Christ
Ephesians 5:29

Discipline in
1 Corinthians 5:1-5

Diversity in
Romans 12:4-5
1 Corinthians 12:12

Gifts in
Romans 12:6-8
Ephesians 4:11-12
1 Timothy 4:13-14
1 Peter 4:10-11

God's household
1 Timothy 3:15
1 Peter 2:5

Growth of
Acts 16:5
Ephesians 4:15-16
Colossians 2:19

Happiness of
Psalm 84:4

Holy sanctuary
Ephesians 2:21

Leadership in
Acts 14:23
Ephesians 4:11-16
1 Timothy 3:1-13

**Members of
one another**
1 Corinthians
12:12-27
Ephesians 4:25

Practices of
Acts 2:42-47
Hebrews 10:24-25

**Purchased through
Christ's death**
Acts 20:28

Reconciliation in
Galatians 6:1
Ephesians 2:14

True religion
James 1:27

Unity in
John 10:16
1 Corinthians 10:17
Ephesians 4:4
Ephesians 4:13

Clean

Definition:
Free from dirt, disease,
or pollution.

Key Verses:
Psalm 24:3-4
Matthew 23:25-26

See Also:
Character
Holiness
Purity

Act of hospitality
Genesis 18:4
Genesis 19:2
Genesis 43:24
John 13:5
John 13:14-16

Free from wickedness
Job 17:9

Law regulations
Leviticus 13:6
Leviticus 14:8-9
Numbers 8:7

Of heart
Psalm 24:3-4
Psalm 51:10
Hebrews 10:22

**Preparation
for worship**
Genesis 35:2
Hebrews 10:22

Coaching

Definition:
Teaching relationship
for the purpose of life
skills development
or motivation and
techniques to effect
change.

Key Verses:
Proverbs 9:9
1 Corinthians 4:14-16

See Also:
Discipleship
Mentoring
Train

Be an encourager
Deuteronomy 1:38
Deuteronomy 3:28
1 Thessalonians 3:2

**Calls for an attitude
of service**
Matthew 20:25-28
1 Peter 5:2-3

Demands hard work
1 Thessalonians 2:9

**Offers appropriate
correction**
Acts 18:24-26

**Perceives unseen
potential**
Acts 9:26-27

**Provides direction
with gentleness**
Matthew 11:28-30
1 Thessalonians
2:7-8

Requires confidence
1 Corinthians 4:16

Codependency

Definition:
A relationship addic-
tion in which both

partners exhibit, foster, and excuse unhealthy or unreasonable behavior in each other.

Key Verses:
Jeremiah 17:5-8
Galatians 1:10

See Also:
Addiction
Dependency

**Abide in Christ
to produce fruit**
John 15:5

**Answer skeptics with
reason and grace**
1 Peter 3:15

**Believers should
continually mature**
Hebrews 5:12
Hebrews 6:1

**Confront those who
make mistakes**
Matthew 18:15-17

**Do not put anyone
in God's place**
Exodus 20:3

**Don't be squeezed
into the world's mold**
Romans 12:2

**Israel relied on
themselves rather
than God**
Jeremiah 2:13

Love God supremely
Deuteronomy 6:5

**Maintain a
balanced life**
Ecclesiastes 7:18

**Make God
your helper**
Psalm 146:5

**Make pleasing
God your goal**
2 Corinthians 5:9

Make wise friends
Proverbs 13:20

**Please God
not people**
Galatians 1:10

**Repentance of
Israel predicted**
Ezekiel 6:9

**Respond with grace
to those who fail**
Galatians 6:1

**The Lord will guide
and provide for you**
Isaiah 58:11

**The Lord will
never forsake you**
Psalm 27:10

Trust in God
Psalm 20:7
Psalm 62:7-8
Jeremiah 17:5-7

Cognitive-Behavioral Therapy

Definition:
Approach to psychotherapy that emphasizes how changing thought patterns and processes alter behavior.

Key Verses:
Romans 12:2
Philippians 4:8

See Also:
Coaching
Counseling
Thoughts

Comfort

Definition:
To soothe and express care in times of trouble.

Key Verses:
Psalm 119:50
2 Corinthians 1:3-4

See Also:
Peace
Prosperity
Safety

For those who mourn
Matthew 5:4

From Christ
Matthew 11:28-30
Luke 7:13
John 14:1

John 16:33
2 Corinthians 1:3-4
2 Thessalonians
2:16-17
Revelation 7:17

From God
Psalm 86:17
Psalm 103:1-22
Isaiah 40:11
Isaiah 51:3
Isaiah 66:13
Lamentations 3:22
Jonah 4:6
2 Thessalonians
2:16-17
2 Thessalonians 3:16

From the Holy Spirit
John 14:15-27

From the Scriptures
Romans 15:4

In difficult times
Psalm 23:4

In hope
Isaiah 35:10
John 14:1-4
2 Corinthians 4:7-18
1 Thessalonians
4:13-18

In suffering
Romans 8:18-39

Purpose for
2 Corinthians 1:3-7

Commitment

Definition:
A pledge, promise, or

agreement to maintain association with a person or thing.

Key Verses:
Exodus 34:6-7
Proverbs 3:3

See Also:
Dependability
Love
Loyalty
Marriage

Reason for
2 Timothy 2:10

Reward for
Mark 8:35

Role in suffering
1 Peter 4:19

To Christ
Matthew 4:20-22
Matthew 8:19
Mark 1:16-20
Luke 9:23
1 Corinthians
15:30-31
Galatians 2:20

To faith
1 Corinthians
9:24-27

To God
Joshua 24:14
Ecclesiastes 5:4
Acts 21:10-14
Romans 12:1
2 Corinthians 6:3-13
Philippians 2:17

To God's people
Romans 1:11-12
2 Corinthians 8:5
1 Thessalonians
2:8-9

To idolatry
Jeremiah 44:24-30

To love
Song of Songs 6:3
Song of Songs 8:6

To obedience
Deuteronomy 5:1
Joshua 24:15

To the Lord
Genesis 22:1-14

Unto death
2 Timothy 4:6

Communication

Definition:
Transmission and reception or exchange of information through words, signs, symbols, or behavior.

Key Verses:
Proverbs 15:23
Ephesians 4:29

See Also:
Intimacy
Prayer

Acceptable to God
Psalm 19:14

Anger creates conflict
Proverbs 15:18

Become attached to love and faithfulness
Proverbs 3:3

Confess sins
Proverbs 28:13

Confidence in
John 7:45-46

Continue to maturity
1 Corinthians 13:11

Controlling
Psalm 141:3
Proverbs 10:19
Proverbs 13:3

Difficulty in
Exodus 4:10

Do not sin with your anger
Ephesians 4:26

Encouragement in
Job 33:2-3
Proverbs 15:4
Proverbs 16:24
Ecclesiastes 10:12
1 Thessalonians 5:11

God enables us to speak
Exodus 4:10-12
Isaiah 50:4
Jeremiah 1:6-10
Matthew 10:18-20

Godly speech
1 Peter 4:11

Honesty in
John 16:25-30
Ephesians 4:15
Ephesians 4:25

Importance of listening
Proverbs 1:5
Proverbs 11:12
Proverbs 13:10
Proverbs 15:31
Proverbs 17:28
James 1:19

Judgment comes to fools
Proverbs 10:13

Live by love
1 Corinthians 13:1-7

Lying condemned
Exodus 20:16
Proverbs 12:22
Colossians 3:9-10

Misuse of
Proverbs 11:9
Proverbs 11:13
Proverbs 18:21
Proverbs 26:24
Matthew 12:34
Luke 6:43-45
Ephesians 4:29
2 Timothy 2:14

Of God
Psalm 107:20
Isaiah 55:11

Opposition to
Ezekiel 3:4-9

Proclaim God's message
2 Timothy 4:2
1 Peter 3:15

Teach others
Colossians 3:16-17

Wisdom in
Proverbs 2:11-12
Proverbs 12:18
Proverbs 15:23
Proverbs 16:23
Proverbs 25:11
Ecclesiastes 3:7

With God
Jeremiah 33:3

Companion

Definition:
A person who associates with or accompanies another.

Key Verses:
Proverbs 13:20
Proverbs 18:24

See Also:
Friendship
Marriage

Avoid evil companions
Psalm 1:1
Proverbs 13:20
Proverbs 24:1
2 Thessalonians 3:14

Benefit of
Ecclesiastes 4:9

Desire for
1 John 1:3

Fellowship offered
Galatians 2:9

Forsaken by
Psalm 55:12-14
2 Timothy 4:9-10

With the godly
Psalm 119:63
Proverbs 2:20

Compassion

Definition:
Awareness of and sympathy with another's suffering with the desire to alleviate it.

Key Verses:
Psalm 116:5
Mark 6:34

See Also:
Caregiving
Counseling
Kindness

Ability to sympathize
Hebrews 4:15

Carry another's burdens
Galatians 6:2

For believers
2 Corinthians 2:4
1 John 3:11-24

For enemies
Luke 6:34-35

For neighbors
Leviticus 19:18
James 2:8
1 Peter 3:8

For the needy
2 Samuel 9:1-13
2 Chronicles 28:15
Psalm 41:1
Proverbs 19:17
Matthew 9:36
Mark 6:34
Luke 10:30-37
Luke 14:1-14
Romans 15:1

For unbelievers
Romans 9:1-4

From unbelievers
Acts 27:3
Acts 28:2

Grieve with others
Psalm 35:13

Lack of
Proverbs 21:13

Need for
Job 6:14

Of God
Exodus 3:7
Psalm 78:38
Psalm 86:15
Psalm 119:156
Isaiah 54:10
Jeremiah 31:3
Lamentations 3:22-23
Lamentations 3:31-33

Of Jesus
Matthew 23:37
Mark 1:40-41
Luke 13:34
Luke 19:41-44

Show affection
Romans 12:10

Competition

Definition:
Striving against a rival toward a mutual goal.

Key Verses:
2 Corinthians 10:3
Ephesians 6:12

See Also:
Disagreement
Opposition
Strife

Condemned
2 Corinthians 10:12

Greatness through humility
Matthew 18:4
Matthew 23:11
Luke 22:26

In ministry
Philippians 1:15

In the family
1 Samuel 1:6-7

Spiritual
1 Corinthians 9:24-27

Complain

Definition:
To express discontent, either peaceably and respectfully or in a harsh, peevish manner.

Key Verses:
Psalm 142:2
Philippians 2:14-15

See Also:
Critical Spirit
Grumbling

Against leaders
Exodus 16:2
Exodus 17:3
Numbers 14:2
Joshua 9:18

Commandment against
1 Corinthians 10:10
Philippians 2:14
James 5:9
Jude 16

Connection with bitterness
Job 10:1
Job 23:2

To God
Psalm 13:1-6
Psalm 64:1
Psalm 142:2
Habakkuk 1:2

Compromise

Definition:
Settlement in a dispute through mutual concession.

Key Verses:
Matthew 5:25
Matthew 6:24

See Also:
Agreeable
Ethics and Integrity

Danger of
1 Samuel 15:9-15

Desire to
Isaiah 30:10-11

Financial
Matthew 6:24

From false teaching
Revelation 2:20

Incomplete obedience
1 Kings 22:43
2 Kings 14:1-4
2 Kings 15:1-4
2 Chronicles 25:2

In leadership
1 Kings 11:8
2 Kings 14:4

Judgment for
2 Chronicles 19:2
Isaiah 5:20
Ezekiel 20:32-38

With idolatry
2 Kings 17:33

Compulsion

Definition:
A repetitive, controlling, often irresistible desire to act against one's better judgment.

Key Verses:
Proverbs 29:11
2 Corinthians 5:14

See Also:
Addiction
Habits

Abstinence from fleshly desires
Romans 13:14
Galatians 5:24
Ephesians 4:22-24
Colossians 3:5
Titus 2:12
1 Peter 2:11

Avoid overeating
Proverbs 23:20

Following Christ
Matthew 16:24-25
Mark 8:34-35
Luke 5:11
Luke 9:23-24
Luke 14:26-27
Luke 14:33
Philippians 3:8

Offer yourself to God
Romans 6:12-13

Personal discipline
1 Corinthians 9:27

Self-control encouraged
Titus 2:2
2 Peter 1:5-7

Compulsive Eating

Definition:
Regular episodes of uncontrolled eating in an attempt to numb emotional needs.

Key Verses:
Proverbs 23:20
1 Thessalonians 4:4

See Also:
Anorexia
Bulimia
Dependency
Gluttony
Overeating
Self-Control

Control your appetite
Proverbs 25:27-28

Do everything for God's glory
1 Corinthians 10:31

Do not be controlled by anything
1 Corinthians 6:12

Do not worry about food
Matthew 6:25

Leads to poverty
Proverbs 23:20-21

Stomach is their god
Philippians 3:19

Warning against
Proverbs 25:16

Conceit

Definition:
Overinflated or vain opinion of one's value, ability, or appearance.

Key Verses:
Isaiah 10:15
Galatians 5:26

See Also:
Arrogance
Boasting
Pride
Self-Exaltation

Characteristic of the ungodly
2 Timothy 3:4

Condemned
Proverbs 3:7
Proverbs 28:26
Jeremiah 9:23-24
Romans 12:16
1 Timothy 6:3-5

God humbles the proud
2 Samuel 22:28
Nehemiah 6:16
Isaiah 2:12-17
Isaiah 3:16-17
Isaiah 16:6-7
Revelation 18:7-8

Hinders wisdom
Proverbs 12:15
Proverbs 14:6
Proverbs 26:12

Spiritual pride
Luke 18:11-12
Romans 11:20-21

Condemnation

Definition:
Remaining under the righteous wrath of God because of sin.

Key Verses:
Mark 16:16
John 3:18

See Also:
Critical Spirit
Eternal Security
Forgiveness

By God
Hebrews 10:29-31

Discipline prevents
1 Corinthians 11:32

For pride
1 Timothy 3:6

No escaping
Matthew 23:33

Of Jesus
Mark 3:2

Of the wicked
Amos 1:3-13
Amos 2:1-6
Mark 16:16

John 3:18
John 3:36
Romans 9:28

Overcoming
John 5:22-24
Romans 5:18-21
Romans 8:1

Confess

Definition:
To proclaim as true;
used especially of
acknowledging sin
to God or proclaim-
ing the deity of Jesus
Christ to men.

Key Verses:
Leviticus 5:5
1 John 1:9

See Also:
Contrite
Repentance
Salvation

Benefits of
Leviticus 26:40-42
Proverbs 28:13
James 5:16
1 John 1:9

Commanded
Leviticus 5:5

Fear of
John 12:42

Of Jesus' lordship
Romans 14:11
Philippians 2:10-11

Of the gospel
2 Corinthians 9:13
1 Timothy 6:12

**Relationship
to baptism**
Matthew 3:6
Mark 1:5

**Relationship
to salvation**
Romans 10:9-10

Confidence

Definition:
Trust in or assurance
of the ability of some-
one or something.

Key Verses:
Jeremiah 17:7
Philippians 3:3

See Also:
Assurance of Salvation
Attitude
Hope

**Based on Christ's
faithfulness**
Romans 8:37-39

Based on love
1 John 3:16-24

**Folly of self-
confidence**
Proverbs 28:26

From God
Genesis 15:1
2 Corinthians 3:4-5
2 Timothy 1:7

In Christ
John 6:20
John 14:1
Philippians 4:13
Hebrews 13:6

In eternal life
2 Corinthians 5:1-7

In God
Joshua 1:9
1 Samuel 17:32-37
Job 42:2
Psalm 20:7
Psalm 118:6-9
Proverbs 3:5
Proverbs 3:26
Proverbs 14:26
Jeremiah 1:17-18

In God's faithfulness
Lamentations
3:22-26

In God's power
Psalm 18:29
Jeremiah 32:17

In God's protection
Psalm 3:6-7
Psalm 9:9-10
Psalm 13:5-6
Psalm 27:1
Proverbs 29:25

In God's provision
Psalm 37:7-11
Daniel 3:16-18

In God's reward
Isaiah 49:4

In leadership
Joshua 1:18

The Biblical Counseling Reference Guide

In obedience
Joshua 1:7

In riches
Proverbs 11:28
Jeremiah 48:7

In temptation
Hebrews 4:14-16

In times of danger
Psalm 27:3
Isaiah 36:13-21

Results of
Jeremiah 17:7-8

Reward for
Hebrews 10:35

Conflict Resolution

Definition:
The process by which
disagreements are
settled or solved and
peace is restored.

Key Verses:
Proverbs 15:18
Romans 14:19

See Also:
Argue
Forgiveness
Quarrel
Restoration

Accept correction
Proverbs 15:12

Accept one another
Romans 15:7

Be a good listener
Proverbs 1:5

**Be careful with
your words**
Proverbs 12:18

Be slow to speak
Proverbs 11:12

Bitterness defiles
Hebrews 12:15

**Conflicting priorities
between siblings**
Luke 10:40-42

Confrontation in
Matthew 18:15-16
Galatians 2:11-21

**Cooperation
requires agreement**
Amos 3:3

**Destroying
each other**
Galatians 5:15

**Discipline produces
good effects**
Hebrews 12:11

Encourage each other
1 Thessalonians 5:11

Execute justice
Leviticus 19:15

**False teachers
create conflict**
Matthew 7:15

Forgiveness in
Colossians 3:13

Forgive others
Mark 11:25

From sinful desires
James 4:1

Gift from the Lord
Proverbs 16:7

**God has given
us all we need**
2 Peter 1:3

**Good friends
improve character**
Proverbs 27:17

Hate creates conflict
Proverbs 10:12

Importance of
2 Timothy 2:23

In the church
Matthew 18:15
1 Corinthians 6:1-8

**Increased conflict
from sin**
2 Samuel 12:7-9

**Jesus condemned
the Pharisees**
Matthew 23:13
Matthew 23:33

**Jesus forgave those
who crucified Him**
Luke 23:34

**Kind words
encourage**
Proverbs 12:25

Listen to rebuke
Proverbs 15:31
Proverbs 17:10

Live in peace
2 Corinthians 13:11

Live unselfishly
Philippians 2:3-4

**Living in peace
with others**
Romans 12:18
Romans 14:19
Ephesians 4:3

Love commanded
1 Peter 1:22
1 Peter 3:8
1 John 3:11
1 John 3:23

Love for enemies
Matthew 5:44

Love is unselfish
1 Corinthians 13:5

Love one another
Romans 13:8

Love your enemies
Luke 6:27-36

**Our sin creates
conflict with God**
Isaiah 59:2

**Paul experienced
conflict and hardship**
2 Corinthians 6:3-10

**Person's actions
reveal his sin**
Mark 7:15

**Please God rather
than men**
Galatians 1:10

Reconciling
Matthew 5:23-24
Luke 12:58

**Repay evil with
blessing**
1 Peter 3:9

**Seeking
reconciliation**
Matthew 5:23-24

**Seeking
understanding**
Proverbs 18:2

Speak gently
Proverbs 15:1

Speak with integrity
Psalm 37:30
Matthew 5:37

Spiritual
2 Corinthians 10:3-4
1 Timothy 1:18
1 Timothy 6:12

**There is a time
for everything**
Ecclesiastes 3:1-8

**The Spirit produces
good fruit**
Galatians 5:22-23

**The tongue is
powerful**
Proverbs 18:21

Through blessing
Romans 12:14

Through doing good
Romans 12:20-21

**Trust God rather
than fearing men**
Proverbs 29:25

Vengeance prohibited
Romans 12:17-19

**Well spoken word
is priceless**
Proverbs 25:11

Within leadership
Acts 15:36-41

With speech
Ephesians 4:29

Conform

Definition:
To change shape or
perspective; to fall
into agreement with
another.

Key Verses:
Romans 8:29
Romans 12:2

See Also:
Friendship
Obedience
Worldly

Confrontation

Definition:
Opposing or encounter-

ing a person in order to resolve disharmony; exposing what is wrong with the goal of establishing truth in order to convict, correct, or change.

Key Verses:
Matthew 18:15-17
Galatians 6:1-2

See Also:
Admonition
Conflict Resolution
Opposition
Reconciliation

Accept confrontation from God
Proverbs 3:11
Hebrews 12:5-6

Accept correction
Proverbs 12:1

Accept positive confrontation
Proverbs 13:18
Proverbs 15:31

A mocker refuses confrontation
Proverbs 15:12

A wise man increases in wisdom from
Proverbs 9:9

A wise son accepts his father's correction
Proverbs 13:1

Be a good listener
James 1:19

Between believers
1 Corinthians 6:1-7

Confrontation demonstrates love
Proverbs 27:5

Confronted by the Word
Colossians 3:16

Confronting an evil person creates
Proverbs 9:7

Confront with the Word
2 Timothy 4:2

Control your tongue
Ephesians 4:29

Don't argue
2 Timothy 2:23

Encourage each other
1 Thessalonians 5:11-14

Failure to do good is sin
James 4:17

Failure to observe rebuke leads to ruin
Proverbs 29:1

Forgive each other
Colossians 3:13

Gentleness in
Galatians 6:1

God confronts Job
Job 38:2

God disciplines His children
Hebrews 12:10

Importance of
Proverbs 13:18

Jesus confronts Peter
Mark 8:33

Jesus confronts unjust accusers
John 8:7-10

Jesus responds to Peter's confrontation
Matthew 16:22-26

Judge yourself
Matthew 7:3

Keep a clear conscience
Acts 24:16

Live by justice
Zechariah 7:9

Live peacefully
Romans 14:19

Live peacefully and allow God to execute
Romans 12:17-19

Love your enemies
Matthew 5:44

Nathan confronted David
2 Samuel 12:1-13

Of a sinning believer
Matthew 18:15
James 5:19-20

Please God rather than men
Galatians 1:10

Positive confrontation contributes to life
Proverbs 6:23

Rebuke is better than flattery
Proverbs 28:23

Speak graciously
Colossians 4:6

Speak with integrity
Ephesians 4:25-26

Wisdom comes from the discerning
Proverbs 16:21

Wisdom from
Proverbs 9:8
Proverbs 12:15
Proverbs 15:32
Proverbs 27:6

Confusion

Definition:
The state of being perplexed or disordered in one's thinking.

Key Verses:
Job 25:2
1 Corinthians 14:33

See Also:
Discernment
Doubt
Indecision

Confusion without guidance
Psalm 82:5

Lord removes confusion
Psalm 107:27-28

Result of drunkenness
Isaiah 28:7

Result of God's judgment
Isaiah 19:14
Ezekiel 7:26-27

Result of lies
Acts 15:24

Conscience

Definition:
The ability, faculty, or power to determine right from wrong and act according to one's discernment.

Key Verses:
Acts 24:16
1 Corinthians 4:4

See Also:
Guilt
Integrity
Thoughts

Before God
Luke 5:8
Acts 23:1

Benefits of
2 Corinthians 7:10-13

Clean conscience
Job 27:6
1 Corinthians 8:12
1 Timothy 1:19
1 Timothy 3:9
Hebrews 9:9
Hebrews 9:14
Hebrews 10:22
Hebrews 13:18

Condemning heart
1 John 3:19-20

Conviction by
Matthew 27:3
Acts 2:37
Romans 2:15

Defiled
Titus 1:15

From God
Ecclesiastes 3:11

Guilty
Psalm 38:4

Importance in worship
Matthew 5:23-24

Obedience to
Romans 2:13-15
2 Corinthians 4:2

Overly sensitive
1 Corinthians
10:27-29

Over sexual sin
Ezra 9:6

Seared
Proverbs 30:20
Jeremiah 6:15
1 Timothy 4:2

Sensitivity to
Romans 14:3
Romans 14:15

Toward God and men
Acts 24:16

Violating
1 Corinthians 8:7-13

Consequences

Definition:
Necessary effects or
results of a given cause
or condition.

Key Verses:
Ezra 9:13
Romans 6:23

See Also:
Condemnation
Justice
Punishment

**Of breaking
God's law**
Romans 2:9

Of delayed judgment
Ecclesiastes 8:11

Of disobedience
Joshua 7:11-12
1 Chronicles 10:13

Of giving
Luke 6:38

Of good and evil
Proverbs 11:19

**Of neglecting
salvation**
Hebrews 2:3

Of obedience
Genesis 22:15-18
Deuteronomy
6:18-19

Of repentance
1 Kings 21:29

Of sin
Genesis 2:17
Psalm 66:18
Proverbs 11:21
Proverbs 13:21
Isaiah 59:2
Romans 5:12
Romans 6:23

Of suffering
Matthew 5:10-12

Contentment

Definition:
The state of being sat-
isfied with what one
has or being joyful in
one's circumstances.

Key Verses:
Proverbs 19:23
Hebrews 13:5

See Also:
Joy
Materialism
Peace
Prosperity

Benefits of
Psalm 37:16
Proverbs 15:16

**Better than
prosperity**
Psalm 37:16-17

**Can't be found
in money**
Ecclesiastes 5:10

**Do not be jealous
of the wicked**
Proverbs 23:17

**Enjoy what God
gives you**
Ecclesiastes 3:12-13
Ecclesiastes 5:18-20
Ecclesiastes 8:15

From God
Psalm 103:5
Psalm 107:8-9

Importance of
Proverbs 30:7-9
Ecclesiastes 5:18
Philippians 4:11-12
1 Timothy 6:6

In every circumstance
Philippians 4:11-13

In God
Psalm 37:4
Psalm 84:10-12

Prayer for
Psalm 90:14

**With one's
social status**
1 Corinthians 7:17

With one's wages
Luke 3:14

With what one has
1 Timothy 6:6-8
Hebrews 13:5

Contrite

Definition:
Penitent or crushed
in spirit as a result of
one's sins.

Key Verses:
Psalm 51:17
Isaiah 57:15

See Also:
Change
Repentance
Sorrow

**Contrition
encouraged**
Joel 1:8
Joel 1:13
Joel 2:12
Matthew 5:4

God favors contrition
1 Kings 8:47-49
Psalm 51:17
Isaiah 30:15
Isaiah 57:15
Isaiah 66:2
Jeremiah 18:8

Joel 2:13
Luke 5:32

**Lack of contrition
for sin**
1 Corinthians 5:1-2

Leads to salvation
2 Corinthians 7:10

Controversy

Definition:
A prolonged (and usu-
ally public) discussion,
debate, or dispute.

Key Verses:
1 Timothy 2:8
Titus 3:9

See Also:
Disagreement
Quarrel
Strife

**Comes from
arrogance**
Proverbs 13:10

Comes from fear
Numbers 14:1-4

Comes from hatred
Proverbs 10:12

Leads to death
1 Kings 16:21-22

**Promoted by
the wicked**
1 Timothy 6:4

Sometimes worthless
Titus 3:9

Coping

Definition:
To successfully manage
and often achieve suc-
cess in spite of chal-
lenges, obstacles, and
disappointments.

Key Verses:
2 Corinthians 4:16-18
Philippians 4:12-13

See Also:
Grief
Hope
Stress
Suffering
Trials

Correction

Definition:
The act or process of
substituting something
right for something
wrong.

Key Verses:
Leviticus 26:23-24
Proverbs 12:1

See Also:
Change
Confrontation
Discipline
Rebuke

Blessing of
Job 5:17
Proverbs 27:5

By church leadership
2 Timothy 4:2

By God
Isaiah 65:6-7
Jeremiah 10:23-24
Hebrews 12:5-6

**Consequences
for rejecting**
Proverbs 10:17
Proverbs 15:10
Proverbs 29:1

**Importance
of heeding**
Psalm 141:5
Proverbs 12:1
Proverbs 25:12
Proverbs 27:9
Acts 18:24-26

Leads to blessing
Psalm 94:12

Leads to repentance
2 Corinthians 7:8-9

Of children
Proverbs 23:13

Poor example of
1 Samuel 2:22-25

Provide
Titus 2:15

Purpose of
Hebrews 12:7

Scripture provides
2 Timothy 3:16-17

Counseling

Definition:
The process of coach-
ing, advising, or help-
ing another.

Key Verses:
1 Kings 22:5
Proverbs 2:1-2, 5

See Also:
Compassion
Premarital Counseling

**Be filled with
the Word**
Colossians 3:16

Be humble
Ephesians 4:2
1 Peter 5:5

Be sympathetic
Romans 12:15

By Jesus
Isaiah 9:6
John 10:10

By the Holy Spirit
Isaiah 11:2
John 14:16-17
John 14:26

**Christ brings
freedom**
John 8:32-36

Comforting others
2 Corinthians 1:3-5
Galatians 6:2

**Correctly handle
the Word**
2 Timothy 2:15

Deliverance in Christ
Romans 7:24-25

Effects of
Proverbs 19:20

Encourage each other
1 Thessalonians 5:11

Goal of
James 5:19-20

God hears and saves
Psalm 145:19

God provides counsel
Psalm 16:7

**God searches
the heart**
Proverbs 21:2

God's provision
Philippians 4:19

God's Word in
Hebrews 4:12

Importance of
Psalm 1:1-2
Proverbs 2:1-11
Proverbs 15:22

Lack of
Ezekiel 7:26

Provide good advice
Proverbs 27:9

Respected advisor
2 Samuel 16:23

**Trust in the
Lord's guidance**
Proverbs 3:5-6

Walk in wisdom
Colossians 4:5-6

Wise speech from a wise heart
Proverbs 16:23

Courage

Definition:
State of mind that allows one to face danger with resolution, bravery, or determination.

Key Verses:
Deuteronomy 31:6
1 Corinthians 16:13

See Also:
Boldness
Hope

Based on God's protection
Exodus 14:13-14

Because of the Lord's faithfulness
1 Chronicles 28:20

Blessing for
Luke 21:19

From trusting in God
Joshua 1:9
Judges 7:7-23
1 Samuel 14:6-14
1 Samuel 17:46-51
Psalm 112:7-8
Isaiah 41:10
Jeremiah 1:17
1 Thessalonians 2:1-2
2 Timothy 1:7

In adversity
Psalm 3:6
Ezekiel 2:6-7
Acts 20:22-24
Ephesians 3:13
Philippians 1:27-30

In doing the Lord's work
1 Corinthians 15:58

In faith
1 Corinthians 16:13

In hope
Revelation 2:25

In prayer
Luke 18:1

Loss of
Joshua 5:1

Prayer for
Psalm 138:3
Acts 4:29

To follow Jesus
Matthew 14:22-31
Acts 21:13

To proclaim the gospel
Acts 14:3

To refuse idolatry
Daniel 3:8-18

Courting

Definition:
The process of attempting to gain someone's affection, attention, or favor; used especially of wooing for the purpose of marriage.

Key Verses:
Song of Songs 2:7
1 Corinthians 7:27-28

See Also:
Dating
Sexual Integrity

Counsel in
Proverbs 19:20

Honesty in
Ephesians 4:15

Importance of marriage
Genesis 2:18

Love in
1 Corinthians 13:4-7
1 John 4:7
1 John 4:11

Only court believers
2 Corinthians 6:14-15

Sacrifice for love
Genesis 29:20

Sexual integrity in
1 Thessalonians 4:3-7
Hebrews 13:4

Covenant

Definition:
A solemn and binding pact, agreement, or contract.

The Biblical Counseling Reference Guide

Key Verses:
Malachi 2:14
Hebrews 10:16

See Also:
Commitment
Marriage

Covet

Definition:
Excessive and blame-worthy desire to possess that which belongs to another.

Key Verses:
Exodus 20:17
Luke 12:15

See Also:
Envy and Jealousy
Greed
Lust
Materialism

Avoided by loving others
Romans 13:9

Can choke God's Word in the heart
Matthew 13:22

Condemned
Exodus 20:17
Deuteronomy 5:21
1 Timothy 3:3
Hebrews 13:5

Keeps many from salvation
Matthew 19:23

Leads to fighting
James 4:2

Leads to sin
Jeremiah 22:17

Never have enough wealth
Ecclesiastes 5:10

Possessions not a life goal
Luke 12:15

Cremation

Definition:
The process by which something (especially a dead body) is consumed by fire so as to reduce it to ashes.

Key Verses:
Ecclesiastes 12:7
1 Corinthians 15:42-44

See Also:
Burial
Death

As an act of defilement
1 Kings 13:1-2
2 Kings 23:16
2 Chronicles 34:5
Amos 2:1

As judgment
Leviticus 20:14
Joshua 7:15
Joshua 7:25

For dead royalty
1 Samuel 31:11-13

Pagan act of child sacrifice
2 Chronicles 28:3

Crime

Definition:
An act contrary to established law that warrants punishment.

Key Verses:
Romans 13:1
1 Peter 2:13-14

See Also:
Justice
Victimization
Violence

Assassination
Esther 2:21

Avoid criminals
Proverbs 1:10-16

Civil disagreements
1 Corinthians 6:1-6

Comes from evil heart
Matthew 15:19

Consequences of
Proverbs 1:18

Criminals do not inherit salvation
1 Corinthians 6:9-10

Government is God's servant to judge
Romans 13:1-4

Murder
Exodus 20:13

Power of the gospel over
1 Timothy 1:9-10

Punishment for
Genesis 6:11-13
Genesis 9:6
Psalm 64:6-7

Worsened by slow judgment
Ecclesiastes 8:11

Crisis

Definition:
A time of intense suspense, instability, or drama.

Key Verses:
Psalm 37:19
Proverbs 27:10

See Also:
Calamity
Disaster
Stress

As a result of sin
Jonah 1:3-4

Avoidance of
Proverbs 22:3
Proverbs 27:12

Fear in
Psalm 107:26

God is a refuge
Psalm 46:1
Psalm 64:1
Psalm 91:3

Seek help from friends
Proverbs 27:10

Should be expected in life
Job 2:9-10
James 1:2-3

Trusting Christ in
Luke 8:23-24
Romans 8:35
2 Corinthians 1:10

Wisdom in
Nehemiah 4:9

Critical Spirit

Definition:
An excessively negative attitude that consistently judges harshly, finds fault, and complains.

Key Verses:
Colossians 4:6
James 3:9-10

See Also:
Criticism

Accept each other
Romans 15:7

Be a good listener
Proverbs 20:5

Become mature
1 Corinthians 13:11

Be filled with the Word
Colossians 3:16

Be patient
Proverbs 19:11
Ecclesiastes 7:8

Between believers
James 4:1-2

Be unselfish
Philippians 2:3-4

Blessings for criticized
Matthew 5:11

Christ experienced opposition
Hebrews 12:2-3

Christ reconciles all
2 Corinthians 5:18-19

Condemned
Matthew 5:44
Luke 6:41
Philippians 2:1-2
Philippians 4:8

Consult the wise
Proverbs 15:12

Control of speech
Proverbs 10:19
Proverbs 15:1
Ephesians 4:29

The Biblical Counseling Reference Guide

Colossians 4:6

Control your tongue
Proverbs 15:4
Proverbs 17:27
James 3:1-12

Correction of
Matthew 18:15

Encourage each other
1 Thessalonians 5:11
Hebrews 3:13

Example of Christ
1 Peter 2:23-24

Fathers to children
Ephesians 6:4

Fitting words
Proverbs 10:32

Folly in
Matthew 7:3

Forgive each other
Colossians 3:13

Harmful effects of
Proverbs 12:18
Proverbs 18:21

Hypocrisy in
Romans 2:1
Romans 14:10

Ignore fools
Proverbs 27:3

Live by love
1 Peter 4:8

Live peacefully
Romans 14:19
1 Peter 3:8-9

Overcoming with good
Romans 12:21

Please God rather than men
1 Thessalonians 2:4

Provide instruction
Proverbs 16:21

Put on compassion
Colossians 3:12

Respond to criticism graciously
Romans 12:14

Speak with integrity
James 5:12

The tongue reveals the heart
Matthew 12:34-35

Criticism

Definition:
The act of analyzing and evaluating the faults and merits of something; used especially of finding fault with something.

Key Verses:
Romans 14:10
James 5:9

See Also:
Critical Spirit

Avoidance of
Romans 14:1

Benefits of heeding
Proverbs 15:31-32
Proverbs 27:6
Proverbs 28:23

Blessings for criticized
Matthew 5:11
Luke 6:22-23

Brings anger
Proverbs 15:1

Condemned
Luke 6:37
Luke 6:41
Romans 14:13
Titus 3:1-3
James 4:11-12
James 5:9

Control of speech
Colossians 4:6

Danger of
Job 6:24-25
James 3:6

From family
Mark 3:20-21

Harmful effects of
Psalm 52:2-4
Psalm 140:3
Proverbs 12:18
Proverbs 15:4
Proverbs 18:21

Hypocrisy in
Romans 2:1

Judge righteously
Matthew 7:1-5

Of leadership
Acts 6:1

Overcoming
1 Corinthians 4:3-4

Responding to
Job 16:1-5

Unjust
Matthew 11:18-19
Mark 2:6-12
Mark 3:1-6

Verbal
Job 19:2

Cross-Dressing

Definition:
Wearing clothing asso-
ciated or identified
with the opposite sex.

Key Verses:
Deuteronomy 22:5
Titus 2:11-12

See Also:
Homosexuality
Identity
Sexual Addiction

Cry

Definition:
To call out loudly,
often with tears.

Key Verses:
Psalm 40:1
Psalm 69:3

See Also:
Brokenhearted

Grief
Hopelessness
Sorrow

From a broken heart
Psalm 6:6-7
Jeremiah 4:19

God hears
Genesis 21:15-19
2 Samuel 22:7
Psalm 10:17
Psalm 40:1
Luke 18:7

Of Jesus
Mark 15:37
John 11:35

**When God
seems silent**
Job 30:20
Psalm 77:1, 7-9
Lamentations 3:8

Cults

Definition:
Sects that hold to
unorthodox or hereti-
cal doctrines while
normally exerting
extensive control over
members.

Key Verses:
John 1:1
2 Timothy 2:15

See Also:
Jehovah's Witness
Mormonism
Occult

Against false teaching
Colossians 2:8

**Answer skeptics with
grace and reason**
1 Peter 3:15

Be merciful
Jude 22

**Beware of false
prophets**
Matthew 7:15

**Condemning
witchcraft**
Deuteronomy
18:10-12

**Consulting the
dead and spirits**
Leviticus 19:31
Leviticus 20:6
Isaiah 8:19

Deception by demons
1 Timothy 4:1

False gospels
Galatians 1:6-8

False prophets
2 Peter 2:1

False teachers
2 Timothy 4:3

Freedom in Christ
Galatians 5:1

**Gospel is power
of God**
Romans 1:16

Idolatry
Isaiah 44:17-20

Idolatry and superstition in Athens
Acts 17:16-34

Restore the fallen
Galatians 6:1-2

Salvation by faith not works
Ephesians 2:8-9

Salvation only through Jesus
John 14:6

Satan's deceptions
John 8:44
2 Corinthians 11:13-15

Separation
2 Corinthians 6:14-17
Ephesians 5:6-8

Warn a sinner
James 5:19-20

Warning against false prophets
Matthew 7:15

Warn those in danger
Proverbs 24:11-12

Watch out for troublemakers
Romans 16:17-18

Danger

Definition:
Exposure or vulner-ability to harm, injury, or loss.

Key Verses:
Proverbs 22:3
Romans 8:35

See Also:
Fear
Safety

Avoidance of
Proverbs 22:3
Proverbs 27:12

Cannot separate you from God
Romans 8:35-39

Constant
Psalm 119:109

From natural forces
Luke 8:23

God protects from
Psalm 57:1
Psalm 138:7
Proverbs 19:23

No fear of
Psalm 23:4
Proverbs 1:33
Proverbs 3:25

Of Christian workers
1 Corinthians 15:30

Dating

Definition:
Romantic social inter-action with a member of the opposite sex.

Key Verses:
Psalm 119:9
2 Timothy 2:22

See Also:
Courting
Love
Marriage
Sexual Integrity

Avoid the angry
Proverbs 22:24

Date believers only
2 Corinthians 6:14-15

Devotion to the Lord
1 Corinthians 7:35

Flee evil desires
2 Timothy 2:22

For unmarried
1 Corinthians 7:8

Guard your heart
Proverbs 4:23

Importance of marriage
Genesis 2:18

Marriage limitations
Romans 7:2

Rejoice in the wife of your youth
Proverbs 5:18

Sacrifice for love
Genesis 29:20

Sexual integrity in
Psalm 119:9

1 Thessalonians
4:3-7
Hebrews 13:4

Deafness

Definition:
The inability to hear,
either physically or
spiritually.

Key Verses:
Proverbs 28:9
Isaiah 35:5

See Also:
Aging
Apathy
Apostasy
Rebellion

Caused by demons
Mark 9:25

Ears made deaf
Exodus 4:11
Isaiah 6:10

Healing of
Isaiah 35:5-6
Matthew 11:2-5

In old age
2 Samuel 19:35

Kindness to the deaf
Leviticus 19:14

Spiritual
Jeremiah 6:10
Ezekiel 12:2
Zechariah 7:11
Acts 28:26
2 Timothy 4:4

Death

Definition:
The end of physical
life; the cessation of
vital body function.

Key Verses:
John 11:25-26
1 Corinthians
15:42-44

See Also:
Euthanasia
Heaven
Hell
Salvation

Abolished by Christ
Isaiah 25:8
1 Corinthians 15:26
2 Timothy 1:10
Revelation 21:4

Appearance
Matthew 17:3

Because of sin
Genesis 2:17
Genesis 3:19
1 Samuel 4:12-18
Romans 5:12-13
Romans 5:17
Romans 6:23
1 Corinthians 15:56

Brevity of life
Job 7:16
Job 14:1
James 4:14

Brings blessing
Ecclesiastes 4:1-2
2 Corinthians 5:2

Philippians 1:21
Philippians 1:23
Revelation 14:13

Call to Lord
Psalm 18:4-6

Christ's death
Romans 4:25

Courage before
Psalm 23:4

Dead in Christ raised
1 Thessalonians 4:16

Description of
Job 10:20-22

Desire for
1 Kings 19:4
Job 10:1

Equality in
Job 21:23-26
Psalm 49:14
Psalm 89:48
Ecclesiastes 2:16
Ecclesiastes 5:15
Luke 16:22

Eternal life
Matthew 25:46

Faith without action
James 2:26

Fear of God
Job 13:20-21

Finality of
Job 16:22

**For rebellion
against God**
Ezekiel 33:11

The Biblical Counseling Reference Guide

For those who worship the Beast
Revelation 14:11

For ungodliness
2 Kings 9:30-37

Glorification in
Philippians 3:20-21

God controls
Genesis 6:7
Genesis 15:15

God delivers from
Psalm 18:4-6
Psalm 68:19-20
Psalm 116:8

God has power over
Deuteronomy 32:39
Revelation 6:1-8

God is with His people unto
Genesis 46:4
Revelation 6:9

God's displeasure with
Ezekiel 18:23

Heaven
John 14:2-4

Hell
Luke 16:22-24

Honoring
Jeremiah 34:4-5

Inevitability of
Psalm 89:47-48
Ecclesiastes 11:8
Isaiah 28:15

Hebrews 9:27
James 1:10-11
1 Peter 1:24-25

In peace
Luke 2:29

In sin
Ephesians 2:1-2
Colossians 2:13

Jesus' power over
Mark 5:38-42
John 11:1-44

Judgment from God
1 Chronicles 10:13
Psalm 78:50

Judgment to come
2 Corinthians 5:10
Hebrews 9:27

Last breath
Luke 23:46

Length of life
Job 14:5
Psalm 39:4

Life in Christ
Matthew 10:39
Colossians 3:2-3

Martyrdom
Acts 7:54-60

Of a leader
2 Samuel 1:19

Of a loved one
2 Samuel 12:16-23

Of Jesus
Mark 15:37-39
John 19:28-30

1 Timothy 2:5-6
Hebrews 10:12
Hebrews 10:14
Hebrews 10:17

Of the wicked
Job 11:20
Job 18:17
Job 27:15
Proverbs 10:25
Matthew 25:41

Persecution
2 Corinthians 4:8-11

Power of
Ecclesiastes 8:8

Prayer at a time of
Matthew 26:39

Preparation for
2 Kings 20:1
Isaiah 38:1
2 Timothy 4:6-8

Reaction to
2 Chronicles 22:10

Reality of
Ecclesiastes 7:1-2

Reassurance
Psalm 16:9-10

Recognition of resurrected Christ
Luke 24:35

Resurrection
Psalm 49:15
Isaiah 26:19
Daniel 12:2
Daniel 12:13

1 Corinthians
15:42-44
1 Corinthians 15:51
1 Corinthians
15:54-57
2 Corinthians
4:14-18
2 Corinthians 5:1
2 Corinthians 5:8
1 Thessalonians
4:13-14
1 Thessalonians 4:17

Seasons of life
Ecclesiastes 3:1-2

**Some things are
worse than death**
Revelation 9:6

Death Penalty

Definition:
Government or societal policy of taking
the life of convicted
murderers.

Key Verses:
Genesis 9:6
Deuteronomy 17:6

See Also:
Capital Punishment
Consequences
Justice

Debate

Definition:
To dispute by engaging in a quarrel or to

argue by presenting
opposing points.

Key Verses:
Acts 15:2
1 Peter 3:15

See Also:
Apologetics
Argue
Communication

Debt

Definition:
Money, goods, or services owed.

Key Verses:
Matthew 6:12
Romans 13:7-8

See Also:
Business Ethics
Finances
Money
Salvation

Canceling
Deuteronomy 15:1
Matthew 18:23-27

**Do not charge
interest**
Exodus 22:25
Deuteronomy 23:19
Psalm 15:5

**God is responsible
for our wealth**
Genesis 14:22-24

**Judgment on
the wicked**
Psalm 109:11

Of love
Romans 13:8

**Oppression of
the poor**
Nehemiah 5:3

Pay wages on time
Deuteronomy
24:14-15

Regulations for
Deuteronomy 24:6

Responsibility in
Romans 13:7-8

**Righteous are
gracious at giving**
Psalm 37:21

Severity of
Proverbs 22:27

Deception

Definition:
Intentional misleading
or causing to believe
something false.

Key Verses:
Leviticus 19:11
Psalm 55:23

See Also:
Lying
Manipulation

Accountability for
Hebrews 4:13

Avoidance of
Job 27:3-4
Psalm 26:4
Psalm 101:7
Psalm 141:3

By Abram
Genesis 12:12-13

By God's prophets
Jeremiah 27:14-15

By Satan
John 8:44
Revelation 12:9

Comes from the heart
Jeremiah 17:9
Matthew 12:34
Matthew 15:19

Condemned
Exodus 20:16
Exodus 23:1
Deuteronomy 5:20
Psalm 119:29-30
Proverbs 24:28
Micah 6:12
Colossians 3:9

Consequences of
Genesis 20:1-18
Leviticus 6:1-7
Job 15:6
Psalm 5:9
Proverbs 11:3
Proverbs 12:19
Proverbs 19:5
Proverbs 21:6
Proverbs 29:12
Ephesians 4:25
Revelation 21:8

Defiance of the truth
James 3:14

Folly of
Proverbs 26:18-19

God desires integrity
Psalm 15:1-2
Psalm 51:6
Proverbs 6:16-19
Proverbs 12:22
John 4:23-24

God does not lie
Numbers 23:19

Jesus is the truth
John 14:6

Of Jacob
Genesis 27:21-24

Prayer amidst
Psalm 120:2

Punishment for
Jeremiah 28:1-17

Decision Making

Definition:
The process of choosing or forming judgments about an attitude or action.

Key Verses:
Romans 12:1-2
Philippians 1:9-10

See Also:
Choice
Maturity
Wisdom

Based on others' benefit
Romans 14:21
1 Corinthians 10:23
Philippians 1:9-10

Based on popular opinion
Galatians 1:10

Discerning the will of God
1 Kings 22:5
Psalm 16:7
Psalm 37:4-5
Psalm 37:23
Psalm 40:8
Proverbs 16:9
Proverbs 19:20-21
Romans 12:1-2
Ephesians 5:10

Faith and action
James 1:22

Flesh and Spirit
Galatians 5:17

For God's glory
1 Corinthians 10:31
Colossians 3:17

Guidance by the Holy Spirit
John 14:26
John 16:13
1 Corinthians 2:14-16

Guidance by the Lord
Psalm 73:24
Isaiah 42:16
Isaiah 58:11

Guidance by the Scriptures
Psalm 119:105

Importance of
Joshua 24:15

Interests of others
Philippians 2:3-4

Obedience
1 John 5:3

Relationship to sin
James 4:17

Trust in the Lord
Proverbs 3:5-6

Wisdom from God
Psalm 25:9
Psalm 32:8
Proverbs 28:26
John 8:12

Wrong and right
Isaiah 7:15

Dedication

Definition:
A pledge, promise, or actions taken to maintain association with a person or thing.

Key Verses:
Romans 12:1
1 Corinthians 15:58

See Also:
Commitment
Loyalty

Defense Mechanism

Definition:
An automatic reaction for self-protection that normally occurs without conscious decision.

Key Verses:
Ecclesiastes 3:7
Mark 8:35

See Also:
Abuse
Anxiety
Childhood Sexual
  Abuse
Denial
Molestation

Deliverance

Definition:
Rescue from evil, danger, or threat of harm.

Key Verses:
Psalm 18:2
Romans 7:25

See Also:
Forgiveness
Salvation

Delusion

Definition:
False belief concerning one's self or reality.

Key Verses:
Psalm 4:2

2 Thessalonians
  2:10-12

See Also:
Deception
Lying

Dementia

Definition:
Deteriorating reasoning and mental capacity, normally associated with advanced age or a disease like Alzheimer's.

Key Verses:
Ecclesiastes 12:6
1 Corinthians 13:12

See Also:
Aging
Caregiving
Chronic Illness

Demons

Definition:
Spirits that are subservient to Satan and hostile to the will of God.

Key Verses:
Romans 8:38-39
James 2:19

See Also:
Occult
Satan, Demons, and
  Satanism
Spiritual Warfare

The Biblical Counseling Reference Guide

Activities
Revelation 9:11

Affliction by
1 Samuel 16:15-16
1 Samuel 18:10
Matthew 8:28
Mark 5:8-9
Mark 9:18
John 13:27
2 Corinthians 12:7

Angels under judgment
2 Peter 2:4
Jude 6

Belief in God
James 2:19

Cast out
Matthew 8:29-32
Mark 1:23-26
Mark 9:25-29

Destination of
Matthew 25:41

Disguised as an angel of light
2 Corinthians 11:14-15

Exorcism of
Matthew 10:1
Luke 11:14
Acts 19:13-16

Followers of Satan
Revelation 12:7-9

Hindering ministry
1 Thessalonians 2:18

Power over the world
1 John 5:19

Relationship to anger
Ephesians 4:26-27

Relationship to apostasy
1 Timothy 4:1

Relationship to false teaching
1 Timothy 4:1-6
1 John 4:1-6

Relationship to idols
Deuteronomy 32:17
1 Corinthians 10:20

Resisting
James 4:7

Role in temptation
1 Peter 5:8-9

Separate from
1 Corinthians 10:21
2 Corinthians 6:17

Submission to Christ
Matthew 12:22
Mark 3:11
Mark 9:25
Romans 8:37-39

Under Christ's authority
1 Peter 3:22
Revelation 12:10

War against God
Revelation 16:13-14

Denial

Definition:
Defensive reaction to avoid confronting a problem, personal challenge, or reality.

Key Verses:
2 Timothy 3:4-5
Titus 1:16

See Also:
Defense Mechanism
Lying

Dependability

Definition:
Capable of being trusted or relied on.

Key Verses:
1 Samuel 26:23
2 Corinthians 1:12

See Also:
Endurance
Instability
Trust

Commanded
Deuteronomy 25:13-16
Proverbs 11:13
Luke 16:10
1 Corinthians 4:2

Of God
Joshua 21:45
Joshua 23:14-15
2 Chronicles 6:4
2 Chronicles 6:14-15

Psalm 136:1-26
Hebrews 6:18

**Stand firm in
the faith**
1 Corinthians 16:13
Philippians 1:27

Dependency

Definition:
Habitual reliance on
someone or something
such that extreme
stress or discomfort
is produced when
the person or thing is
removed.

Key Verses:
2 Kings 18:21
Psalm 62:7

See Also:
Addiction
Alcohol and Drug
   Abuse
Codependency

**Enslavement
to passions**
Titus 3:3

**Folly of depending
on self**
Isaiah 30:12-13
Hosea 10:13-14
Romans 9:16

For protection
2 Kings 18:20-22

On ethnicity
Romans 2:17-24

On God
2 Chronicles 14:11
Psalm 62:7
Isaiah 50:10

On other people
Jeremiah 17:5

**Slave to what
masters you**
2 Peter 2:19

Depersonalize

Definition:
To remove personal
identification or con-
nection.

Key Verses:
Romans 14:7
Colossians 4:6

See Also:
Defense Mechanism

Depression

Definition:
An emotional state
characterized by pro-
longed feelings of
hopelessness, gloom,
insecurity, and guilt
accompanied by leth-
argy.

Key Verses:
Psalm 27:13
1 Thessalonians
   5:16-17

See Also:
Anger

Envy and Jealousy
Fear
Grief
Guilt
Phobia
Self-Worth

Anger
1 Samuel 18:10-11
Jonah 4:9

Anguish
Psalm 38:8

Anxiety
Proverbs 12:25
1 Peter 5:7

Bitterness and joy
Proverbs 14:10

Darkness
Job 5:14
Ecclesiastes 5:17
Isaiah 50:10

Distress
Psalm 77:1-4

Grief
Lamentations
   3:32-33
Psalm 31:9

Guidance
Isaiah 42:16

Hidden
Proverbs 14:13

Hope
Psalm 42:5-6
Psalm 55:4-8
Proverbs 13:12

The Biblical Counseling Reference Guide

Ecclesiastes 9:4

Hope in God
Psalm 27:13-14
Psalm 34:8
Psalm 42:8-11
Psalm 43:5
Psalm 130:5
2 Corinthians 4:8-11
Hebrews 6:18-19

In discouragement
Job 4:5-6

**Joyful heart helps
heal the body**
Proverbs 17:22

Renewal
2 Corinthians 4:16

Rest
Matthew 11:28-29

Result of grief
Nehemiah 2:2

Result of sin
Genesis 4:6-7
Psalm 32:3-4

**Result of troubles
in life**
Psalm 102:3-11

Think godly thoughts
Philippians 4:8

Time for everything
Ecclesiastes 3:4

Troubles
Psalm 25:17

Trust in the Lord
Psalm 16:8

John 14:1

**Unrealistic
view of life**
1 Kings 19:3-10

Desertion

Definition:
The act of finally and
unexpectedly aban-
doning, leaving, or
forsaking someone or
something; used espe-
cially of family respon-
sibilities.

Key Verses:
Joshua 1:5
1 Corinthians 7:13-16

See Also:
Abandonment
Betrayal
Responsibility

By friends
Jeremiah 38:22

By God
Isaiah 54:7

False accusation of
Jeremiah 37:13-14

**God cares for
the deserted**
Psalm 68:6

Of a wife
Isaiah 54:6

Of Jesus
Matthew 26:56
Mark 14:50

Out of fear
1 Samuel 13:7-8

**To follow another
person**
2 Samuel 20:2
2 Kings 25:11
Jeremiah 38:19
Jeremiah 39:9

Desire

Definition:
Unsatisfied longing,
craving, or appetite for
something or some-
one.

Key Verses:
Psalm 73:25
1 John 2:17

See Also:
Ambition
Infatuation
Lust

Condemned
1 Peter 2:11
1 John 2:15-16

For God
Psalm 42:1-2
Psalm 63:1
Psalm 73:25
Psalm 143:6
Isaiah 26:9
Philippians 1:23
Philippians 3:7-11

For God's will
1 Peter 4:1-2

For power
Mark 10:35-37

Insatiability of
Ephesians 4:19

Obstacle to faith
Mark 4:19

Of the devil
John 8:44

Of the flesh
Ephesians 2:3

Relationship to prayer
James 4:2

Satisfied by God
Psalm 37:4
Psalm 145:16

Spiritual milk
1 Peter 2:2

Despair

Definition:
Loss of all hope or confident expectation.

Key Verses:
Psalm 88:15
2 Corinthians 4:7-9

See Also:
Depression
Hopelessness
Sorrow

Destruction

Definition:
A state of ruin, brokenness, or uselessness.

Key Verses:
Proverbs 14:11
Galatians 6:8

See Also:
Calamity
Disaster
Judgment

Of Babylon
Revelation 18:21

Of the wicked
Numbers 21:3
Deuteronomy 3:6
Joshua 6:21
Joshua 8:24-29
Isaiah 34:2
Malachi 4:1

Result of God's judgment
2 Chronicles 15:6
Jeremiah 25:9
Zephaniah 1:2-3

Detachment

Definition:
Separation from, indifference toward, or general lack of personal concern or interest.

Key Verses:
John 17:16
Romans 14:7

See Also:
Affection
Friendship

Diligence

Definition:
Persistent or persevering devotion to a task or activity.

Key Verses:
Proverbs 21:5
Hebrews 6:11

See Also:
Commitment
Patience
Work

Commanded
Romans 12:11

Importance of
Hebrews 12:1-3

In doing good
Deuteronomy 6:17
Galatians 6:9
Titus 3:14

In following God
Hebrews 4:11

In labor
Ruth 2:7

In preaching
2 Timothy 4:1-2

In the Lord's work
1 Corinthians 15:58
2 Timothy 4:5

In work
Ecclesiastes 9:10

**Make the most
of the time**
Ephesians 5:15-16
Colossians 4:5

Of a wife
Proverbs 31:14-15

Supplies provision
Proverbs 13:4
Proverbs 28:19

To guard yourself
Deuteronomy 4:9

Disabilities

Definition:
Inability or disadvan-
tage, often referring to
profound impairment
that inhibits life.

Key Verses:
Isaiah 40:31
2 Corinthians 12:9-10

See Also:
Chronic Illness
Depression
Disease
Evil and Suffering

Disagreement

Definition:
Difference in opinion,
conflict, quarrelling,
dissent.

Key Verses:
Philippians 2:14
James 4:1

See Also:
Argue
Conflict Resolution
Opposition
Quarrel

Alternative to
1 Timothy 2:8

Importance of ending
Proverbs 17:14
Matthew 5:25

In the church
Acts 15:1-3
1 Corinthians 1:10
1 Corinthians 11:16
Galatians 2:11-21

Loved by offenders
Proverbs 17:19

Reconciliation in
Deuteronomy 20:10
Luke 12:58
1 Corinthians 6:1-7

Disappointment

Definition:
An emotion of empti-
ness following unmet
expectations or hopes.

Key Verses:
Isaiah 51:6
Romans 5:5

See Also:
Discouragement

Failure
Pessimism
Regret
Sorrow

Affects the spirit
Proverbs 13:12

In an ungodly son
Proverbs 17:25

In friends' behavior
2 Timothy 4:16

**Result of God's
judgment**
Deuteronomy 28:39
Isaiah 17:10-11
Micah 6:15
Zephaniah 1:13
Haggai 1:9

**Righteous not
disappointed**
Psalm 112:7-8

Temporary
Hebrews 11:13

Disaster

Definition:
Sudden and cata-
strophic destruction,
failure, loss, or distress.

Key Verses:
2 Samuel 22:19
Psalm 37:19

See Also:
Calamity
Destruction
Evil and Suffering

Comes unexpectedly
Ecclesiastes 9:12

**Never to occur
by flood again**
Genesis 9:8-16

Protection from
Psalm 57:1
Isaiah 37:36

**Result of God's
judgment**
Genesis 19:15-22
Isaiah 8:6-7
Isaiah 15:1
Jeremiah 4:18
Ezekiel 7:2-5
Revelation 8:6-13
Revelation 18:17-19

Discernment

Definition:
The ability to under-
stand and judge clearly
and wisely.

Key Verses:
Proverbs 10:13
1 Corinthians 2:14

See Also:
Guidance
Justice
Trust
Wisdom

**Comes through
training in
righteousness**
1 Corinthians
2:14-16

Hebrews 5:14

Commanded
Leviticus 10:10
Matthew 10:16
1 Corinthians
3:18-20
1 John 4:1-6

For the obedient
John 7:17

**In understanding
God's Word**
Psalm 119:125
Acts 17:11

Lack of
Deuteronomy 32:28
Matthew 16:1-4

**Not based on
outward appearances**
John 7:24

Of false teachers
Deuteronomy
18:21-22
Revelation 2:2

Of God
Proverbs 21:2-3

Of God's judgments
Micah 4:12
Ephesians 1:18-19

Of Jesus
Luke 6:8
John 2:24-25

Of words
Job 12:11
Job 34:1-3

Relationship to love
Philippians 1:9-10

Request to God
1 Kings 3:9

Discipleship

Definition:
The process by which
one follows the teach-
ing and training of a
respected mentor.

Key Verses:
Mark 8:34
Luke 14:33

See Also:
Admonition
Coaching
Mentoring

Blessings in
Revelation 1:3

Care for God's people
John 21:15-19

Cost of
Matthew 10:37-39
Matthew 16:25
Mark 10:28-31
Luke 14:23-26
Luke 14:33
Luke 18:28-30

Faithfulness in
1 Corinthians 4:2

Follow Christ
Mark 1:17
John 10:27
John 12:24-26

John 14:15
1 Corinthians 11:1
Galatians 2:20
Philippians 3:12-16
1 Peter 2:21-25

Grace in
2 Timothy 2:1-4

Hunger for righteousness
Matthew 5:6

Imitate godly persons
1 Corinthians 4:15-16

Importance of
1 Corinthians 9:24-27

Love God
Deuteronomy 6:5
Joshua 23:11
Mark 12:30

Love one another
John 13:35

Make disciples
Matthew 28:18-20

Obedience in
Deuteronomy 5:1
John 15:8
Colossians 1:9-12
Hebrews 6:1

Perseverance in
John 8:31
Acts 2:42
Acts 20:22-24
2 Timothy 3:12

Righteousness in
Psalm 15:1-5
Hebrews 12:1-2

Search for God with whole heart
Jeremiah 29:10-14

Service in
Matthew 9:9
Matthew 23:8-12
Mark 9:35
Romans 1:1
Romans 12:10
1 Corinthians 9:19-23
Galatians 5:13
Philippians 2:3-4
Colossians 3:23-24
Titus 1:1

Strengthen the disciples
Acts 14:21-22
Acts 15:36
Acts 18:23

Suffering in
2 Corinthians 6:3-13

Discipline

Definition:
Training or chastisement intended to develop a certain attitude or behavior.

Key Verses:
Job 5:17
Hebrews 12:11

See Also:
Compassion

Parenting
Reproof
Train

Benefits of heeding
Job 5:17
Proverbs 10:17
Proverbs 12:1
Proverbs 13:24
Proverbs 29:17
2 Timothy 2:5

By God
Isaiah 65:6-7
John 15:2

Despising
Psalm 32:8-9
Proverbs 5:12-13
Jeremiah 32:33

For disobedience
Judges 8:16
1 Chronicles 21:13
Ezra 7:26
Nehemiah 9:30
Amos 3:2
Zephaniah 3:2

For obedience
Romans 6:12-13

For sexual immorality
1 Corinthians 5:5

Grief resulting from
2 Corinthians 2:6-7

In the church
Matthew 18:15-17
1 Corinthians 5:11
1 Timothy 1:3-5

Leading to happiness
Psalm 94:12

Leading to repentance
2 Corinthians 7:8-9

Love in
Jeremiah 31:20

Mercy in
Ezra 9:13

Of Jesus
Hebrews 5:8-9

Purpose of
Hosea 6:1
Hebrews 12:7

Restoration
Galatians 6:1

Role in prayer
1 Peter 4:7

Spiritual
1 Corinthians
9:24-27

The Lord disciplines the ones He loves
Proverbs 3:11-12
Hebrews 12:5-11
Revelation 3:19

Will benefit children
Proverbs 19:18
Proverbs 22:15
Proverbs 23:13-14
Ephesians 6:4

Discouragement

Definition:
The emotional state of hopelessness that hinders plans, activity, or progress.

Key Verses:
Psalm 61:2
Jeremiah 8:18

See Also:
Bitterness
Pessimism
Self-Pity

Because of illness
Isaiah 38:9-12

Because of persecution
2 Corinthians 4:7-12

Condemned
Ephesians 3:13

Courage in
John 16:33

God gives victory
1 Corinthians
15:57-58

Peace in
John 14:27

Result of defeat
Joshua 7:2-12

Result of losses in life
Ruth 1:21

Through comparing yourself to others
Psalm 73:1-14

Turn to God for help
Psalm 61:2
Psalm 142:3

Discrimination

Definition:
The act of distinguishing or judging between things; used especially of unjust distinguishing based on preconceived categorization rather than individual merit.

Key Verses:
Romans 2:11
James 2:3-4

See Also:
Bigotry
Prejudice

Acceptance of others
Romans 14:1
Romans 15:7
Galatians 2:9-10

Condemned
1 Corinthians 4:6

God does not discriminate
Acts 10:34-35
Romans 10:12
Ephesians 6:9
Colossians 3:25

Disease

Definition:
Abnormal function of the human body caused by heredity, outside agent, or other factor and resulting in recognizable symptoms.

Key Verses:
Psalm 103:2-3
Matthew 4:23

See Also:
Affliction
Chronic Illness
Suffering
Terminal Illness

Afflicted by Satan
Job 2:6-7

Caused by sin
John 5:14

For God's glory
John 9:1-3
John 11:4

For our good
2 Corinthians 12:7-10

God heals
Exodus 15:26
Deuteronomy 7:15
2 Kings 5:1-14
Psalm 103:2-3
Philippians 2:25-27
James 5:15-16

Jesus heals
Matthew 4:23-24
Matthew 8:14-15
Matthew 9:20-22
Matthew 14:14
Mark 7:32-35
Luke 4:40

Judgment from God
Leviticus 26:15-16
Leviticus 26:25
Deuteronomy 28:21-22
Deuteronomy 28:27
2 Chronicles 21:15
2 Chronicles 26:19-21
Isaiah 3:16-17
Jeremiah 29:17
Ezekiel 5:17
1 Corinthians 11:27-30

Makes one unclean
Leviticus 13:9-17
Leviticus 22:4-5
Deuteronomy 24:8

Dishonesty

Definition:
Lack of integrity, truth, or trustworthiness.

Key Verses:
Leviticus 19:35
Proverbs 13:11

See Also:
Cheating
Deception

Honesty
Lying

Destroys the wise
Ecclesiastes 7:7

God judges
Psalm 101:7
Proverbs 11:1
Proverbs 20:10
Micah 6:11
Acts 5:1-11
1 Thessalonians 4:6
James 5:4-5

Hated by the righteous
Proverbs 13:5

Hatred for the righteous
Amos 5:10

Leads to misery
Proverbs 12:19-22

Leads to poverty
Proverbs 21:6
Jeremiah 17:11

Maintain honesty
Leviticus 19:35-36

Mature are not deceived
Ephesians 4:14-15

Of a ruler
Matthew 2:7-8

Of hearts
Psalm 12:2

Of merchants
Leviticus 19:13
Hosea 12:7
Amos 8:5-6

Disobedience

Definition:
Failure to submit, obey, or follow a command.

Key Verses:
Romans 5:19
Ephesians 5:6

See Also:
Obedience
Rebellion
Submission

Do not associate with
2 Thessalonians
3:14-15

Fleeing from God
Jonah 1:3

God judges
Genesis 19:26
Leviticus 10:1-2
Numbers 14:22-24
Numbers 20:10-12
Deuteronomy
11:26-28
Deuteronomy
28:15-68
1 Samuel 28:18
Isaiah 42:24
Jeremiah 17:13
Jeremiah 44:1-3
Ezekiel 18:24
Ezekiel 20:21

Zechariah 1:4-6
Ephesians 5:6
2 Thessalonians 1:8
Hebrews 2:2-3

In the Garden of Eden
Genesis 3:1-11

Obey God's commands
Ezekiel 20:18-19

Of God's people
Jeremiah 7:22-26
Zephaniah 3:2

Partial obedience
1 Kings 22:43

Repentance of
Ezra 10:2-3

Warning against
Genesis 2:17
1 Samuel 12:15
Jeremiah 12:17
Matthew 5:19

Disorder

Definition:
A mental malady that interferes with normal function of the body.

Key Verses:
1 Corinthians 14:40
James 3:16

See Also:
Chronic Illness
Disease
Health

Disrespect

Definition:
Discourtesy or lack of esteem for others.

Key Verses:
Deuteronomy 27:16
Romans 12:10

See Also:
Honor
Insult
Respect

For elders
2 Kings 2:23-24
Job 30:1
Isaiah 3:5
Lamentations 5:12

For God
Jeremiah 2:5-8
Malachi 1:6

For God's house
Ezekiel 25:3-4

For God's Word
Jeremiah 36:20-32

For Jesus
John 18:19-24

For parents
Proverbs 30:17

For the Lord's servants
Deuteronomy 17:12

Dissociative Identity Disorder

Definition:
Separation of one's personality into distinct, segmented personas rather than a unified core identity.

Key Verses:
Lamentations 1:20
John 8:31-32

See Also:
Counseling
Identity
Personality

Distress

Definition:
State of pain and suffering or danger and risk of loss.

Key Verses:
Psalm 18:6
Psalm 107:6

See Also:
Suffering
Trials

Divination

Definition:
Forecasting the future by interpreting signs and omens or using allegedly supernatural abilities.

Key Verses:
Deuteronomy 18:10
1 Samuel 15:23

See Also:
Occult
Satan, Demons, and Satanism

Divorce

Definition:
Legal dissolution of a marriage.

Key Verses:
Malachi 2:16
1 Corinthians 7:15-17

See Also:
Adultery
Conflict Resolution
Marriage
Reconciliation

Amounts to treachery
Malachi 2:15

Avoided
1 Corinthians 7:12-17

Based on abandonment
1 Corinthians 7:15

Condemned
Malachi 2:16
Matthew 5:31-32
Matthew 19:1-12
Mark 10:2-12
1 Corinthians 7:10
1 Corinthians 7:14

Death frees from marriage vows
Romans 7:1-3

Example of
Jeremiah 3:1

Favor in wife
Proverbs 18:22

For unlawful marriages
Ezra 10:1-44

Gravity of
Genesis 2:24
Malachi 2:13-16

Husbands should love their wives
Ephesians 5:25

Leads to adultery
Matthew 19:3-9
Mark 10:11-12
Luke 16:18

Limitations on remarriage
Deuteronomy 24:1-4

Married to the Lord
Isaiah 54:5

Private
Matthew 1:19

Remarriage
1 Corinthians 7:10-11

Unity in marriage
Matthew 19:6

Unmarried
1 Corinthians 7:8-9

Vows
Numbers 30:9

Domestic Violence

Definition:
Physical harm and injury purposefully inflicted within family relationships, normally a pattern of repeated behavior.

Key Verses:
Psalm 11:5
Ephesians 5:25

See Also:
Assault
Spouse Abuse
Verbal and Emotional
Abuse

Doubt

Definition:
Hesitancy or indecision because of uncertainty or lack of trust.

Key Verses:
Matthew 21:21
James 1:6

See Also:
Indecision
Instability
Trust

Condemned
Matthew 14:31
Matthew 21:21
John 20:24-31
Hebrews 3:12

Dangers of
Matthew 14:22-32

Have mercy on doubters
Jude 22-23

In Jesus
John 12:37-38

In persecution
Judges 6:11-13

In the goodness of God
Job 10:3

In times of danger
Isaiah 36:1-20

Of God's promises
Luke 1:34

Of Moses
Exodus 4:1-17
Exodus 6:12

Of Sarah
Genesis 16:1-16
Genesis 18:1-15

Of the gospel
John 8:45-47
1 Corinthians 1:18

Of the resurrection
Matthew 28:17

Overcoming
Matthew 17:20

Mark 9:23-24

Providing an answer to doubters
Acts 2:36

Remembering God in
Psalm 42:5

Drug Abuse

Definition:
Improper use of a substance that alters body function; used especially of chemical dependence or narcotic addiction.

Key Verses:
Proverbs 23:31-32
1 Corinthians 10:23

See Also:
Alcohol and Drug
Abuse

Dysfunctional Family

Definition:
A family in which healthy functions have been exchanged for abnormal ones so that the family is a danger to itself.

Key Verses:
Genesis 37:3-4
Romans 15:5

See Also:
Alcohol and Drug
Abuse

Communication
Marriage
Rebellion
Unbelieving Mate

Child-raising in
Deuteronomy 6:5-9
Proverbs 13:24
Proverbs 22:6
Ephesians 6:4

**God cares for those
who are hurt**
Psalm 68:5

**God overcomes
family fights**
Genesis 50:20

Instruction
Proverbs 1:8

Reconciliation in
Matthew 5:23-24

**Rejoice with your
household in God's**
Deuteronomy 12:7

**Unwise to disrupt
household**
Proverbs 11:29

Eating Disorders

Definition:
Malady characterized
by harmful eating
habits and unhealthy
attitudes regarding
food, body image, and
self-worth.

Key Verses:
Psalm 102:4-5
Psalm 146:7

See Also:
Anorexia and Bulimia
Compulsive Eating
Gluttony
Overeating

Emotional Abuse

Definition:
Systematic misuse or
neglect of verbal or
nonverbal commu-
nication that inhibits
another person's devel-
opment.

Key Verses:
Proverbs 12:18
1 Peter 2:17

See Also:
Abuse
Communication
Verbal and Emotional
Abuse

Empathy

Definition:
The ability to inter-
nalize the thoughts,
feelings, and experi-
ences of another with-
out sharing the same
objective reality.

Key Verses:
2 Corinthians 1:4
Hebrews 2:17-18

See Also:
Caregiving
Compassion
Golden Rule

Employment

Definition:
The performance of
work on a regular basis
that results in wages.

Key Verses:
Colossians 3:23
2 Thessalonians 3:7-8

See Also:
Business Ethics
Finances
Responsibility
Work

Appeal to authority
Daniel 1:8-14

**Cannot serve both
God and money**
John 16:13

Deserves wages
Leviticus 19:13
Deuteronomy
24:14-15
Matthew 10:10
1 Corinthians 9:6-7
1 Timothy 5:18
James 5:4

Difficulty in
Nehemiah 4:19-20
Nehemiah 5:6-7

Done for the Lord
Ephesians 6:6-8
Colossians 3:17
Colossians 3:22-24

Faithfulness in
Proverbs 28:20
Luke 16:10
2 Thessalonians
3:6-10

Futility of
Genesis 3:17-18
Ecclesiastes 2:17

Prosperity the result of obedience
Psalm 128:2

Submit to employers
Ephesians 6:5-9
1 Timothy 6:2
Titus 2:9-10

Treat servants properly
Colossians 4:1

Working together
Nehemiah 4:22

Empty Nest

Definition:
Description of the time period within a marriage relationship following the maturity and independence of children.

Key Verses:
Psalm 128:6
Proverbs 17:6

See Also:
Aging
Loneliness
Marriage
Parenting

Encouragement

Definition:
The act of inspiring, comforting, counseling, or giving confidence or hope.

Key Verses:
1 Thessalonians 5:11
Hebrews 3:13

See Also:
Coaching
Compassion
Discipleship

By church leadership
2 Timothy 4:2

By friends
2 Corinthians 7:6

Commanded
1 Thessalonians 4:18
Hebrews 3:13
Hebrews 10:24-25

Effects on a person
Proverbs 12:25

Encouragement in Christ
Philippians 2:1-2

Encouraging people
1 Corinthians 16:18

For the discouraged
1 Thessalonians 5:14

From angels
Acts 27:23-24

From God
2 Kings 6:16
Haggai 2:4
Acts 23:11
2 Thessalonians
2:16-17

From the Scriptures
Psalm 119:28

Health from
Proverbs 16:24

In midst of trials
John 16:33
2 Corinthians 7:4-7

In speech
Job 16:4-5
Ephesians 4:29

In the Lord
Isaiah 41:10

Ministry of encouragement
Acts 20:1-2
Colossians 4:7-8
1 Thessalonians
2:11-12

Need for
Hebrews 10:24-25

Of mistreated
Hebrews 13:3

**Should be offered
with tact**
  Proverbs 25:20

Definition:
The act or ability to
withstand and perse-
vere through stress or
affliction.

Key Verses:
Psalm 49:12
Hebrews 12:2-3

See Also:
Commitment
Perseverance

Against evil
  Ephesians 6:13

**A godly character
quality**
  2 Peter 1:5-6

Of believers
  James 5:11
  Revelation 13:10

Of God's discipline
  Hebrews 12:7

Of hope in the Lord
  1 Thessalonians 1:3

Of persecution
  2 Timothy 3:11

Of trials
  Matthew 10:22
  Romans 5:3-4
  2 Thessalonians 1:4

James 1:2-4
James 1:12
Revelation 3:10

Run with
  Hebrews 12:1-2

**Through God's
strength**
  Colossians 1:9-11

Enemies

Definition:
One who is hostile
or antagonistic to
another, an opponent.

Key Verses:
Proverbs 25:21
Matthew 5:44

See Also:
Argue
Disagreement
Friendship
Strife

Envy

Definition:
A feeling of desire and
resentment brought
about by the fortune
or ability of another.

Key Verses:
Job 5:2
Philippians 4:11

See Also:
Envy and Jealousy
Jealousy

Be content
  Philippians 4:11-13
  Philippians 4:19
  1 Timothy 6:6

**Blessing can
lead to envy**
  Genesis 37:5
  Genesis 37:11

Comes from the heart
  Mark 7:20-22

Condemned
  Exodus 20:17
  Psalm 37:1
  Proverbs 23:17
  Proverbs 24:19-20
  Galatians 5:19-21
  Galatians 5:25-26
  1 Peter 2:1

Consequences of
  Proverbs 14:30
  Daniel 6:3-5
  Matthew 27:15-18
  James 3:16

Evil of
  James 3:14-16

Godly
  2 Corinthians 11:2

Love is not envious
  1 Corinthians 13:4-5

**No one can withstand
jealous anger**
  Proverbs 27:4

Of accomplishments
  1 Samuel 18:5-11

Of another's success
Acts 13:44-45

Of God
Exodus 34:14

Of prestige
Esther 5:11-13

Of spiritual gifts
Numbers 11:25-29

Of the wealthy
Genesis 26:12-14
Psalm 73:3

**Relationship
to prayer**
James 4:2

Warning against
Luke 12:15

Envy and Jealousy

Definition:
Synonyms indicating
desires to possess or
embody the posses-
sions or abilities of
others.

Key Verses:
Matthew 6:33
James 3:16

See Also:
Envy
Jealousy

Evil of comparison
2 Corinthians 10:12

Indicates worldliness
1 Corinthians 3:3

In families
Genesis 30:1-9

In marriage
Numbers 5:29

Is pointless
Ecclesiastes 4:4

Leads to deception
Genesis 27:8-12

Leads to other sin
1 Samuel 18:9-17

Of siblings
Genesis 27:28-41
Genesis 29:30-31
Genesis 30:1

Seek the kingdom
Matthew 6:33

Toward Jesus
John 11:47-53

Eternal Life

Definition:
Life that is unhindered
by sin and death; used
of present participa-
tion in the kingdom
of God and future life
without end.

Key Verses:
John 3:16
John 3:36

See Also:
Assurance of Salvation
Forgiveness
Salvation

Believe in Jesus for
John 3:16
John 5:24-25
John 10:28
John 14:6
John 17:3
John 20:30-31
1 John 5:11-13
1 John 5:20

**Eternal life and
eternal judgment**
Daniel 12:2

**Eternal life rescues
from death**
John 5:24
2 Corinthians 5:1

God's gift of
Romans 6:23

**The paths to life
and death**
John 3:36
John 12:25

Eternal Security

Definition:
The teaching that
authentic believers in
Jesus Christ are certain
to endure to the end
and are unable to lose
their salvation.

Key Verses:
John 10:28
Romans 8:30

See Also:
Assurance of Salvation
Salvation

The Biblical Counseling Reference Guide

**Based on belief
in Jesus**
John 3:16
John 5:24
Romans 8:1
Romans 10:9
Ephesians 2:8-9
Titus 3:5
1 John 5:11-13

Based on call of Jesus
John 10:27

**Based on
Christ's work**
2 Corinthians 5:21
Philippians 1:6
Hebrews 7:25
Hebrews 10:14

**Based on God's
faithfulness**
John 10:29
Romans 8:38-39
2 Timothy 1:12
1 John 1:9
1 John 2:25
Jude 24-25

**Deeds evidence
salvation**
1 John 1:6

**Relationship
to apostasy**
1 John 2:19

**Relationship to
obedience**
1 John 2:3-6
1 John 3:6
1 John 4:6

**Relationship to
persecution**
1 John 3:13-14

**Relationship to
predestination**
Ephesians 1:4

Role of Holy Spirit in
Romans 5:5
Romans 8:16
Ephesians 1:13-14
Ephesians 4:30

Test yourself
2 Corinthians 13:5

Ethics

Definition:
A standard of moral
principles distinguish-
ing right from wrong.

Key Verses:
Psalm 119:11
Proverbs 13:6

See Also:
Ethics and Integrity
Honesty
Morality

Ethics and Integrity

Definition:
Synonyms indicating
devotion to a high
standard of conduct.

Key Verses:
Micah 6:8
2 Corinthians 1:12

See Also:
Ethics
Honesty
Integrity
Morality

Accountability for
2 Corinthians 5:10
Hebrews 4:13

Anarchy
Judges 21:25

Before God
Acts 5:29

Capital punishment
Genesis 9:6

Commanded
1 Thessalonians 4:7
1 Peter 1:15-16

Commitment to
Psalm 101:1-8
Daniel 6:3-4

Importance of
Psalm 24:1-4
Proverbs 16:2
Matthew 5:13-16
Matthew 5:27-28
2 Corinthians 4:1-2
Colossians 3:8-10

**Increasing
responsibility**
Luke 16:10

In disputable issues
1 Corinthians 10:24

In paying taxes
Mark 12:14-17

Maintaining
Psalm 119:11
Psalm 119:104
Matthew 5:14-16
Matthew 23:28
Romans 5:3-4
Romans 6:11
Romans 12:2
1 Corinthians 11:1
2 Corinthians 5:17
2 Corinthians
6:14-18
Ephesians 4:22-24
Colossians 1:22

Natural law
Romans 2:14-15

Relationship to influences
1 Corinthians 15:33

Relationship to love
1 John 5:2

Security from
Proverbs 10:9
Proverbs 11:3

The Ten Commandments
Exodus 20:1-17

Definition:
Cessation of life for a suffering individual either by withdrawing care or inducing death.

Key Verses:
Leviticus 24:17
Deuteronomy 32:39

See Also:
Death
Murder
Terminal Illness

Choose life
Deuteronomy 30:19

Desire to die
Revelation 9:6

Do not murder
Genesis 9:6
Exodus 20:13

God controls life and death
Deuteronomy 32:39
Job 14:5
Hebrews 9:27

God supports life
Psalm 139:16

Jesus is life
John 14:6

Love protects others
1 Corinthians 13:6-7

Our life belongs to God
Ecclesiastes 12:7
1 Corinthians
6:19-20

Rescue from death
Proverbs 24:11

Suffering and comfort
2 Corinthians 1:5

Definition:
Presentation of the good news of Jesus Christ with an attempt to reconcile an individual to God.

Key Verses:
Romans 1:16
1 Corinthians 15:2

See Also:
Forgiveness
Salvation

Blessing for
Isaiah 52:7

Boldness in
Isaiah 40:9
Romans 1:14-15

Christ will call people to Himself
John 12:32

Commanded
Psalm 9:11
Matthew 28:16-20
Mark 16:15
Luke 24:45-49
2 Timothy 4:5

Doors opened by the Lord
2 Corinthians 2:12

Effectiveness of the Word
Isaiah 55:10-11
Colossians 1:5-6

Effects of
James 5:20

God's desire for
Matthew 4:19

Harvest is ready
John 4:35-38

Importance of
Romans 10:14-15

Prayer for
Luke 10:1-2
2 Thessalonians 3:1

Preparation for
1 Peter 3:15

**Proclaim the
gospel to all**
Matthew 28:19-20
Acts 19:10
Romans 16:25-27
1 Corinthians
9:19-23

Responsibility in
Ezekiel 3:18-19

Results of
2 Corinthians 4:15
1 Thessalonians
1:4-10

Role of God in
1 Corinthians 3:6-9

Role of the Spirit in
Acts 1:8
2 Corinthians 10:1-5

**Salvation comes
through the gospel**
1 Corinthians 15:1-5

**Salvation is
available to all**
Revelation 22:17

Satan's hindrance of
1 Thessalonians
2:17-20

Evil

Definition:
Something harmful or
morally reprehensible.

Key Verses:
Deuteronomy 32:4
Psalm 5:4

See Also:
Satan, Demons, and
Satanism
Sin
Suffering
Worldly

Avoidance of
2 Corinthians 6:14

**Beginning of
human sin**
Genesis 3:2-7

Conquering
Romans 12:21

Consequences of
Ezekiel 18:4
Galatians 6:7

**Do not repay
with evil**
Romans 12:17

**God does not
tempt with evil**
James 1:13-14

God judges
Psalm 7:15-16
Jeremiah 25:11-14
Revelation 18:4-8

The gospel exposes
John 3:19-20

**Wickedness
throughout the world**
Genesis 6:5
2 Timothy 3:12-13

Evil and Suffering

Definition:
Harm or moral repug-
nance and the pain
that proceeds as its
chief effect.

Key Verses:
Romans 8:28
1 Peter 4:19

See Also:
Evil
Suffering

Accept discipline
Hebrews 12:5-11

At crucifixion
John 19:6
John 19:10-11

Avoid evil
Psalm 37:27

Be patient
Psalm 40:1-3

Blessings from
Matthew 5:10

Brevity of life
Job 7:7

Christ's example in
Hebrews 12:2
Hebrews 12:4
1 Peter 2:24
1 Peter 3:18

Contentment during
Philippians 4:12

Deliverance from
Psalm 34:7
2 Peter 2:9

Depression over
Job 10:1

End of
Revelation 21:3-4

Evil and good on all
Matthew 5:45

Generational evil
2 Kings 21:19-21

God created all
Genesis 1:31
Psalm 102:25

God hates evil
Psalm 5:4

God judges all
Ecclesiastes 12:14

God of comfort
Psalm 46:1

2 Corinthians 1:3-4

God works through
Genesis 50:20
Lamentations 3:12
Psalm 119:67
Romans 8:28
2 Corinthians 12:7
Philippians 1:12-13

In Paul's life
2 Corinthians 4:8-11

In sickness
John 11:4

Integrity
Romans 14:16

In the world
John 15:18
John 15:20

Joy in suffering
James 1:2
1 Peter 1:6

Lucifer's fall
Isaiah 14:12

Misconceptions
Job 42:7
Isaiah 5:20

Of Israel
Exodus 15:9

Of Jerusalem
Matthew 23:37

Of Job
Job 1:14-20
Job 2:7

Peace during
John 16:33

Perseverance
Job 6:10
Job 17:9
James 1:12
James 5:11

Remove evil
James 1:21

Results of evil
Proverbs 24:20

Suffer faithfully
1 Peter 4:19

Suffering of Messiah
Isaiah 53:6

Trust in God
Job 13:15

Examine

Definition:
To thoroughly investigate or inspect.

Key Verses:
Psalm 26:2-3
2 Corinthians 13:5

See Also:
Confess
Critical Spirit

Example

Definition:
A model, pattern, or picture of a general truth.

Key Verses:
John 13:15
Philippians 3:17

See Also:
Discipleship
Mentoring

Bad
Ezekiel 20:18

Following
2 Timothy 3:10-15

God's example of forgiving
Ephesians 4:32
Colossians 3:13

God's example of perfection
Matthew 5:48

Imitate God
Leviticus 11:44
Leviticus 19:2
Ephesians 4:31-32
Ephesians 5:1-2

Imitate godly Christians
1 Corinthians 4:16
1 Corinthians 11:1
Philippians 3:17
1 Thessalonians 1:6-7
1 Timothy 4:12
Titus 2:7
Hebrews 13:7
1 Peter 5:2-3

Importance of avoiding bad examples
Deuteronomy 18:9

Jesus' example of humility
Philippians 2:5-11

Jesus' example of love
John 13:34
1 John 3:16

Jesus' example of service
Matthew 20:26-28
Luke 22:27

Jesus' example of suffering
Matthew 16:21-23
Hebrews 12:1-2
1 Peter 2:21-23

Of obedience and discipline
Jeremiah 35:1-16

Of prayer
Matthew 6:5-13
Luke 11:1-4

Of suffering
Matthew 5:11-12
James 5:10

Excuses

Definition:
Justification given to avoid punishment or receive forgiveness.

Key Verses:
Romans 1:20
Romans 2:1

See Also:
Avoidance
Dishonesty

Blameshifting
Genesis 3:12-13

Care for temporal matters
Matthew 8:21-22
Luke 9:59-62

For idolatry
Exodus 32:24

Given by the lazy
Matthew 25:24-25

Illustrated in kingdom parable
Luke 14:16-24

Inability to speak eloquently is no excuse
Exodus 4:10

No excuse for not seeing God's existence
Romans 1:20

Stature or weakness is no excuse
Judges 6:15
Jeremiah 1:7

Exercise

Definition:
Physical effort for

fitness or deliberate use for a specific purpose.

Key Verses:
1 Corinthians 9:26-27
1 Timothy 4:8

See Also:
Discipline
Stress

Exorcism

Definition:
To remove an evil spirit.

Key Verses:
Matthew 17:18
Luke 9:1

See Also:
Deliverance
Occult
Satan, Demons, and
  Satanism

Expectation

Definition:
Anticipation or assumption of future events or conditions.

Key Verses:
Proverbs 13:12
Romans 8:19

See Also:
Faith
Hope
Trust

Failure

Definition:
Lack of success

Key Verses:
Joshua 23:14
Psalm 73:26

See Also:
Dependency
Prosperity
Purpose in Life
Success

Forget what is past
Philippians 3:13-14

From disobedience
Hebrews 4:6-7

Show compassion for those who fail
Proverbs 24:17-18

Through lack of faith
Matthew 14:28-31

To heal
Matthew 17:16

Your adequacy comes from God
2 Corinthians 3:5

Faith

Definition:
Intellectual assent to someone or something's truth, and trust in its ability.

Key Verses:
Romans 10:17
Hebrews 11:1

See Also:
Hope
Trust

Amidst pain
Job 2:10

Armor of
1 Thessalonians 5:8

Cling to
1 Timothy 1:18-19

Confidence in the Lord
Psalm 27:1
Psalm 131:3
Psalm 147:10-11
Proverbs 3:5
Proverbs 29:25
Isaiah 41:10
Daniel 3:16-17
Nahum 1:7
Luke 12:22-24

Contending for
Jude 3

During war
1 Chronicles 19:13

Effects of
Romans 5:1-2
1 Peter 1:7-9
1 John 5:4

Examples of
Hebrews 11:1-40

The Biblical Counseling Reference Guide

For the future
2 Corinthians
4:16-18

God will guide you
Proverbs 3:5-6

Importance of
Matthew 23:23
Hebrews 4:2

In dangerous times
2 Chronicles
32:10-15

In Jesus
Matthew 8:2-4
Matthew 14:22-31
Mark 4:36-41

In prayer
Mark 11:24

In resurrection
Job 19:25-26
John 11:25-26

In terminal illness
Job 13:15

In the justice of God
Job 16:19

In the unseen
Romans 8:24-25

Lack of
Mark 6:4-6

Means of salvation
Galatians 3:6-9

**Necessary to
please God**
Hebrews 11:6

Of children
Mark 10:13-16

Power of
Isaiah 7:9
Matthew 9:22
Matthew 17:20
Matthew 21:21
Mark 9:23
Luke 17:6

Prayer for
Luke 17:5

Relationship to love
Galatians 5:6

**Relationship
to prayer**
James 1:6

**Relationship to
righteousness**
Genesis 15:1-6
Romans 1:17
Galatians 2:16
Philippians 3:9
Hebrews 10:38

**Relationship
to works**
James 2:26

Results in blessing
Jeremiah 17:7

Shield of
Ephesians 6:16

Testing of
2 Corinthians 13:5
James 1:2-3

Walking by
2 Corinthians 5:7

Work of
1 Thessalonians 1:3

False Doctrine

Definition:
Teaching contrary to
the faith founded in
Jesus Christ, taught
by the apostles, and
received by the church.

Key Verses:
Galatians 1:8
2 Peter 2:1

See Also:
Apologetics
Belief
Cults

Family

Definition:
A group of individu-
als (usually related)
who are united under
a single household
and form a recognized
social unit.

Key Verses:
1 Timothy 5:8
Hebrews 2:11

See Also:
Children
Father
Marriage
Mother
Parenting

Adulterous wife
Hosea 1:2

Alienation from
Psalm 69:8

Betrayal by
Luke 21:16

Blessing from God
Genesis 2:24
Genesis 9:1
Genesis 15:1-6
Genesis 18:17-19
1 Samuel 1:20
1 Samuel 2:21
Psalm 128:3-6

**Blessing on
godly families**
Psalm 112:1-3

Care for
John 19:26-27
1 Timothy 5:4

**Children a gift
from God**
Psalm 127:3-5

**Children should
obey parents**
Colossians 3:20

Duties within
1 Corinthians
7:32-34
2 Corinthians
12:14-15
Ephesians 5:22-26
Ephesians 6:1-4
Colossians 3:18-21
1 Timothy 5:3-8

Enmity in
Proverbs 15:27
Micah 7:6
Matthew 10:21
Matthew 10:32-36
Mark 13:12
Luke 12:49-53
Luke 21:17
2 Timothy 3:2

Godly
Isaiah 59:21
Titus 1:6
1 Peter 3:1-7

**God promised Abram
a large family**
Genesis 17:1-21

Honor for parents
Deuteronomy 5:16
Ephesians 6:2-3

**Importance of
provision**
1 Timothy 5:8

**Instruction of
children**
Deuteronomy
11:16-21
Psalm 78:4-7
Joel 1:3

Jesus more important
Luke 14:26

Love for
Romans 12:10

Peace in
Genesis 13:8
Proverbs 17:1

Praying for children
Job 1:4-5

Rejection by
Mark 3:20-21
John 7:5

Salvation of
Acts 16:31-34

**Sexual
relationships in**
1 Corinthians 7:3-5

Spiritual
Matthew 12:48-50
Mark 3:31-35
Luke 8:19-21
John 1:12
Romans 8:15
2 Corinthians 6:18
Hebrews 2:11
3 John 4

Unity in
Nehemiah 3:12

Famine

Definition:
An extreme shortage
or scarcity of food
within a geographic
area.

Key Verses:
Psalm 104:14
Psalm 146:7

See Also:
Calamity
Death
Hunger
Poverty

Fleeing from
Genesis 12:10
Genesis 26:1-3
Ruth 1:1

God provides food
1 Kings 17:7-16
Psalm 33:18-19

God's judgment
Deuteronomy 28:38
2 Samuel 21:1
Jeremiah 14:1-6
Jeremiah 14:15
Jeremiah 29:17-19
Lamentations 1:11
Ezekiel 5:17
Hosea 9:1-2
Joel 1:11
Joel 1:17-18
Amos 4:6
Matthew 24:7
Luke 21:11
Revelation 18:8

Relief from
Acts 11:28-30

Result of warfare
2 Kings 6:24-25
2 Kings 25:1-3

Fasting

Definition:
The practice of abstaining from something (especially food or kinds of foods) for a period of time; usually connected to religious devotion or observance.

Key Verses:
Isaiah 58:6-7
Matthew 6:16

See Also:
Hunger
Prayer
Worship

Act of repentance
Deuteronomy 9:11-18
1 Samuel 7:6
Ezra 10:6
Daniel 9:3
Joel 1:13-14
Jonah 3:7

Act of worship
Acts 13:2-3
Acts 14:23

Can be an empty religious exercise
Isaiah 58:1-7
Zechariah 7:1-6
Luke 18:11-12

Connected to vow or oath
Acts 23:12-13

Expression of grief
1 Samuel 31:13
2 Samuel 1:12
2 Samuel 3:35
1 Chronicles 10:11-12

In time of trouble
Esther 4:16
Psalm 35:13
Psalm 69:10-11

Psalm 109:24
Daniel 6:18
Acts 27:33-36

In times of joy
Zechariah 8:19

Of Jesus
Matthew 4:1-2
Luke 4:1-2

Proper
Matthew 6:16
Matthew 9:14-15
Mark 2:18-20
Luke 5:33-35

Father

Definition:
A male parent or ancestor. Also used of God to describe the first person of the Trinity.

Key Verses:
Psalm 68:5
Psalm 103:13

See Also:
Children
Family
Mother

Abandonment by
Psalm 27:10

Care for children
Job 1:4-5
Proverbs 13:22
John 10:29

Example of
2 Kings 15:34
Ezekiel 20:18
John 8:41

Failure as
1 Samuel 2:12
1 Samuel 2:22-25

**Father of a fool
has no joy**
Proverbs 17:21

God as Father
Deuteronomy
1:30-31
Psalm 103:13-14
Proverbs 3:11-12
John 20:16-18
Romans 8:15
2 Corinthians 6:18
Galatians 4:6

Honor for
Exodus 20:12
Proverbs 1:8

Imitate God as Father
Ephesians 5:1

Prayer of
1 Chronicles 29:19

Read God's Word
Nehemiah 8:13

Rebellion against
2 Samuel 15:1-14
2 Chronicles
32:20-22

Spiritual
1 Thessalonians
2:11-12

Submission to
Hebrews 12:9

Wisdom from
1 Kings 2:1-9
Proverbs 4:1-10

Favoritism

Definition:
Unfair preference
or partiality of one
person or thing over
another.

Key Verses:
Exodus 23:2
Acts 10:34-35

See Also:
Injustice
Prejudice

Condemned
1 Corinthians 4:6

Consequences of
Job 32:21-22

God does not show
Acts 10:34-35
Romans 10:12
Ephesians 6:9
Colossians 3:25

In the family
Genesis 37:1-4

Of God to His people
Isaiah 44:2
Daniel 1:9-10

Of Jacob
Genesis 29:30

Genesis 37:3

Of Rebekah
Genesis 27:6-17

Fear

Definition:
An intense, agitated
emotional reaction
to a specific object of
impending pain or
danger.

Key Verses:
Psalm 56:3
Isaiah 41:10

See Also:
Anxiety
Phobia

**Can be overcome
by God**
Psalm 34:4
Psalm 46:1

Caused by God
Genesis 35:5
Leviticus 26:36
Joshua 2:24

Condemned
Deuteronomy 31:6
Deuteronomy 31:8
Jeremiah 1:6-8
Matthew 10:26-28
Mark 4:35-41
Luke 12:4-12
John 6:20
Philippians 1:27-30
1 Peter 3:14

Confidence in the Lord
  Deuteronomy 1:21
  Psalm 23:1-4
  Psalm 27:1-3
  Psalm 118:6
  Proverbs 29:25
  Isaiah 41:10-13

Experienced
  Job 18:11
  Job 30:15
  Job 31:34
  Psalm 55:4-5

Fear of God
  Deuteronomy 6:13
  Deuteronomy 13:4
  1 Samuel 12:24
  Job 28:28
  Psalm 103:11
  Proverbs 1:7
  Proverbs 14:27
  Ecclesiastes 12:13
  Isaiah 8:13
  Luke 12:4-5
  James 2:19

In battle
  1 Samuel 13:5-7

In difficult times
  1 Kings 19:1-5
  Luke 8:22-25

Leads to worship
  Revelation 11:13

Of angels
  Luke 1:11-12
  Luke 2:8-10

Of Gideon
  Judges 6:11-16

Of Job
  Job 3:25

Of nature
  Matthew 14:30

Of people
  Isaiah 51:7
  Isaiah 51:12
  Proverbs 29:25
  Galatians 2:11-14

Of punishment
  1 Kings 1:50-53

Of religious leaders
  John 12:42

Of the supernatural
  Matthew 14:26

Peace in
  John 14:27

Realized
  Job 4:14

Relationship to love
  1 John 4:18

Trust in the Lord
  Psalm 56:3-4
  Psalm 112:7

Victory over
  Judges 7:1-20
  1 Samuel 14:6
  1 Samuel 17:37
  Psalm 56:11
  Isaiah 12:2
  Luke 4:18
  2 Timothy 1:7

Fetish

Definition:
An object with supposed unusual power or a sexualized object, body part, or activity.

Key Verses:
Ezekiel 16:58
Galatians 5:19

See Also:
Purity
Sexual Addiction
Sexual Integrity

Finances

Definition:
A system of money management that includes banking, circulation, credit, investments, economics, and accounting.

Key Verses:
Luke 14:28
2 Corinthians 9:7

See Also:
Greed
Money
Prosperity

Against greed
  Proverbs 28:20
  Ephesians 5:5
  Colossians 3:5
  James 4:3

Against injustice
Jeremiah 5:27-28

Against materialism and consumerism
Ecclesiastes 5:11

Against stingy behavior
Proverbs 28:22

Be humble
Proverbs 22:4

Cannot satisfy
Ecclesiastes 5:10

Cannot serve both God and money
Matthew 6:24

Careful consideration
Haggai 1:5-6

Collect treasures in heaven
Matthew 6:20

Contentment
Philippians 4:11-12

Debtor serves lender
Proverbs 22:7

Diligence and laziness
Proverbs 12:24

Dishonest gain
Proverbs 13:11

Disputes between believers
1 Corinthians 6:1-8

Fool and money
Proverbs 17:16

From God
Deuteronomy 8:17-18
Job 42:10
Psalm 24:1
Proverbs 10:22
Philippians 4:19

Generosity
Deuteronomy 15:11
Psalm 37:21
Proverbs 11:24-25
Proverbs 19:17
Matthew 6:1
Matthew 19:16-21
Romans 12:13
2 Corinthians 8:3-5
2 Corinthians 9:7

Giving to God
Mark 12:41-44

God oversees all
James 4:13-14

God's gifts
2 Corinthians 9:10

God's ownership
Psalm 50:12
Proverbs 22:2
Haggai 2:8

God's provision
Philippians 4:19

Importance of faithfulness
Luke 16:10-11

Justice
Proverbs 3:27-28
Proverbs 8:20-21

Laziness
Proverbs 6:10-11
Proverbs 10:4

Offerings
Deuteronomy 26:10
1 Corinthians 16:2

Parable against greed
Luke 12:13-21

Parable concerning stewardship
Matthew 25:14-30
Luke 16:1-13
Luke 19:11-17

Pay debts
Romans 13:7-8

Provide for family
1 Timothy 5:8

Spirituality and greed
1 Timothy 6:3-5

Tithing
Genesis 14:20
Numbers 18:26
Deuteronomy 14:22-23
Deuteronomy 14:28-29
Malachi 3:8-10
Matthew 23:23
Luke 11:42
Hebrews 7:4

Treasure in heaven
Matthew 6:21

The Biblical Counseling Reference Guide

Warning against greed

Luke 12:15
1 Timothy 6:10
Hebrews 13:5

Work hard

Lamentations 3:27-29
Colossians 3:23-24

Worry

Matthew 6:25-34
Philippians 4:6

Fixation

Definition:
Extreme fascination or preoccupation with a subject or object.

Key Verses:
Colossians 3:2
1 Peter 1:13

See Also:
Obsessive Compulsive Disorder

Flashbacks

Definition:
A memory, sometimes suppressed, recalled unwillingly and vividly in the mind.

Key Verses:
2 Corinthians 10:5
Hebrews 3:1

See Also:
Abuse

Anxiety
Fear
Stress

Flattery

Definition:
The practice of praising or complementing excessively and insincerely, often with selfish motives.

Key Verses:
Job 32:21
Proverbs 29:5

See Also:
Bribery
Dishonesty
Manipulation

Brings destruction
Proverbs 26:28

Of limited benefit
Proverbs 28:23

Refuse to use
1 Thessalonians 2:5-6

Used as a trap
Proverbs 29:5
Matthew 22:16-21
Mark 12:13-17
Luke 20:21-25

Used by the wicked
Psalm 5:9
Psalm 36:1-2
Proverbs 2:16
Proverbs 5:3-4

Proverbs 7:5
Proverbs 7:21

Used to deceive
Psalm 12:2-3
Romans 16:18
Jude 16

Used to gain acceptance from others
Genesis 33:10

Fool

Definition:
A person who lacks wisdom or sound judgment.

Key Verses:
Psalm 14:1
Proverbs 1:7

See Also:
Ignorance
Knowledge
Wisdom

Forgiveness

Definition:
The act or process of absolving, dismissing, or pardoning from guilt.

Key Verses:
Colossians 3:13
Hebrews 9:22

See Also:
Conflict Resolution
Grace

Guilt
Reconciliation

Be merciful
Matthew 5:7
James 2:12-13

Benefits of
Psalm 32:1
Romans 4:7-8

Better than sacrifice
Matthew 9:13

Between believers
Matthew 18:15

Cautious with angry people
Proverbs 22:24

Combats darkness
Ephesians 5:11
Ephesians 6:11-16

Commanded
Matthew 5:39
Matthew 6:12
Mark 11:25
Luke 6:36-37
Luke 17:3-4
Acts 7:60
2 Corinthians 2:6-10
Ephesians 4:32
2 Timothy 4:16

Covers multitude of sins
Proverbs 10:12
Proverbs 17:9
Proverbs 19:11
1 Peter 4:8

Danger of bitterness
Acts 8:23
Hebrews 12:15

Difficulty receiving from others
Proverbs 18:19

From God
Psalm 25:11
Psalm 32:5
Psalm 99:8
Psalm 103:2-4
Psalm 103:8-12
Psalm 130:3-4
Proverbs 28:13
Isaiah 1:18
Isaiah 43:25
Isaiah 44:22-23
Isaiah 53:6
Isaiah 55:7
Jeremiah 31:34
Jeremiah 50:20
Daniel 9:9
Micah 7:18-19
Luke 7:39-50
Acts 10:43
Romans 5:8-10
Ephesians 1:7
1 Timothy 1:12-14
Hebrews 10:17-18
James 5:15-16
1 John 1:9
1 John 2:1-2

From Jesus
Matthew 8:1-11
Matthew 9:2-6
Luke 23:34

From Joseph
Genesis 45:5

God executes justice
Deuteronomy 32:35

Message of
Acts 13:38

Ministry of
2 Corinthians 5:18

Of debts
Deuteronomy 15:1

Of family members
Genesis 45:14-15
Genesis 50:15-21

Produces forgiveness
Matthew 6:14-15
Matthew 18:23-35
Colossians 3:12-13

Relationship to worship
Matthew 5:23-24

Repeated
Matthew 18:21-22

Retribution under the Law
Deuteronomy 19:21

Through Christ
Romans 3:25-26
Romans 6:23

Through the Holy Spirit
Titus 3:5

Vengeance condemned
Romans 12:17-19
1 Peter 3:9

Fornication

Definition:
Sexual immorality.
Used especially of
sexual intercourse
between unmarried
people.

Key Verses:
1 Corinthians 6:13
1 Thessalonians 4:3

See Also:
Adultery
Immorality
Morality
Sexual Addiction

Abstinence from
1 Thessalonians
4:1-8

Bestiality forbidden
Deuteronomy 27:21

Condemned
1 Corinthians
6:12-13
Galatians 5:19

**Enslaved to what
defeats them**
2 Peter 2:19

**Homosexuality
condemned**
Leviticus 18:22

**Illustrated in
spiritual relationships**
James 4:4

Love is not selfish
1 Corinthians 13:4-5

Lust condemned
Matthew 5:27-28

**Overcoming
through Christ**
Job 31:1
Psalm 51:10
Psalm 101:3-4
Psalm 139:23-24
Romans 7:24-25
Romans 8:9
Romans 12:1-2
1 Corinthians
3:16-17
1 Corinthians
6:16-20
1 Corinthians 10:13
Colossians 3:1-5
James 1:21

Punishment for
Hebrews 13:4

**Rebuke the
sinning believer**
Matthew 18:15-16

**Sexual immorality
condemned**
Ephesians 5:3-4

Source of temptation
James 1:14-15

**Wicked given over
to impure life**
Ephesians 4:17-19

Forsake

Definition:
To leave, renounce,
abandon, or desert.

Key Verses:
Deuteronomy 31:8
Isaiah 55:7

See Also:
Abandonment
Confess
Desertion
Repentance

Fortune-Telling

Definition:
A person who predicts
the future.

Key Verses:
Micah 3:11
Acts 16:16

See Also:
Occult
Satan, Demons, and
Satanism

Freedom

Definition:
Liberty of action; the
state of being unre-
strained or unfettered.
Used especially of civil
liberty.

Key Verses:
Isaiah 61:1
1 Corinthians 8:9

See Also:
Bondage
Liberty
Oppression

Bought by God
Exodus 6:6

Bought by the Son
John 8:36

Call to
Galatians 5:13

From sin
Romans 6:1-2
Romans 6:14

From slavery
Romans 8:15
Galatians 4:7

From the Law
Romans 7:6

In Christ
1 Corinthians 9:19
Galatians 5:1
Colossians 1:13-14

In disputable issues
1 Corinthians
10:23-26

In the Spirit
2 Corinthians 3:17

Of youth
Ecclesiastes 11:9

Truth will set you free
John 8:31-32

Wise use of
1 Peter 2:16

Friendship

Definition:
A kind relationship
that exists between
two people and is
characterized by affec-
tion, loyalty, and com-
munication.

Key Verses:
Proverbs 17:17
John 15:13

See Also:
Companion
Hospitality

**Abandonment
by friends**
Psalm 38:11
Psalm 88:8

Ability to listen
Proverbs 20:5

Among God's people
John 13:35

Avoid evil friends
Psalm 1:1
Proverbs 13:20
Proverbs 24:1
2 Thessalonians 3:14

Based on money
Proverbs 14:20
Proverbs 19:4

Benefits of
Proverbs 27:9-10
Proverbs 27:17
Ecclesiastes 4:9-12

Betrayal of
Psalm 41:9
Psalm 55:12-14
Jeremiah 9:4-5
Jeremiah 20:10

Matthew 26:48-49

Faithfulness in
2 Kings 2:2
Job 6:14
Proverbs 17:17
Proverbs 18:24

Fellowship offered
Galatians 2:9

Forsaken
Psalm 55:13-14
2 Timothy 4:9-10

Gossip separates
Proverbs 16:28
Proverbs 17:9

Honesty in
1 Samuel 20:8-9
Proverbs 27:5-6

In the church
Acts 2:42-47

Jesus' model of
John 15:13

Model of
1 Samuel 18:1

Of John
3 John 14
Revelation 1:9

Protection in
1 Samuel 19:1-2

Sacrifice in
Romans 16:3-4

Unity in
Amos 3:3

The Biblical Counseling Reference Guide

With angry people
Proverbs 22:24-25

With God
Isaiah 41:8-9
James 2:23

With Jesus
Matthew 17:1
Luke 7:34
John 11:1-3
John 15:10-17

With the disreputable
Acts 9:26-27

With the godly
Psalm 119:63
Proverbs 13:20

With the world
James 4:4

Frustration

Definition:
An emotion of discontent following thwarted, impeded, or nullified plans.

Key Verses:
Romans 8:20
Galatians 6:9

See Also:
Anger
Disappointment
Discouragement

At dashed hopes
Job 6:11

By the Lord
Psalm 146:9
Proverbs 22:12
1 Corinthians 1:19

Of creation
Romans 8:20

Ruined plans
Job 17:11-12
Ecclesiastes 4:6

Sexual
2 Samuel 13:2

Troubled life
Job 7:3

Fury

Definition:
Intense, uncontrolled, and violent anger or rage.

Key Verses:
Proverbs 6:34
Revelation 19:15

See Also:
Anger
Rage
Wrath

Avoidance of
Psalm 37:8
Proverbs 15:1

Condemned
James 1:19

Control of
Ephesians 4:26

Folly of
Proverbs 29:22

Harmful effects of
Matthew 5:22

In response to domestic violence
2 Samuel 13:21

In the home
Esther 1:12

Of leaders
Proverbs 16:14
Proverbs 20:2
Daniel 2:12

Futility

Definition:
The state or quality of being ineffective or useless.

Key Verses:
Psalm 94:11
Ephesians 4:17

See Also:
Disappointment
Failure
Purpose in Life

Life without a companion
Ecclesiastes 4:7-8

Of idolatry
1 Kings 18:29
Psalm 4:2
Isaiah 44:14-20

Powerless to cleanse sin
Jeremiah 2:22

To trust Christ if there is no resurrection
1 Corinthians 15:13-19

Trust in those powerless to save
Hosea 12:1

Future

Definition:
All that has not yet happened and is yet to come.

Key Verses:
Ecclesiastes 7:14
Jeremiah 29:11

See Also:
Prophecy

Gambling

Definition:
The act of wagering money or valuables on a game of chance.

Key Verses:
Proverbs 16:33
Ecclesiastes 5:10

See Also:
Addiction
Greed
Money

Danger of greed
Proverbs 15:27
Proverbs 28:25
Proverbs 29:4

Danger of money
Matthew 6:24
Luke 16:13

Financial responsibility
Proverbs 13:11
Proverbs 17:16
Ecclesiastes 7:12
Matthew 25:27
Luke 19:23

Leads to violence
Judges 14:12-20

Love of money is a root of evil
1 Timothy 6:9-10

Money cannot satisfy
Ecclesiastes 5:10

Warning against greed
Jeremiah 6:13
Matthew 23:25
Luke 12:15
Romans 1:29
1 Corinthians 6:10
Ephesians 5:3-5

Generosity

Definition:
The state or quality of being liberal with giving or sharing.

Key Verses:
Psalm 37:21
2 Corinthians 9:6

See Also:
Charity
Love
Mercy

Blessings for
Psalm 41:1
Psalm 112:5
Proverbs 22:9
Acts 20:35

Commanded
Romans 12:8
2 Corinthians 9:6-11
1 Timothy 6:17-18

Give from what you have
Proverbs 3:27-28
2 Corinthians 8:12

In poverty
2 Corinthians 8:2-5

Of God
Ephesians 1:7-8
Ephesians 1:17-19

Of the righteous
Psalm 37:25-26
Acts 2:44-46

Rich through Christ
2 Corinthians 8:9

Secrecy of
Matthew 6:1-4

Toward the needy
Psalm 112:9

Proverbs 19:17
Matthew 5:42
1 Corinthians 16:1-2

Work in order to give to those in need
Ephesians 4:28

Gluttony

Definition:
Sin characterized by excessive eating and drinking.

Key Verses:
Proverbs 25:28
Proverbs 28:7

See Also:
Compulsive Eating
Overeating

Cannot satisfy
Numbers 11:18-20
Philippians 3:19

Condemned
Numbers 11:31-34
Proverbs 23:1-7
Luke 12:45

Harmful effects of
Proverbs 23:20-21
Proverbs 25:16

Overcoming
Romans 13:13-14

God

Definition:
The personal, spiritual, and holy Being who

created and sustains the world, and exists in the three persons of one essence.

Key Verses:
Deuteronomy 4:39
Matthew 22:37-38

See Also:
Holy Spirit
Jesus Christ
Worship

Ability of
Genesis 18:14
Mark 10:27

Adoption by
Romans 8:15

Appearance to Abram
Genesis 17:1

Attributes and actions
Exodus 15:11-18
Exodus 33:18-23
Numbers 23:19
Nehemiah 9:6-37
Titus 1:2
1 John 1:5

Belief in
John 12:44
John 14:1
James 2:19

Birth of Christ
Matthew 1:18
Matthew 1:23
Matthew 1:25
Luke 2:11

Blessing of
Genesis 6:8
Genesis 14:18-20
Genesis 35:9
Matthew 6:4

Compassion of
Psalm 116:5
Jeremiah 31:3
Daniel 9:9
Micah 7:18-19

Creation by
Genesis 1:1
Genesis 1:26-31
Genesis 2:4
Psalm 104:24
Isaiah 48:13
John 1:1-3
Hebrews 11:3
Revelation 4:11

Direction by
Psalm 23:1-4
Proverbs 3:5-6

Eternality of
Deuteronomy 32:40
Psalm 90:2
Daniel 4:34
Revelation 10:6

Faithfulness of
Deuteronomy 7:9
Joshua 23:14
1 Chronicles 16:34
Psalm 100:5
Isaiah 49:15
2 Timothy 2:13
Hebrews 10:23

Father and Son
Matthew 11:27

Luke 2:48-49
John 5:16-27
John 8:14-20
John 14:9-13
John 17:1
Philippians 2:5-11
Hebrews 1:1-3
Hebrews 5:5-10
1 John 2:22-24

Fear God

Genesis 22:12
Exodus 20:20
Deuteronomy 6:13
Deuteronomy 6:24
Proverbs 9:10
Acts 9:31

Fear of

Psalm 64:9

Glory of

Exodus 40:34
Revelation 21:23

Goodness of

Psalm 84:11
Psalm 119:68
Mark 10:18

Grace of

1 Corinthians 1:4
Titus 2:11
Hebrews 4:16

Greatness of

Deuteronomy 10:14
1 Chronicles
   29:10-13
Psalm 145:3
Isaiah 40:28-31
Isaiah 55:9

Holiness of

Exodus 3:5
Leviticus 11:44
Leviticus 19:2
Psalm 99:9
Isaiah 6:1-5
1 Peter 1:15-16
Revelation 4:8

Holy Spirit

Genesis 1:2
Psalm 51:11
Joel 2:28
Mark 3:29
John 14:26
John 15:26
Acts 1:8
Galatians 5:22-23
Ephesians 4:30

Hope in

Psalm 42:11
Colossians 1:27
Revelation 21:3-4

Immutability of

1 Samuel 15:29
Malachi 3:6
James 1:17

In the flesh

John 1:1
John 1:14

Invisibility of

John 1:18
1 Timothy 6:15-16

Jealousy of

Exodus 34:14
Deuteronomy 4:24
Isaiah 42:8

Jesus Christ

John 1:1-14
Philippians 2:5-8
Colossians 1:16
1 John 5:20

Justice of

Genesis 6:13
Genesis 18:25
Deuteronomy 32:4
Psalm 98:9
Jeremiah 17:10
Romans 2:11
Romans 3:4
James 4:12
1 Peter 1:17

Kindness of

Romans 2:4
Ephesians 2:6-7

Lord's ways

Isaiah 55:9

Love of

Psalm 117:2
Lamentations 3:22
John 3:16
Romans 5:8
1 John 4:8
1 John 4:16
1 John 4:19

Mercy of

Exodus 34:6
Deuteronomy 4:31
Romans 9:16
Ephesians 2:4-5
Hebrews 8:12

Name of

Exodus 3:13-15

Nearness of
Psalm 119:151
Jeremiah 23:23-24

No other God
Isaiah 45:5

Obedience
John 14:23
1 Peter 1:2

Omnipresence of
1 Kings 8:27
Psalm 139:7-12

Omniscience of
Genesis 16:13
Job 31:4
Psalm 147:5
Proverbs 24:12
Hebrews 4:13
1 John 3:20

Ownership of
Deuteronomy 10:14
1 Chronicles 29:16

Patience of
Numbers 14:18
2 Peter 3:9

Peace of
2 Corinthians 13:11
Philippians 4:6-7

Plans
Job 42:2
Jeremiah 29:11

Power of
2 Chronicles 20:6
Isaiah 40:21-26
Jeremiah 10:10
Jeremiah 32:17

Zechariah 4:6
Matthew 19:26
Ephesians 1:20-21

Protection of
2 Samuel 22:31
Psalm 46:1
Proverbs 18:10
Proverbs 30:5

Provision of
Genesis 22:14
1 Chronicles
29:11-12
John 17:7
James 1:17

Redeemer
Isaiah 47:4

Reign of
Isaiah 9:6-7
Psalm 113:4-6
Hebrews 1:8
Revelation 19:6

Relationship with
Genesis 21:33
Exodus 15:26
Deuteronomy
10:12-11:1
Jeremiah 17:14
Matthew 6:6-15
John 14:1-21
Acts 10:34-43
Romans 8:28-30
2 Corinthians 1:3-4
Colossians 3:1-25
James 1:17
James 4:8

Righteousness
Psalm 89:14

Psalm 119:137
Jeremiah 23:6

Scripture is from
2 Timothy 3:16-17
2 Peter 1:21

Sovereignty of
Job 38:4-12
Psalm 89:11
Psalm 135:6
Proverbs 21:1
Isaiah 43:13
Isaiah 45:5-12
Daniel 4:17
Daniel 4:35
Romans 9:18-20

Support by
Deuteronomy 33:27
1 Peter 5:10

Trinitarian activity
Matthew 28:19
Mark 12:36
Luke 1:35
Luke 3:21-23
Luke 10:21
John 14:26
John 15:26
John 16:15
Acts 2:32-36
Acts 7:55
Romans 1:1-4
Romans 5:1-8
2 Corinthians 13:14
Galatians 4:4-6
1 Peter 1:2

Trustworthiness of
Psalm 9:10
Psalm 33:4
Proverbs 3:5-6

Uniqueness of
Deuteronomy 4:35
Deuteronomy 4:39
Job 9:10
1 Samuel 2:2
1 Samuel 12:13-25
Isaiah 44:6
Isaiah 46:9-11
Mark 12:32
Romans 11:33-36
1 Corinthians 8:4
1 Timothy 1:17
Revelation 15:4

Wrath of
Psalm 89:46
Romans 1:18

Golden Rule

Definition:
"Do unto others as you would have others do unto you," as taught by Jesus in Matthew 7:12.

Key Verses:
Leviticus 19:18
Matthew 7:12

See Also:
Ethics and Integrity
Respect

Abuse of
Psalm 109:5

Be merciful
Matthew 5:7

Do not take revenge
Proverbs 24:29

Forgive others
Matthew 18:21-22

Illustrated
Deuteronomy 22:1-3

Love for enemies
Luke 6:27-36

Love for neighbor
Leviticus 19:18
Matthew 7:12
Romans 13:9
Galatians 5:14

Seek the good of others
1 Corinthians 10:24
1 Thessalonians 5:15

Gospel

Definition:
The good news that God has provided salvation to sinners through Jesus Christ.

Key Verses:
Romans 1:16-17
1 Corinthians 15:3-5

See Also:
Evangelism
Salvation

Benefits of following
Mark 8:35
Mark 10:29-30
Ephesians 1:13

Benefits of supporting
Philippians 1:4-6

Consequences of rejecting
2 Thessalonians 1:8

Effects of
Colossians 1:6
1 Peter 4:6

Message of
1 Corinthians 15:1-5
2 Timothy 2:8

Perversion of
Galatians 1:6-9

Power of God for salvation
Romans 1:16

Preaching of
Matthew 24:14
Matthew 28:18-20
Mark 13:10
Mark 14:9
Luke 9:6
Acts 8:25
1 Corinthians 1:17

Purpose of
Acts 15:7

Righteousness from
Romans 1:17

Suffering for
1 Thessalonians 2:2
2 Timothy 1:8

Support for preaching
1 Corinthians 9:14

The Biblical Counseling Reference Guide

Gossip

Definition:
To spread personal rumors (often with intimate details) in order to harm the reputation of another.

Key Verses:
Proverbs 16:28
Proverbs 26:20

See Also:
Lying
Slander

Appeal of
Proverbs 26:22

Avoidance of
Psalm 101:5
Proverbs 20:19
1 Timothy 5:19

Blessing upon those afflicted by gossip
Matthew 5:11-12
Luke 6:22-23

Condemned
Exodus 23:1
Leviticus 19:16
Proverbs 4:24
Proverbs 12:22
Micah 6:12
Romans 1:29
2 Corinthians 12:20
Ephesians 4:29
1 Timothy 3:11
1 Timothy 5:13
Titus 3:2
1 Peter 3:9

3 John 9-10
Revelation 14:5

Destruction caused by
Proverbs 17:9

Do not slander
Titus 2:3

Effects of
Psalm 5:9
Psalm 52:2-4
Psalm 64:8
Psalm 140:3
Proverbs 16:28
Proverbs 26:20

Enemies slander
Lamentations 3:60-62

Folly of
Proverbs 10:18

Guarding the tongue
Psalm 15:1-3
Psalm 39:1

Practice of the ungodly
Jeremiah 9:5

Prayer amidst
Psalm 109:1-3
Psalm 120:1-2

Response to
Romans 12:14
Colossians 4:6

Government

Definition:
The organization of

individuals to provide leadership, establish rules of conduct, and administer justice for a political unit.

Key Verses:
Isaiah 9:7
Romans 13:1

See Also:
Authority
Capital Punishment
Justice

Authority from God
John 19:10-11

Believer in ruling position
Daniel 2:48-49
Daniel 6:3
Romans 16:23

By the Lord
Judges 8:22-23
1 Samuel 10:17-19

By the wicked
2 Kings 21:11
Proverbs 28:28
Mark 10:42

Civil disobedience
Exodus 1:15-21
Acts 4:19-20
Acts 5:29

Corruption in
Psalm 94:20
Matthew 14:1-11
Acts 24:26

Disengaged government
Acts 18:12-17

Established through righteousness
Proverbs 16:12

God can bring down
Psalm 76:12

Godly influence in
Esther 10:3

God rejects ruler
Jeremiah 30:20
Lamentations 2:6
Hosea 13:11

Importance of honesty in
Proverbs 17:7

Instability in
Proverbs 28:2
Isaiah 3:4

Joseph in
Genesis 41:37-45

Justice in
2 Samuel 8:15
1 Chronicles 18:14
Proverbs 14:34

Oppression in
Exodus 2:23-25
Amos 1:13
Malachi 3:5
Matthew 27:11-26

Perversion of justice
Habakkuk 1:3-4

Pray for rulers
1 Timothy 2:1-4

Relationship to church
1 Corinthians 6:1

Seek God's choice of leaders
Hosea 8:4

Servant leadership
1 Kings 12:7

Submission to
Matthew 22:15-22
Luke 20:21-25
Romans 13:1-7
Titus 3:1-2
1 Peter 2:13-17

Wars against God
Psalm 2:1-3
Revelation 16:13-14

Working with
Nehemiah 2:1-8
Acts 16:35-40

Grace

Definition:
Undeserved favor, goodness, or blessing extended by God to a person.

Key Verses:
Romans 11:6
Ephesians 2:8-9

See Also:
Legalism
Mercy
Salvation

Agent of salvation
Ephesians 2:7-8

For those with integrity
Psalm 84:11

In speech
Ephesians 4:29
Colossians 4:6

Leading to good works
2 Corinthians 9:8

Of God
Exodus 34:6-7
Nehemiah 9:17
Psalm 78:38
Psalm 103:9-10
Psalm 145:8-9
Romans 5:17
Ephesians 1:7-8

Receiving from Christ
John 1:16

To preach to the nations
Romans 1:5

Toward apostates
Hosea 14:4

Gratitude

Definition:
The state of being thankful.

Key Verses:
Colossians 3:16-17
Hebrews 12:28

The Biblical Counseling Reference Guide

See Also:
Thankfulness

At God's restoration of Israel
Jeremiah 33:10-11

Commanded
Psalm 136:1-26
Philippians 4:6
Colossians 2:6-7
1 Thessalonians 5:18

For answered prayer
John 11:40-41

For food
John 6:11

For friends
Ephesians 1:16
1 Thessalonians 3:8-10

For God's gift of Christ
Romans 7:24-25
2 Corinthians 9:15

For God's revelation
Daniel 2:19-23

For hospitality
2 Kings 4:13

For kindness
Ruth 2:10
2 Samuel 10:2

For loyalty
2 Samuel 9:1

For ministry
1 Thessalonians 2:13

For salvation
Luke 7:36-50
Colossians 1:12
1 Timothy 1:12-14

For spiritual victory
1 Corinthians 15:57

Given by only a few
Luke 17:12-19

Of Christ
Matthew 26:27
1 Corinthians 11:24

Sacrifice of
Leviticus 7:12

To God
Psalm 106:1
Ephesians 5:20
Colossians 3:15-17
Hebrews 13:15

Greed

Definition:
Excessive or insatiable desire to possess money or power; avarice.

Key Verses:
Proverbs 28:25
Luke 12:15

See Also:
Gambling
Lust
Money

Accompanying power
1 Samuel 8:3

Can't satisfy
Ecclesiastes 5:10

Condemned
Isaiah 56:11
Jeremiah 22:17
Matthew 6:19-21
1 Corinthians 5:11
Titus 1:7

Consequences of
2 Kings 5:20-27
Proverbs 28:22
Ephesians 5:5
1 Timothy 6:6-11

Effects of
Psalm 52:7
James 5:1-6

Example of Paul
1 Thessalonians 2:5

Folly of
Jeremiah 17:11
Matthew 16:26
Luke 12:13-21

Greedy succumb to temptation
1 Timothy 6:9-10

Judgment on
Habakkuk 2:6
Habakkuk 2:9
James 5:1-3

Leads to betraying friends
Matthew 26:14-16

Leads to quarrelling
Genesis 13:5-7
Genesis 26:19-22

James 4:1-2

Manifestations of
2 Peter 2:3

Righteous give
Proverbs 21:26

**Seek the kingdom
of God**
Matthew 6:33

Warning against
Luke 12:15

Grief

Definition:
Deep, enduring, and
intense sorrow or suf-
fering caused by an
emotional loss.

Key Verses:
Psalm 57:1
1 Thessalonians
4:13-14

See Also:
Bereavement
Death
Loneliness

After God's judgment
Lamentations 1:4-5

Anguish
Psalm 6:3
Psalm 118:5

**Because of a
wayward child**
Proverbs 10:1

Benefits of
2 Corinthians
7:10-11

Blessings for
Matthew 5:4

Comfort in
Psalm 10:14
Psalm 57:1
Psalm 62:5
Psalm 119:28
Psalm 147:3
Lamentations
3:19-26
Lamentations 3:32
Romans 8:28
2 Corinthians 1:3-4

Comforting
John 11:19

Grief expressed
1 Samuel 15:35
Psalm 73:21-22
Lamentations
3:49-51
Matthew 17:23
Acts 8:2

Grief will turn to joy
Psalm 30:5
Psalm 30:11
John 16:18-20

Grief with hope
1 Thessalonians 4:13

Hope in God
1 Timothy 5:5

**Improper response
to the grieving**
Proverbs 25:20

Joy and mourning
Proverbs 14:13
Lamentations 5:15

Need for
Ecclesiastes 3:1-8
Ecclesiastes 7:3-4

Numbered days
Job 14:5

Of Jacob
Genesis 37:34

Of Jesus
Luke 19:41-44
John 11:35

Of the Holy Spirit
Isaiah 63:10
Ephesians 4:30

Over death
Genesis 37:33-35
Genesis 50:1-4
2 Samuel 1:12
2 Samuel 12:22-23
2 Samuel 19:1-8

Perseverance
Romans 5:3
Hebrews 10:36

Perspective in
Genesis 50:20
2 Corinthians 4:18

Prayer in
Psalm 142:1
Psalm 143:7-8

Rejoice
Romans 12:15

The Biblical Counseling Reference Guide

**Response to
horrible news**
1 Samuel 4:16-19

**Result of physical
suffering**
Job 6:2
Job 17:7

Sacrifice
Psalm 51:17

Salvation from
Psalm 138:7
Jeremiah 17:14

**Sowing tears and
reaping joy**
Psalm 126:5

Suffering
Job 36:15
Psalm 119:107
Isaiah 53:3
1 Peter 2:19

**The Lord saves
the grieving**
Psalm 34:17-18

Trouble
Job 11:16
Psalm 25:17

**Wisdom and
knowledge**
Ecclesiastes 1:18

Grumbling

Definition:
Discontented com-
plaining, often in a
caustic manner.

Key Verses:
John 6:43
Philippians 2:14

See Also:
Argue
Complain

Guidance

Definition:
Direction, supervision,
or advice obtained in
order to make a proper
decision.

Key Verses:
Psalm 32:8
John 16:13

See Also:
Advice
Decision Making
Mentoring
Purpose in Life

By angels
Exodus 23:20
Hebrews 1:14

By God
Genesis 12:1-8
Genesis 24:11-21
Genesis 46:1-4
Exodus 16:2-5
2 Samuel 5:17-19
2 Samuel 22:33
Psalm 25:4-5
Psalm 32:8
Psalm 139:23-24
Proverbs 16:9
Isaiah 30:19-21

Isaiah 46:10-11
Matthew 2:12-14
Matthew 2:19-21
2 Corinthians 2:12
Hebrews 11:8
James 1:5-6

By the Holy Spirit
Job 32:8
Psalm 139:7-10
Ezekiel 36:26-27
Matthew 3:16–4:1
Luke 4:1-2
John 16:13
Romans 8:26-27

By the Scriptures
Joshua 1:6-9
Psalm 119:104-105

From elders
Numbers 10:29-33

From mentors
1 Timothy 3:14-15

Given to the prophets
Amos 3:7

In adversity
Psalm 27:11

In choosing a leader
Acts 1:24-26

In leadership
Jeremiah 10:23

In ministry
Acts 16:6-7

Lack of
Amos 8:11-12

Sought by the nations
Micah 4:2

The will of God
Proverbs 19:21
Acts 18:20-21
Ephesians 1:11-12
Ephesians 5:17

Trust in the Lord
Proverbs 3:5-6

Guilt

Definition:
Culpability or responsibility for committing an act deemed worthy of punishment. Also used of the feelings associated with guilt.

Key Verses:
Psalm 32:5
James 2:10

See Also:
Forgiveness
Salvation
Shame
Sin

Affliction
Job 10:15

Avoidance of
John 3:20

Because of apostasy
Matthew 27:3
Hebrews 10:28-31

Because of disobedience
2 Samuel 24:10
Jeremiah 3:24-25
Jonah 1:10-12
James 2:10

Because of manslaughter
Deuteronomy 19:4-7

Because of murder
Exodus 2:11-14
2 Samuel 1:1-16

Because of oppressing the innocent
Jeremiah 2:34-35

Because of sin
Genesis 3:8-13
Genesis 4:8-10

Blameless
Psalm 19:12-13

Can produce repentance
2 Corinthians 7:10

Carried by Messiah
Isaiah 53:6-10

Cleansing from
Acts 24:16
Hebrews 9:14
Hebrews 10:22

Conscience
Romans 2:15
1 Peter 3:16

Conviction by the Holy Spirit
John 16:13

Effects of
Psalm 38:4
Psalm 51:3-4

Everyone is sinful
Proverbs 20:9
Isaiah 53:6
Isaiah 64:6
Romans 3:10-11

False
1 Samuel 20:1

Forgiveness of
Psalm 32:5
Psalm 103:12
Proverbs 28:13
Isaiah 1:18
Jeremiah 31:34
Jeremiah 50:20
John 8:6-11
Romans 4:7
Romans 5:9
Romans 8:1
Romans 8:33-34
Colossians 2:13
1 Timothy 1:12-14
Hebrews 8:12
Hebrews 10:15-18

Guilt expressed
Job 10:15
Psalm 69:5
Jeremiah 30:15
John 16:8

In abusing communion

1 Corinthians
11:27-30

Judgment for

Micah 6:11
Nahum 1:3

Offering for

Leviticus 6:6-7

On the basis of witnesses

Deuteronomy 19:15

Relationship to confession

1 John 1:9

Relationship to ignorance

Leviticus 5:17

Relationship to scapegoat

Leviticus 16:20-22

Responsibility for

Deuteronomy 24:16
Romans 14:12

Restitution for

Proverbs 6:30-31

The Lord upholds the innocent

Genesis 39:11-20

Universality of

Romans 1:20
Romans 3:10-20

Habits

Definition:
An almost involuntary pattern of behavior acquired by frequent repetition.

Key Verses:
Matthew 7:26-27
Romans 8:9

See Also:
Addiction
Compulsion

Accountability for

Genesis 6:5
2 Corinthians 5:9-10
Hebrews 4:13

Can be overcome with Christ

Psalm 139:23-24
Proverbs 3:5-6
Romans 6:1-2
Romans 6:6
Romans 6:11
Romans 12:1-2
Romans 13:14
1 Corinthians
6:19-20
1 Corinthians 10:13
Galatians 5:16
Ephesians 2:2
Ephesians 4:22-24

Come from the heart

Psalm 119:11
Matthew 15:19

Confession and repentance

2 Kings 17:13
Proverbs 28:13

Effects of

Galatians 6:7-8
2 Peter 2:19

Good

Psalm 1:1-6
John 14:15
Romans 12:1-2
Romans 12:9-13
Romans 13:14
Galatians 5:16
Ephesians 4:22-24
Philippians 4:8
1 Thessalonians
5:16-18
1 Timothy 6:11
1 Timothy 6:18
Titus 2:3
Titus 3:14
2 Peter 1:3-8

Of praying

Romans 1:9
Ephesians 1:16
Colossians 1:9
1 Thessalonians
5:16-18

Relationship to maturity

1 Corinthians 13:11

Harm

Definition:
To cause injury or damage.

Key Verses:
Proverbs 3:29
Romans 13:10

See Also:
Abuse
Critical Spirit
Verbal and Emotional
  Abuse

Haste

Definition:
The quality of making rash or thoughtless decisions without reflecting upon the consequences.

Key Verses:
Psalm 119:60
Proverbs 29:20

See Also:
Decision Making
Procrastination

In departing
  1 Samuel 21:8

In going to court
  Proverbs 25:8

**To embrace a
loved one**
  Luke 15:20

To heal child
  2 Kings 4:29

**To prepare food
for guests**
  Genesis 18:7

To seek the Lord
  Zechariah 8:21

**To tell of Christ's
resurrection**
  Matthew 28:7

Hatred

Definition:
Violent or intense dislike, animosity, or enmity.

Key Verses:
Proverbs 10:12
Matthew 5:43-44

See Also:
Anger
Disrespect
Malice

Because of Jesus
  Matthew 10:22
  Matthew 24:9

Condemned
  Leviticus 19:17
  Matthew 5:43-44
  Galatians 5:19-20
  Colossians 3:8
  1 John 2:9-11
  1 John 4:20-21

For divorce
  Malachi 2:16

Of evil
  Psalm 45:7

Of the righteous
  Esther 5:10-14
  Psalm 69:4

John 15:18-25
John 17:14

**Relationship
to murder**
  1 John 3:15

**Relationship
to the world**
  1 John 2:15-17
  1 John 3:11-15

Wicked hate the light
  John 3:20

Healing

Definition:
To restore to wholeness and health.

Key Verses:
Proverbs 12:18
Matthew 4:23

See Also:
Medicine
Restoration

Health

Definition:
The condition of a person with regard to the soundness of their mind or body.

Key Verses:
Psalm 147:3
Isaiah 53:5

See Also:
Disease
Medicine

Bad health sometimes for God's glory
John 9:1-7

Bad health sometimes result of sin
Psalm 38:3
Ecclesiastes 7:17
1 Corinthians 11:29-30

Benefit of exercise
1 Timothy 4:8-9

From God
Deuteronomy 7:15
Job 2:3-6
Psalm 21:4
Psalm 23:3
Proverbs 20:12
Isaiah 38:1-6

In old age
Deuteronomy 34:7

Jesus' power over
Luke 7:21
Luke 13:10-13

Long-term illness
Mark 5:25-26

Of the wicked
Job 21:7
Psalm 73:3-4

Poor physical condition
Galatians 4:13-14

Restored by God
Job 33:25
Isaiah 38:16

Use of medication
1 Timothy 5:23

Heart

Definition:
Muscular, blood-pumping organ in the chest; used figuratively to describe the emotional center or core of a person.

Key Verses:
Jeremiah 17:9
Ezekiel 36:26

See Also:
Compassion
Courage
Love

Heaven

Definition:
The dwelling place of God as distinguished from earth and usually considered to be beyond the sky.

Key Verses:
Matthew 6:20
Philippians 3:20

See Also:
Assurance of Salvation
Eternal Life
Eternal Security
Hell
Salvation

Description of
Revelation 22:1-5

God created
Genesis 1:6-7

God's dwelling place
1 Kings 8:30

God's throne
Isaiah 66:1
Acts 7:49

Hope of
1 Corinthians 2:9
2 Corinthians 5:2
Colossians 1:12
2 Peter 3:13

Lit by God's glory
Revelation 21:23

New heaven and new earth
Revelation 21:1-2

No sorrow in
Isaiah 60:19-20
Revelation 21:4

People from every nation in heaven
Revelation 7:9

The Lord is preparing
John 14:1-3
Hebrews 11:16

Treasures in
Matthew 6:19-24

Wonder of
2 Corinthians 12:4

Hell

Definition:
The future dwelling place of the ungodly, characterized by eternal torment and separation from God.

Key Verses:
Matthew 10:28
Revelation 20:15

See Also:
Assurance of Salvation
Eternal Security
Heaven
Salvation

A place of torment
Matthew 8:12
Matthew 13:49-50
Luke 16:22-23

Destination of those who harm the righteous
Psalm 63:9

Everlasting punishment
2 Thessalonians 1:9

God's enemies cast into hell
Matthew 25:41
2 Peter 2:4
Revelation 19:20
Revelation 20:7-15

Hell gives up its dead
Revelation 20:13-15

Road is wide to destruction
Matthew 7:13

Weeping in
Matthew 13:49-50

Holiness

Definition:
A primary attribute of God related to His moral character and "otherness," to which Christians are being conformed by the work of the Holy Spirit.

Key Verses:
Romans 6:22
Hebrews 12:14

See Also:
Character
God
Righteousness

Accomplished when Christ returns
1 Corinthians 1:8

Based on God's promise
2 Corinthians 7:1

Benefits of
1 Timothy 4:8

By God's Word
John 17:17

Commanded
Genesis 17:1

Leviticus 11:44-45
Leviticus 19:2
Deuteronomy 18:13
Romans 12:9
1 Corinthians 3:16-17
Ephesians 5:1
Philippians 2:14-15
Philippians 4:8-9
Colossians 3:5-7
1 Thessalonians 4:1-8
Hebrews 12:14
James 1:21
1 Peter 1:14-16
1 John 3:3

Effect on sin
Luke 5:8

Hate evil and love good
Amos 5:15

In body
1 Corinthians 6:19-20

In light of the Lord's return
Romans 13:12-14

In speech
Zephaniah 3:9

Noah was a holy man
Genesis 6:9

Of a priesthood
1 Peter 2:5

Of God
Leviticus 11:45
Isaiah 6:1-5

The Biblical Counseling Reference Guide

Daniel 9:14

Of His people
Leviticus 20:26
1 Peter 2:9

Of Jesus
1 John 3:4-6

Power to be
Romans 6:11-14
Romans 6:22
Romans 12:1-2
Ephesians 4:20-24
Philippians 2:13-15
1 Thessalonians
5:22-23
Titus 2:11-12
1 Peter 2:1
2 Peter 1:3

**Purified for
sincere love**
1 Peter 1:22

**Relationship to
confession**
1 John 1:7-10

Walking in
Hosea 14:9

Holy Spirit

Definition:
The third person of
the Trinity, often
associated with God's
supernatural work-
ings on earth such as
miracles, supernatural
gifts, the sanctifica-
tion of believers, and

the inspiration of
Scripture.

Key Verses:
John 14:16-18
Ephesians 1:13

See Also:
God
Jesus Christ
Spiritual Gifts
Trinity

**Active in Christ's
death**
Hebrews 9:14

**Active in Christ's
ministry**
Matthew 3:16
Luke 3:21-22
Luke 4:1
Luke 4:18

Active in Israel
1 Samuel 16:14

Active in salvation
Romans 8:15
Ephesians 1:13-14

Activity in creation
Genesis 1:1-2
Genesis 1:26-27

Aids in true worship
John 4:23

At Pentecost
Acts 2:1-4
Acts 2:32-33

Baptism in
Matthew 28:19

Acts 1:4-5

Blasphemy against
Matthew 12:32
Mark 3:29

Can be resisted
Acts 7:51

Conviction by
John 16:7-8

Do not stifle
1 Thessalonians 5:19

Down payment of
2 Corinthians
1:21-22
2 Corinthians 5:5

Eternal life from
Galatians 6:8

Filling with
Exodus 31:1-5
Romans 8:9-11
1 Corinthians
3:16-17
Ephesians 5:18

Freedom of
John 3:8

Fruit of
Galatians 5:22-23

Gifts from
Joel 2:28
Romans 12:6-8
1 Corinthians 12:4
1 Corinthians
12:7-11
1 Corinthians
12:28-30

Guidance by
Psalm 139:23-24
John 16:13
Romans 8:26-27

Guiding the early church
Acts 13:2

In leadership
Numbers 27:18

Inspiring apostles
Matthew 10:20

Inspiring prophets
2 Samuel 23:2
Isaiah 61:1

Insulted
Hebrews 10:29

Involved in Christ's birth
Luke 1:35

Involved in prayer
Romans 8:26-27

Involved with believers
Luke 2:26
Romans 8:16
Romans 15:30
1 Corinthians 2:12
Galatians 5:22-25
Ephesians 1:13-14
1 Thessalonians 5:19

Joy from
Acts 13:52
1 Thessalonians 1:6

Knowledge of
1 Corinthians 2:9-10

Live by
Galatians 5:16

Lying to
Acts 5:3

Ministry of
John 14:16-17
1 Corinthians 12:4-6
1 Corinthians 12:13
2 Corinthians 13:14
Galatians 3:3

Omnipresent
Psalm 139:7

Power from
Acts 1:8
Ephesians 3:16

Prayer in
Ephesians 6:18
Jude 20

Promise of
Romans 5:5

Provides enablement
Zechariah 4:6

Provides wisdom
Acts 6:10
1 Corinthians 2:1-10
1 Corinthians 2:13
Isaiah 11:2

Relationship to assurance
Ephesians 1:13-14
Ephesians 4:30
1 John 3:24
1 John 4:13

Relationship to prophecy
2 Peter 1:21
1 John 4:1-3

Renewal by
Titus 3:5

Revelation by
1 Corinthians 2:10

Role in illumination
1 Corinthians 2:14

Role in sanctification
2 Thessalonians 2:13

Speaks to the churches
Revelation 2:7
Revelation 2:11
Revelation 2:17
Revelation 2:29
Revelation 3:6
Revelation 3:13
Revelation 3:22

Submission to
Romans 8:5-6

Temple of
1 Corinthians 3:16
1 Corinthians 6:19-20

Transformation by
2 Corinthians 3:18

Trinitarian relationship
John 16:13-15
1 Corinthians 2:11

Truth of
1 John 5:6

The Biblical Counseling Reference Guide

Understanding from
Genesis 41:38-39
Luke 12:12
John 14:26

Unity of God
Deuteronomy 6:4

Work of
Ezekiel 36:26-27

Homosexuality

Definition:
Sexual attraction and contact between two people of the same sex.

Key Verses:
Romans 1:26-27
1 Corinthians 6:9-11

See Also:
Bisexual
Identity
Same-Sex Attraction
Transsexual
Transvestite

Avoidance of
1 Corinthians 6:18

Body belongs to God
1 Corinthians 6:19-20

Bold sin
Isaiah 3:9

Can be overcome in Christ
Romans 6:11-14
1 Corinthians 10:13

Condemned
Genesis 13:13
Genesis 19:5-13
Leviticus 18:22
Judges 19:22-24
Romans 1:26-28
1 Corinthians 6:9-11
1 Timothy 1:8-11

Example of
Genesis 19:4-7
Judges 19:16-28

Freedom from
1 Corinthians 6:9-11

Hypocrisy
Jeremiah 23:14

Judgment on
Leviticus 20:13
Romans 1:24-27
2 Peter 2:6
Jude 7

Marriage
Genesis 2:24
Malachi 2:15

Patient rebuke
2 Timothy 2:25-26

Relation of male to female
Genesis 2:22

Honesty

Definition:
Straightforwardness in speech and conduct; truthfulness or integrity.

Key Verses:
Proverbs 24:26
Ephesians 4:25

See Also:
Character
Dependability
Integrity
Justice

Benefits of
Proverbs 10:9
Proverbs 20:7
Proverbs 24:26
Ephesians 4:15

Comes from the heart
Matthew 12:33-37

Commanded
Leviticus 19:35
Deuteronomy 25:13

Focus on
Philippians 4:8

In avoiding a bribe
1 Kings 13:8

In business
2 Kings 12:15
Proverbs 13:11
Ezekiel 45:10
Luke 3:12-13

In conduct
2 Corinthians 1:12

In speech
Ephesians 4:25

In work
2 Chronicles 34:12

Lack of
Jeremiah 5:1

Of Samuel
1 Samuel 12:1-5

Prayer for
Proverbs 30:7-9

Role in worship
John 4:23-24

The Lord desires
Proverbs 11:1
Proverbs 16:11
Proverbs 20:10

**The wicked
hate honesty**
Proverbs 29:10
Amos 5:10

Honor

Definition:
To respect, esteem, praise, or bestow special privilege upon.

Key Verses:
Exodus 20:12
1 Timothy 1:17

See Also:
Respect
Reward
Worship

Based on humility
Proverbs 15:33
Proverbs 18:12
Proverbs 29:23
Matthew 23:12
Mark 10:40-45

Luke 14:8-11

Do not seek
Luke 14:11
John 5:41

For church leaders
1 Timothy 5:17

For parents
Exodus 20:12
Deuteronomy 5:16
Matthew 15:4

For the Lord
Psalm 148:1-14

For the righteous
Job 29:7-10
Daniel 5:29

**For those who
follow God**
Romans 2:10

From God
1 Kings 3:13
Ecclesiastes 6:2

**From pursuing
righteousness**
Proverbs 21:21

From wisdom
Proverbs 3:16

Refused
Acts 10:25-26

Shown to wives
1 Peter 3:7

Hope

Definition:
Eager expectation or

anticipation of the future; used especially of optimistic assurance based upon God's faithfulness.

Key Verses:
Jeremiah 29:11
Hebrews 6:19-20

See Also:
Confidence
Desire
Faith
Security

**Based on God's
faithfulness**
Lamentations
3:21-23

Benefits of
Proverbs 13:12

Brings God delight
Psalm 147:11

Certainty of
Proverbs 23:18

Defense of
1 Peter 3:15

Does not disappoint
Romans 5:5

For God's glory
Philippians 1:20

For salvation
Romans 8:24

**For the repentant
heart**
Job 11:14-18

The Biblical Counseling Reference Guide

From God
Psalm 62:5
Jeremiah 29:11
Romans 15:13
2 Thessalonians
2:16-17

From the Scriptures
Romans 15:4

Gateway of
Hosea 2:15

**Hopelessness
without God**
Ephesians 2:12

In calling
Ephesians 1:18
Ephesians 4:4

In Christ
Hebrews 6:17-20

In Christ's return
Titus 2:11-14

**Inciting faith
and love**
Colossians 1:3-5

In faith
Hebrews 10:23

In God
Job 13:15
Psalm 25:3
Psalm 39:7
Psalm 42:5-6
Psalm 130:7
Lamentations
3:23-24
Romans 5:2
1 Timothy 4:10

1 Peter 1:21

In God's promise
Psalm 119:116

In God's Word
Psalm 119:74

In His sovereignty
Psalm 71:5

In His unfailing love
Psalm 33:18
Psalm 33:22

In riches
1 Timothy 6:17

**In the midst
of suffering**
Romans 5:3-5
2 Corinthians
4:16-18

None for the godless
Job 8:13

Of eternal life
Job 19:25-26
John 3:16
John 11:25
Acts 24:15
Titus 1:2

Of having children
Romans 4:18

Of heaven
Colossians 1:5

Of rest
Hebrews 4:1

Of righteousness
Galatians 5:5

Of salvation
1 Thessalonians 5:8

Producing boldness
2 Corinthians 3:12

Relationship to faith
Hebrews 11:1

Security of
Psalm 9:18
1 Corinthians 13:13
Hebrews 6:19

**Through the
resurrection**
1 Peter 1:3

With patience
Romans 8:25

Hopelessness

Definition:
A feeling of sadness,
despair, and pessimism
regarding the future.

Key Verses:
Psalm 42:5-6
Romans 8:24-25

See Also:
Depression
Hope
Suicide Prevention

Because of hardships
2 Corinthians 1:8

Courage in
Isaiah 57:10

Effect of pain
Psalm 38:7

Encouragement from the Lord
Isaiah 61:1-3

Hope from the Scriptures
Psalm 119:81

Hope in the Lord
Psalm 25:3
Psalm 33:17-18
Psalm 39:7

Meaninglessness of labor
Ecclesiastes 2:20

Need for friends
Job 6:14

Perseverance in
2 Corinthians 4:8

Prayer during
Psalm 88:1-18

Hospitality

Definition:
The practice of receiving guests in a cordial, friendly, and loving manner.

Key Verses:
Mark 9:37
Romans 12:13

See Also:
Friendship
Generosity
Kindness

Betrayal in
Psalm 41:9

Commanded
Exodus 23:9
Leviticus 19:10
Leviticus 24:22
Deuteronomy 10:19
Luke 6:31
Romans 12:13
Philemon 22
Hebrews 13:2
1 Peter 4:9
3 John 5-8

Example of
Genesis 18:1-8
Genesis 19:1-3
Genesis 24:12-33
1 Kings 13:15
2 Kings 4:8-10
Mark 8:1-8
Galatians 4:14

Hospitality given
Luke 10:38-42
Acts 10:21-23
Acts 16:34

Importance of
Romans 12:13

Limit to
2 John 10-11

Love one another
Matthew 7:12

Of Peter
Galatians 1:18

Refusal of
Numbers 20:14-21

To foreigners
Exodus 2:16-20
Ruth 2:14

To Jesus
Mark 14:13-15

To ministers
1 Corinthians 16:5-6
2 Corinthians 1:16

To the less fortunate
Luke 14:12-14

Will be rewarded
Matthew 10:40-42

Hostility

Definition:
Enmity; mutual distrust, dislike, or ill will.

Key Verses:
Romans 8:7
Ephesians 2:14

See Also:
Anger
Hatred
Malice

Against God's servants
Exodus 16:2
Acts 17:5-7

Against God's Word
Jeremiah 36:22-24

End of
2 Samuel 2:26-28
Isaiah 11:13

Ephesians 2:16

In the family
Genesis 16:11-12

Of God
Psalm 78:49

To God
Leviticus 26:23-24
Romans 8:7
Colossians 1:21

To God's people
2 Thessalonians 3:15

Human Nature

Definition:
The essential character, qualities, and inclinations of being a person in the race of mankind.

Key Verses:
Psalm 51:5
Ephesians 2:3

See Also:
Pride
Relationship
Sin

Humanism

Definition:
A perspective centered on human interests, dignity, capabilities, and worth.

Key Verses:
Romans 1:25
1 Corinthians 1:25

See Also:
God
Materialism

Humility

Definition:
The quality of being humble; meekness; lack of pride.

Key Verses:
Colossians 3:12
1 Peter 5:5

See Also:
Inferiority
Meekness
Pride

Associate with the humble
Romans 12:16

Before God
Job 40:2-4
Job 42:5-6
James 4:10

Benefits of
2 Chronicles 7:14
Proverbs 3:34
Proverbs 22:4
Isaiah 57:15
Zephaniah 2:3

Boasting only in the Lord
Jeremiah 9:23-24

1 Corinthians 1:31

Commanded
Proverbs 27:2
Jeremiah 45:5
Luke 18:9-14
Romans 12:3
Ephesians 4:1-3
Philippians 2:3-4
Colossians 3:12
1 Peter 3:8
1 Peter 5:5-7

Desired by God
Micah 6:8

Encouragement toward
Philippians 2:1-7

Example of
Genesis 32:10
Matthew 8:5-10
John 1:27
John 3:30
1 Corinthians 15:9

God favors
Isaiah 66:2

God humbles the proud
2 Samuel 22:28
Daniel 4:37

Greatness in
Matthew 18:4
Matthew 23:11-12

Importance of
Matthew 18:2-4
Luke 14:11

Leadership through
Matthew 20:25-26

Matthew 23:11
Mark 9:35
Luke 9:46-48

Leads to honor
Proverbs 15:33
Proverbs 18:12
Proverbs 29:23

Love is humble
1 Corinthians 13:4

Of Christ
Isaiah 53:2-3
Matthew 11:29
Matthew 26:39
Mark 10:45
John 13:1-17
Philippians 2:5-8

Of Moses
Numbers 12:3

Of Paul
2 Corinthians
12:7-10

**People will
become proud**
2 Timothy 3:2

Reason for pride
James 1:9

**Relationship
to worship**
Psalm 51:15-17
James 4:6-10

Wisdom in
Proverbs 11:2
2 Corinthians
10:12-14

Hunger

Definition:
The desire or need
for food; uneasiness
caused by a need or
desire.

Key Verses:
Psalm 107:8-9
Revelation 7:16

See Also:
Famine

After a long fast
Matthew 4:2
Luke 4:2

Because of sin
Lamentations 1:11
Lamentations 4:4-5
Ezekiel 4:16-17
Amos 4:6

**Can eat when
you wish**
Deuteronomy 12:20

Cause of sin
Proverbs 6:30-31

**Famine displaces
families**
Genesis 12:10

**Feed the hungry in
Christ's service**
Matthew 25:37-40
Romans 12:20

For God's Word
Amos 8:11-12

For righteousness
Matthew 5:6

For spiritual milk
1 Peter 2:2

God provides
Isaiah 55:1-2

God will remove
Revelation 7:16

**Grumbling against
God because of**
Exodus 16:2-3

Imposed by leader
1 Samuel 14:24

Jesus feeds the 4000
Matthew 15:32-38
Mark 8:1-9

Jesus feeds the 5000
Matthew 14:15-21
Mark 6:35-44

Leads to selfishness
1 Corinthians
11:33-34

Of God's servants
1 Corinthians 4:11

Of Jesus
Matthew 21:18
Mark 11:12

Urges worker to work
Proverbs 16:26

Hurt

Definition:
To cause pain and suf-
fering.

The Biblical Counseling Reference Guide

Key Verses:
Psalm 69:29
Lamentations 3:49-51

See Also:
Abuse
Cry
Hope
Pain

Husband

Definition:
A married man.

Key Verses:
Ephesians 5:33
1 Peter 3:7

See Also:
Family
Father
Marriage
Wife

Enjoy life with one's wife
Ecclesiastes 9:9

Harshness condemned
Colossians 3:19

Importance of faithfulness
Proverbs 5:15-19
Hebrews 13:4

Love for one's wife
Ephesians 5:25-33

Sexual responsibility of
1 Corinthians 7:3-5

Show honor to wife
1 Peter 3:7

United to wife
Matthew 19:5

Hypocrisy

Definition:
False pretense or simulation of a belief or behavior that one does not truly hold; used especially pertaining to religious virtues.

Key Verses:
Matthew 6:2
1 Peter 2:1

See Also:
Character
Deception
Dishonesty
Integrity
Lying

Avoidance of
Psalm 26:4
Matthew 6:1
1 Peter 2:1

Condemned
Matthew 6:5
Luke 6:46
Titus 1:16

Danger of
Proverbs 27:6
Romans 2:1

Deception of
Proverbs 26:23

Effects of
Psalm 55:21
Romans 2:21-24

God knows the heart
Revelation 3:1

In God's people
Jeremiah 5:1-2

In righteousness
Matthew 15:7-9
Matthew 23:1-33
Mark 7:6
Luke 20:20
James 1:26

Of disobedience
Ezekiel 33:31

Of fasting
Isaiah 58:3-5
Matthew 6:16

Of idolatry
Ezekiel 14:4

Of legalism
John 7:19

Of liars
1 Timothy 4:2

Protection from
Psalm 28:3

Religious pride
Luke 3:7-8

Repentance from
James 4:8

Spying on freedom in order to enslave
Galatians 2:4

To avoid persecution
Galatians 6:12-13

Toward other believers
Galatians 2:11-13

Identity

Definition:
One's concept of oneself as distinguished from others.

Key Verses:
2 Corinthians 5:17
Galatians 2:20

See Also:
Inferiority
Purpose in Life
Self-Worth

Abraham's sons
Galatians 3:7

Accepted by the Lord
Psalm 27:10

Alive in Christ
Romans 6:11

Apart from achievement
Job 6:13

Before salvation
Ephesians 2:1-3

Born again
John 3:3

Can walk in new way of life
Romans 6:4

Children of God
John 1:12
Romans 8:15-16
Galatians 4:7
Ephesians 1:5
1 John 3:1

Children of light
Ephesians 5:8

Chosen by God
Ephesians 1:4

Christian
Acts 11:26

Cleansed spiritually
1 Corinthians 6:11

Clothed with Christ
Galatians 3:27

Conform to the image of God
Romans 12:2

Filling of Christ
Colossians 2:9-10

Freed from sin
Romans 6:6-7
Romans 6:22

Freed from the law
Romans 6:14
Romans 7:4
Galatians 3:13

From behavior
Proverbs 20:11

From God
Deuteronomy 26:18
Psalm 139:13-14
Proverbs 16:4
Jeremiah 32:38
Ezekiel 36:26-27

God's workmanship
Ephesians 2:10

Heirs according to the promise
Galatians 3:29

Hidden with Christ in God
Colossians 3:3

Holy before God
1 Corinthians 6:19-20
Ephesians 5:8-17
Colossians 1:22
1 Peter 2:9

In Christ
Romans 6:11
Romans 8:1
2 Corinthians 1:21-22
2 Corinthians 5:17
2 Corinthians 5:20-21
Galatians 2:20
Ephesians 1:3
Ephesians 1:18
Ephesians 2:3
Ephesians 2:19-22
Colossians 1:2
Colossians 1:10-16
Colossians 2:11
Colossians 3:1-3
1 Peter 1:23

2 Peter 1:3-4
Revelation 14:1

In depravity
Romans 5:12
Ephesians 2:3

**In fellowship
with others**
1 John 1:7

In God's flock
John 10:1-6

In God's plan
Romans 8:29
Ephesians 1:11-12

Jesus' disciple
John 13:34-35
Revelation 22:4

Know yourself
Proverbs 27:19

**New birth into
a living hope**
1 Peter 1:3

Of Jesus Christ
Mark 15:1-2
Luke 9:18-20

**Saved from
God's wrath**
Romans 5:9

**Sealed with the
promised Holy Spirit**
Ephesians 1:13-14

Sins are forgiven
Ephesians 1:7

**Slaves to
righteousness**
Romans 6:19

Idleness

Definition:
The state of being
inoperative, inactive,
unemployed, or not
in use.

Key Verses:
1 Thessalonians 5:14
2 Thessalonians 3:6

See Also:
Laziness
Procrastination
Work

**Ant an example
against idleness**
Proverbs 6:6-8

**Do not give work
to the lazy**
Proverbs 10:26

Effects of
Proverbs 6:9-11
Proverbs 10:4-5
Proverbs 12:24
Proverbs 13:4
Proverbs 14:23
Proverbs 19:15
Proverbs 20:13
Proverbs 21:25
Ecclesiastes 4:5
Ecclesiastes 10:18

Idle without a job
Matthew 20:6-7

**The lazy give excuses
not to work**
Proverbs 22:13
Proverbs 26:13

**Willingness to
work commanded**
2 Thessalonians
3:10-11

Idolatry

Definition:
To worship or revere
a graven image; meta-
phorically to order
one's life around some-
thing other than God
Himself.

Key Verses:
Exodus 20:4
1 Corinthians 10:14

See Also:
God
Judgment
Worship

Ignorance

Definition:
Lack of knowledge,
training, or under-
standing of something.

Key Verses:
Hebrews 5:2
1 Peter 1:14

See Also:
Knowledge
Wisdom

About God
Isaiah 44:18
Jeremiah 10:14
Acts 17:23
Acts 17:30
1 Corinthians 15:34

Blasphemy in
Jude 10

Danger of
Proverbs 19:2

Deal gently with
Hebrews 5:2

Effects of spiritual ignorance
Hosea 4:5-6

No excuse for
Romans 1:19-25

Of truth
1 Timothy 1:7

Sinning in
Acts 3:17

Spiritual
Luke 23:34

Trust God during
Proverbs 3:5
Hebrews 11:8

Illness

Definition:
An unhealthy or diseased condition or state.

Key Verses:
Psalm 41:3
James 5:14-15

See Also:
Caregiving
Chronic Illness
Evil and Suffering
Health

Image

Definition:
An exact likeness or recreation of another; a picture in the mind.

Key Verses:
Genesis 1:27
Colossians 1:15

See Also:
God
Idolatry
Self-Worth
Worship

Imitate

Definition:
To mimic, become like, or follow another.

Key Verses:
1 Corinthians 4:16
3 John 11

See Also:
Conform
Discipleship
Example

Immaturity

Definition:
Lack of physical, mental, or spiritual development.

Key Verses:
1 Corinthians 13:11
James 1:4

See Also:
Carnality
Child Training

Due to disobedience
Hebrews 5:12-14

Due to partial understanding
Acts 18:24-26
Acts 19:1-7

Easily deceived
Ephesians 4:14

Leads to strife
1 Corinthians 3:3

Overcome through wisdom
Proverbs 9:6

Immorality

Definition:
Wickedness or behavior contrary to what is right and moral.

Key Verses:
Matthew 15:19
1 Corinthians 5:9-11

Avoidance of
Proverbs 6:23-24
Acts 15:20
Acts 15:29
Acts 21:25
1 Corinthians 6:18
1 Corinthians 7:2
Colossians 3:5
1 Thessalonians 4:3

Comes from the heart
Matthew 15:19
Mark 7:21

Condemned
Romans 13:13
1 Corinthians 6:9-10
1 Corinthians 6:13
1 Corinthians 10:8
Galatians 5:19-21
Ephesians 5:3
Ephesians 5:5
Hebrews 13:4
Revelation 21:8
Revelation 22:15

Discipline for
1 Corinthians 5:9-11

Failure to repent
Revelation 2:21
Revelation 9:21

Sexual
Numbers 25:1
1 Corinthians 5:1

Immortality

Definition:
The state or quality of being free from death; eternal life.

Key Verses:
1 Corinthians
15:53-54
2 Timothy 1:9-10

Conquer death through resurrection
1 Corinthians
15:42-55

Eating from the tree of life
Genesis 3:22

Eternal dwelling with God
2 Corinthians 5:1

Eternal life or eternal judgment
Daniel 12:2

In Jesus Christ
John 3:14-16
John 10:28
John 11:25-26
Romans 6:23
1 Peter 1:3-4

Mortality of people
Hebrews 1:10-12

Nothing can separate us from God
Romans 8:38-39

Of God
1 Timothy 6:15-16

Of martyrs
Revelation 20:4-6

Of the righteous
Matthew 25:46
John 5:28-29

Take hold of
1 Timothy 6:12

Through keeping Jesus' Word
John 8:51

Importance

Definition:
Degree of value, significance, or consequence.

Key Verses:
Matthew 6:25
Mark 12:33

Of commandments
Matthew 22:37-38
Matthew 23:23
Mark 12:28-29

Of leaders
Galatians 2:6

Of others
Philippians 2:3-4

Of popularity
1 Corinthians 4:3

Of the gospel
1 Corinthians 15:3-4

Impulse

Definition:
A sudden, spontaneous inclination to act without reflection.

Key Verses:
Proverbs 20:25
James 1:19

See Also:
Inclination
Temptation

Avoidance of harmful
Psalm 119:128

**Benefits of
self-control**
Proverbs 16:32
Proverbs 29:11

Danger of
Proverbs 13:3
Proverbs 20:25
Proverbs 25:28
Romans 7:5
Romans 8:6

**Self-control
encouraged**
Galatians 5:22-23
1 Thessalonians
4:4-5

1 Thessalonians
5:6-8
1 Timothy 3:2
Titus 1:8
Titus 2:2
1 Peter 1:13
1 Peter 5:8

Incest

Definition:
Sexual contact between members of the same family, most often an adult and child.

Key Verses:
Leviticus 18:6
Psalm 37:39-40

See Also:
Abuse
Childhood Sexual
    Abuse
Rape
Verbal and Emotional
    Abuse

Condemned
Leviticus 18:9-17
Leviticus 20:17
Ezekiel 22:11
1 Corinthians 5:1

**Deliverance
for victims**
Psalm 10:14

Patience in
Romans 12:12

**The Lord brings
justice**
Psalm 9:12
Psalm 9:18
Psalm 72:2

**The Lord cares
for victims**
Psalm 10:17
Psalm 22:24

Inclination

Definition:
A disposition, preference, or leaning toward something; used especially pertaining to natural dispositions.

Key Verses:
Genesis 6:5
Deuteronomy 5:29

See Also:
Impulse
Temptation

Of believers
Romans 8:9
Galatians 5:16
Galatians 5:22-23

Of flesh and Spirit
Romans 8:5
Galatians 5:17
Jude 19

Of unbelievers
Genesis 6:5
Genesis 8:21
1 Corinthians 2:14

The Biblical Counseling Reference Guide

Galatians 5:19-21

Results of following
Romans 8:6
Romans 8:13
Galatians 6:8

Toward obedience
Deuteronomy 5:29

Definition:
The quality of being not consistent, incompatible, not predictable, erratic, or irregular.

Key Verses:
Numbers 23:19
1 John 2:4

See Also:
Disobedience
Hypocrisy
Rebellion
Trust

From employers
Genesis 31:41

God is consistent
Numbers 23:19
1 Samuel 15:29
Malachi 3:6
James 1:17

In worship
1 Kings 18:21
Psalm 78:57

Of doubters
James 1:6

Of the spiritually immature
Ephesians 4:14

Stability praised
Romans 4:20

Definition:
The inability to make up one's mind; hesitancy or irresolution.

Key Verses:
Job 12:13
Psalm 32:8

See Also:
Decision Making
Purpose in Life

Cannot be slaves of two masters
Matthew 6:24

Hesitant to leave
Genesis 19:15-16

Indecisive people not fit for God's kingdom
Luke 9:62

Instability of
James 1:6-8

Worshipping God and idols
1 Kings 18:21
2 Kings 17:41

Definition:
The killing of a newborn child.

Key Verses:
Leviticus 18:21
Luke 18:16

See Also:
Abortion
Death
Euthanasia

As an act of fear
Matthew 2:16

As an act of oppression
Exodus 1:16
Acts 7:19

During warfare
Isaiah 13:18
Lamentations 2:20
Nahum 3:10

Practice of idolatry
2 Kings 16:3
2 Kings 21:6
2 Chronicles 28:3
Ezekiel 20:31

Definition:
Extreme, unreasonable, and irrational affection or admiration for someone or something.

Key Verses:
Deuteronomy 5:21
Proverbs 4:23

See Also:
Desire
Love
Lust

Leads to sin
Judges 14:1-3
2 Samuel 11:2-5

Self-control encouraged
Proverbs 25:28
Proverbs 29:11
Galatians 5:22-23
1 Thessalonians 4:4
1 Thessalonians 5:6-8
1 Timothy 3:2
Titus 1:8
Titus 2:2
1 Peter 1:13
1 Peter 4:7
1 Peter 5:8

Used as a trap
1 Samuel 18:20-29

Inferiority

Definition:
The state or quality of being lower in value, quality, rank, or position.

Key Verses:
Matthew 12:12
1 Corinthians 1:26-29

See Also:
Oppression
Resentment

In blessing
Hebrews 7:7

Intrinsic value
Luke 12:6-7

Not inferior to others
Job 12:3
Job 13:2
2 Corinthians 11:5
2 Corinthians 12:11

Of a kingdom
Daniel 2:39

Of drink
John 2:10

Of people
Deuteronomy 32:21

Infertility

Definition:
The inability to conceive or give birth to a child after one or more years of attempting.

Key Verses:
Proverbs 13:12
Isaiah 54:1

See Also:
Adoption
Childlessness

Adoption
Exodus 2:10

Affliction associated with
1 Samuel 1:7-8

Cause of anguish
Genesis 30:1
1 Samuel 1:1-7

God can overcome
Genesis 18:13-14
Genesis 21:1-3
1 Samuel 1:20

God controls the womb
Genesis 16:1-4
Genesis 20:17-18
Genesis 29:31
Genesis 30:1-2
Genesis 30:22

God gives greater blessings than children
Isaiah 56:3-5

Husband's love
1 Samuel 1:5

Judgment from God
Hosea 9:14

Love, mentor younger ones
Isaiah 54:1-8

Of Sarah
Genesis 11:30

Of the righteous
Luke 1:7

Pain in childlessness
1 Samuel 1:7-8

The Biblical Counseling Reference Guide

Perseverance in
Proverbs 13:12

Praying for a child
1 Samuel 1:11

Rejoicing in
Isaiah 54:1

Sharing the joy
Luke 1:57-58

Supernatural pregnancy
Luke 1:24-25

Take delight in the Lord
Psalm 37:4

Influence

Definition:
The ability to affect or shape outcome or development.

Key Verses:
1 Corinthians 15:33
2 Corinthians 5:11

See Also:
Discipleship
Reputation

Avoidance of negative influences
Deuteronomy 18:9-13
Psalm 1:1-2

Do not be an evil influence
Matthew 18:6

Mark 9:42
Luke 17:1-2
1 Corinthians 8:7-13

Effects of
Proverbs 13:20

Evil
Deuteronomy 13:6-10
1 Kings 11:1-8
1 Kings 22:51-53
2 Chronicles 21:6
2 Chronicles 33:9
Micah 1:13
Acts 13:50
Acts 14:2
1 Corinthians 8:10-13
1 Corinthians 15:33
2 Thessalonians 3:6
3 John 9-10

Godly
Matthew 5:13-16
Philippians 2:14-15
1 Thessalonians 1:7-8
1 Thessalonians 2:11-12
2 Timothy 1:5
2 Timothy 3:14-15

Influence to lead others to Jesus
John 12:9-11
Acts 10:24-27
Acts 17:4
1 Corinthians 10:32-33

In government
Esther 4:12-14

Esther 10:3

Of ancestors
Ruth 4:11
Jeremiah 16:10-12

Of a spouse
1 Corinthians 7:16
1 Peter 3:1-2

Of Satan
John 13:2

Of teachers
Luke 6:40

On youth
2 Chronicles 13:7
Proverbs 22:6

Through good works
1 Peter 2:12

Injure

Definition:
To harm.

Key Verses:
Psalm 147:3
Isaiah 53:5

See Also:
Abuse
Restoration

Injustice

Definition:
Unfairness or inequity in a legal decision; perversion of what is right or fair.

Key Verses:
2 Chronicles 19:7
Psalm 12:5

See Also:
Oppression
Persecution
Prejudice

Condemned
Exodus 23:1-9
Leviticus 19:15
Deuteronomy
16:19-20
Deuteronomy
24:17-18
Proverbs 17:15

God is just
Zephaniah 3:5

God judges
Exodus 22:21-24
Deuteronomy 27:19
Isaiah 10:1-4
Amos 5:11-15

Of the wicked
Job 24:2-3
Habakkuk 1:1-4

Innocence

Definition:
Ignorance, naivety, or freedom from evil or wrongdoing.

Key Verses:
Exodus 23:7
Romans 16:19

See Also:
Children

Guilt
Ignorance
Virtue
Wisdom

Concerning evil
Romans 16:19

**Do not judge
the innocent**
Exodus 23:7
Matthew 12:7

False claim of
Matthew 27:24

God's blessing on
2 Samuel 22:21-25

Innocent of blame
1 Samuel 22:11-15
Jonah 1:14
Ephesians 5:25-27
Philippians 2:15
Philippians 3:6
Colossians 1:22
1 Thessalonians 3:13
2 Peter 3:14

**Keep from
willful sins**
Psalm 19:13

Of Jesus
Luke 23:15-16
John 19:1-6
1 Peter 2:21-22

Persecution in
Genesis 39:11-20

Insanity

Definition:
A legal and social term for the state of being incapacitated by one's mental state so that normal behavior is not possible.

Key Verses:
Mark 5:15
Acts 26:24

See Also:
Counseling
Mental Illness

False accusation of
Mark 3:20-21
John 10:20
Acts 26:24-25

Pretending to be
1 Samuel 21:12-14

**Result of an
evil spirit**
1 Samuel 18:10-11

**Result of God's
judgment**
Deuteronomy 28:28
Deuteronomy 28:34
Daniel 4:31-34
Matthew 17:15

Insensitive

Definition:
Lacking in tact or concern for the feelings of others.

The Biblical Counseling Reference Guide

Key Verses:
Proverbs 18:19
1 Corinthians 9:22

See Also:
Apathy
Communication
Confrontation
Tact
Wisdom

To conscience
Hosea 12:8
Ephesians 4:19
1 Timothy 4:1-2

To God
Psalm 95:8-10

To God's judgment
Isaiah 42:25

To Jesus' miracles
Matthew 11:20-24

To spiritual needs
Acts 28:27

Insomnia

Definition:
Chronic inability to sleep; may be characterized by restlessness, inability to fall asleep, or inability to sustain sleep.

Key Verses:
Psalm 119:148
2 Corinthians 11:27

See Also:
Fear

Guilt
Prayer

Could not sleep
Esther 6:1

Result of concern for another
Song of Songs 3:1-2
Daniel 6:16-23

Result of dreams
Daniel 2:1

Result of riches
Ecclesiastes 5:12

Suffering of the righteous
2 Corinthians 11:27

To meditate on Scripture
Psalm 119:148

To pray over troubles
Psalm 77:2-8

Troubled nights
Job 7:3-4
Ecclesiastes 2:23

Instability

Definition:
The state or quality of being in flux, prone to change, inconsistent, or unenduring.

Key Verses:
Psalm 40:2
Proverbs 29:4

See Also:
Dependability
Trust

Abandoning first love
Revelation 2:4

Do not be led astray
Hebrews 13:9

Inconsistent loyalty
Hosea 6:4

Of doubters
James 1:6

Of immature believers
Ephesians 4:14

Result of God's judgment
1 Kings 14:15

Turning from Christ
Galatians 1:6-9

Undependable servant
Matthew 6:24

Instruction

Definition:
The act or process of imparting knowledge, customs, or attitudes.

Key Verses:
Proverbs 13:18
Proverbs 22:15

See Also:
Children
Family

Father
Mother
Discipleship

Need for discipline
Proverbs 13:24
Proverbs 19:18
Proverbs 29:15
Proverbs 29:17

**Preparing others
before your death**
1 Kings 2:1
1 Chronicles 22:6

**Responsibility
of fathers**
Ephesians 6:4

**Teach children
the fear of God**
Psalm 34:11

**Teach God's Word
to children**
Deuteronomy 4:9
Deuteronomy 6:6-7
Deuteronomy
11:18-19
Psalm 78:5

Insult

Definition:
To treat with offense,
indignity, or reproach.

Key Verses:
Proverbs 12:16
1 Peter 2:23

See Also:
Gossip
Malice

Ridicule
Slander

Action of wicked men
1 Samuel 10:27
2 Peter 3:3-4

Against the innocent
Matthew 26:68

Attacking actions
2 Samuel 6:20

Attacking character
Acts 17:18
Titus 1:12

Because of Christ
1 Peter 4:14

Condemned
1 Peter 2:1

Effect on the heart
Psalm 69:20

**Geographical
prejudice**
John 1:46

God's judgment on
2 Kings 2:23-24

Integrity

Definition:
Unyielding devotion
to a code of conduct;
soundness, forthright-
ness, and honesty in
conduct.

Key Verses:
Proverbs 10:9
Titus 2:7-8

See Also:
Character
Ethics
Immorality
Lying
Morality
Stealing

**Against the
world system**
Colossians 2:8
1 John 2:15

Amidst loss
Job 2:3

Benefits of
2 Chronicles 12:12
Psalm 112:5
Proverbs 10:9
Proverbs 11:3
Proverbs 19:1
Proverbs 20:7
Proverbs 24:26

Commanded
Luke 6:31
Ephesians 4:1
Colossians 3:9-10
Titus 2:7

Commitment to
Job 27:4-6
Philippians 4:8

Creates protection
Proverbs 13:6

Dishonest business
Hosea 12:7

Enablement for
Proverbs 3:26

2 Peter 1:3-10

Encouragement toward
Psalm 15:1-5
Psalm 101:1-8

Example of
2 Kings 12:15

Financial
Romans 13:8

Follow the Word
Psalm 19:7-9
Psalm 119:9

God sees all
Psalm 26:2-3
Hebrews 4:13

Importance of
1 Timothy 1:19

In avoiding a bribe
1 Kings 13:8

In business
Proverbs 16:11

In judgment
Zechariah 8:16-17

In leadership
Exodus 18:21
Daniel 6:1-4
Titus 1:7

In speech
Ephesians 4:25

In suffering
Job 2:9

Live with
Psalm 40:8

Of God
Numbers 23:19

Of God's people
Revelation 14:5

Relationship to vows
Numbers 30:1-2

Vindication for
Psalm 7:8

Wicked hate those with
Amos 5:10

Intervention

Definition:
To disrupt the natural course of events, pattern of behavior, or usual consequences by interfering or confronting.

Key Verses:
Proverbs 24:11-12
Isaiah 59:16

See Also:
Addiction
Alcohol and Drug Abuse
Counseling
Habits

Intimacy

Definition:
The state or quality of being closely familiar or acquainted with someone.

Key Verses:
Ephesians 1:17
Philippians 2:1-2

See Also:
Communication
Friendship
Marriage

Based in love
1 Corinthians 13:4-7

Be a good listener
Proverbs 20:5

Benefits of
Ecclesiastes 4:8-12

Faithful friend
Proverbs 27:6

Gossip destroys intimacy
Proverbs 17:9

Marital
Genesis 4:1
Ephesians 5:31

Prayer for
Romans 15:5-6

Relationship to forgiveness
Ephesians 4:32

With believers
James 5:16

With friends
1 Samuel 18:3-4
Proverbs 17:17

With God
Exodus 33:11

Deuteronomy 6:5
Psalm 9:10
Psalm 16:11
Psalm 25:1-3
Psalm 73:23-28
Psalm 139:1-2
Psalm 139:23-24
Psalm 143:8
Jeremiah 31:3
Matthew 6:8
2 Corinthians 12:9
Ephesians 5:1-2

With Jesus
Galatians 2:20

Intoxication

Definition:
The state or quality of being strongly influenced by something, especially alcohol or other chemicals.

Key Verses:
Isaiah 5:11-12
Ephesians 5:18

See Also:
Addiction
Alcohol and Drug
  Abuse
Habits

Condemned
1 Thessalonians
  5:6-8

Not addicted to wine
1 Timothy 3:2-3
Titus 1:7
Titus 2:2-3

Practicing abstinence
Proverbs 31:4-5
Jeremiah 35:1-6
Luke 7:33

Sensible living
Titus 2:12

Islam

Definition:
A monotheistic religion that began under the leadership of Muhammad in the Arabian Peninsula during the seventh century C.E.

Key Verses:
Romans 5:8
Philippians 2:6-8

See Also:
Bible Reliability
God
Jesus Christ

**Covenant
through Isaac**
Genesis 17:21

Deity of Jesus
Luke 2:11
John 1:1

Evil passions
James 4:1

**Failure of human
wisdom**
Psalm 118:22

God's love
1 John 4:8
1 John 4:18-19

Great Commission
Matthew 28:19-20

Ishmael's blessing
Genesis 17:20

Jesus' authority
Matthew 18:12-13
Matthew 28:18
John 3:16-17
John 8:28
John 11:43-44
1 Timothy 2:5

**Jesus is the Word
from God**
John 1:14

Jesus the Creator
John 1:3

**Origin and use
of Scripture**
2 Timothy 3:16-17

**Prophecy
concerning Jesus**
Deuteronomy 18:15
Deuteronomy 18:18

**Response to
adversaries**
Matthew 5:9
Matthew 5:44
Romans 12:14
Romans 12:20

Salvation in Jesus
Acts 3:18-23
Acts 4:12

The Biblical Counseling Reference Guide

Romans 5:8
Galatians 1:8
Ephesians 2:8-9
Titus 3:5
Hebrews 8:12
Hebrews 10:10
2 Peter 3:9
1 John 3:1
1 John 5:13

Jealousy

Definition:
The quality of being hostile toward or intolerant or suspicious of rivals.

Key Verses:
Deuteronomy 4:24
Proverbs 27:4

See Also:
Envy
Materialism
Resentment

Between brothers
Genesis 4:3-7
Genesis 37:3-4
Luke 15:28-30

Condemned
Proverbs 23:17
1 Corinthians 3:3
2 Corinthians 12:20
Galatians 5:19-20

Danger of
Proverbs 27:4

In ministry
Acts 13:45

Philippians 1:15

Motivation by
Ecclesiastes 4:4

Of accomplishments
1 Samuel 18:8

Of God
Exodus 20:5
Exodus 34:14
Deuteronomy 32:16
Deuteronomy 32:21
Psalm 78:58
Ezekiel 16:42
Zechariah 8:2

Of Moses
Numbers 12:1-9

Of possessions
Genesis 26:12-14

Of the wealthy
Psalm 73:3-12

Results in violence
Acts 17:5
1 John 3:12

Jehovah's Witness

Definition:
A worldwide religion with a self-contained authority structure and errant teachings, such as denial of the Trinity, frequent predictions of Armageddon, and their own flawed translation of Scripture.

Key Verses:
John 1:1-3
1 John 5:13

See Also:
Cults
God
Jesus Christ

Jesus Christ

Definition:
The Son of God who was born to the Virgin Mary, was crucified for sins, rose from the dead, ascended into heaven, and is returning in judgment.

Key Verses:
John 1:1
1 John 5:1

See Also:
God
Holy Spirit
Messiah

Alpha and Omega
Revelation 1:8
Revelation 22:13

Anointing
Matthew 3:16

Belief in
John 3:16
John 20:31

Birth narrative
Matthew 2:1
Matthew 2:11

Luke 1:31
Luke 2:6
Luke 2:21

Blessing through Abraham
Genesis 22:18

Bread of life
John 6:35

Childhood
Luke 2:40
Luke 2:51-52

Compassion of
Matthew 14:14

Cornerstone
Ephesians 2:20

Creation by
Colossians 1:16-17

Davidic covenant
Psalm 89:3

Death of
Zechariah 12:10
Romans 5:6

Deity and humanity
John 1:14

Deity of
John 1:3-4
John 1:12
John 8:58
John 10:30
John 20:28
Romans 9:5
Philippians 2:6
Colossians 1:15
Colossians 2:9
1 Timothy 6:15

Titus 2:13
Hebrews 1:3
2 Peter 1:1
1 John 5:20
Revelation 1:17

Descendant of David and Abraham
Matthew 1:1

Enablement through
2 Peter 1:3

Eternality of
Hebrews 7:3

Example of
2 Corinthians 8:9
Ephesians 5:2
Hebrews 3:1
Hebrews 12:2
1 Peter 2:21
1 John 3:16

Fulfilled prophecy
Micah 5:2-4
Matthew 2:4-6

Giver of eternal life
Romans 6:9
Romans 6:23

Grace of
Matthew 9:10-12
John 13:3-5

Great Commission
Matthew 28:19

Head of the church
Ephesians 5:23
Colossians 1:18

Help from
Hebrews 2:18

High Priest
Hebrews 4:14-15
Hebrews 7:23-24

Holy one of God
Luke 4:34

Humanity of
Galatians 4:4
Hebrews 2:14
Hebrews 2:17

Humility of
Philippians 2:6-7

Identification with
Romans 6:4-6
Romans 6:11
Romans 10:12

Identity of
Matthew 16:16

Immanuel
Isaiah 7:14

Importance of following
Deuteronomy 18:15

Institutes the New Covenant
Jeremiah 31:34

Intercession of
Romans 8:34
Hebrews 7:25-28
Hebrews 8:1-2

Judgment seat of
2 Corinthians 5:10

King of kings
Revelation 1:5
Revelation 17:14

Revelation 19:16

Lamb of God
John 1:29
Revelation 13:8

Living Stone
1 Peter 2:4

Lordship of
Romans 10:9
1 Corinthians 15:28
Ephesians 1:20-23
Philippians 2:9-11

Love of
2 Corinthians 5:14

Love of God in
Romans 8:38-39

**Mediator between
God and man**
1 Timothy 2:5

Messiah
Matthew 26:63-65
Luke 2:11
Luke 9:20

Ministry of
Matthew 4:23
Mark 1:34
Luke 4:18-21

Mission of
Luke 19:10

Obedience of
Philippians 2:8

Power over death
John 11:1-44

Power over demons
Mark 3:11

Power over sickness
Luke 7:21

Praise to
Matthew 21:9
John 1:41
John 4:25

Prayer of
John 17:1-26

Preaching concerning
Acts 2:31
Acts 3:22
Acts 13:38
Romans 1:1-4
1 John 1:1

Preeminence of
John 1:2
Colossians 1:17
Hebrews 1:1-4
Hebrews 1:8

Preexistence
Psalm 90:2

Prophecy concerning
Genesis 49:10
Deuteronomy 18:15

Prophecy fulfilled
Matthew 3:3
Matthew 5:17
Matthew 8:17
Luke 22:37

Propitiation of
Romans 5:18
1 John 2:2
1 John 4:10

**Reconciliation
through**
Romans 5:1

Rejection of
Mark 8:31
John 1:11

Resurrection of
Acts 2:23-24
Ephesians 1:20

Return of
Acts 1:11
Philippians 3:20

Revealer of God
John 1:18
John 14:9
Hebrews 1:2

**Root of the
Offspring of David**
Revelation 22:16

Sacrifice
Romans 5:8
Romans 6:23
Galatians 3:13
Hebrews 9:28
1 Peter 2:24
1 Peter 3:18

Salvation by
Colossians 3:1
1 John 4:14
Revelation 7:17

Salvation in
Romans 8:1
Romans 10:13
1 Corinthians 15:3-4
2 Corinthians 5:17
Ephesians 1:5

1 John 2:1

Service of
Mark 10:45

Sin and separation
Isaiah 59:2

Sinlessness of
1 Peter 2:22
1 John 3:5

Son of God
Matthew 27:54
Mark 1:11
Mark 15:39
Acts 9:20
Hebrews 1:5
2 Peter 1:17

Substitutionary atonement of
2 Corinthians 5:21

Suffering of
Hebrews 5:8
1 Peter 2:23

Superiority to angels
Hebrews 1:6

Supernatural knowledge of
John 2:24

Sympathy of
Hebrews 4:15

Teachings of
Matthew 9:15
Matthew 11:28
Matthew 24:30
Matthew 24:36
Luke 5:17

The Creator
Genesis 1:1
Nehemiah 9:6
Isaiah 40:28
John 1:1-3

The Word of God
John 1:1
Revelation 19:13

Triumph of
Revelation 5:5

Trust in
Psalm 9:10

Unity of God
Exodus 34:14
Isaiah 43:10
Isaiah 44:6
Ephesians 4:4-6

Virgin birth of
Isaiah 7:14
Matthew 1:18-25
Luke 1:34-35

Way to the Father
John 14:6

Worthiness of
Revelation 5:9

Jewish Fulfillment

Definition:
The unique place in history of the Jewish people, including revelation received from God, divine preservation, and purpose in relation to the entire world.

Key Verses:
Romans 8:3-4
Hebrews 3:3

See Also:
Jesus Christ
Messiah
Prophecy

Abraham in Canaan
Genesis 14:13

Abraham's condition
Genesis 18:11

Covenant through Moses
Exodus 19:5-6
Exodus 19:19-20
Exodus 24:5-8

Covenant with Abraham
Genesis 12:1-3
Genesis 12:7
Genesis 22:18
Isaiah 51:1-2
Galatians 3:16

Covenant with David
2 Samuel 7:12-16
Psalm 89:3-4

Covenant with Israel
Deuteronomy 1:8
Deuteronomy 4:25-27
Deuteronomy 7:7-9
Deuteronomy 14:2
Deuteronomy 26:18-19
Deuteronomy 28:1-15

Deuteronomy
28:62-63
Deuteronomy
30:3-5
1 Kings 8:44-49
Jeremiah 31:3
Ezekiel 3:7
Ezekiel 12:15
Romans 9:3-5

Faith in God
2 Chronicles 20:20

Jesus is David's descendant
Matthew 1:1
Matthew 21:9
Acts 13:22-23

Jesus is Messiah
John 1:41
John 1:45

Miraculous birth of Jesus
Matthew 1:20-23
Matthew 2:1-2

New Covenant initiated by Jesus
Isaiah 59:20-21
Jeremiah 31:31-37
Ezekiel 36:24-28
Luke 22:20
Hebrews 9:15
Revelation 5:5

Origin of name *Israel*
Genesis 32:28

Prophecy concerning Jesus
Deuteronomy 18:15
Psalm 2

Psalm 16:9-10
Psalm 22:7-8
Psalm 22:18
Psalm 31:5
Psalm 34:20
Psalm 41:9
Psalm 69:21
Psalm 72:8
Psalm 72:11
Psalm 72:17
Isaiah 7:14
Isaiah 9:1
Isaiah 9:6-7
Isaiah 42:6
Isaiah 49:6
Isaiah 52:13-15
Isaiah 53:1-12
Jeremiah 23:5-6
Daniel 7:13-14
Daniel 9:25-26
Micah 5:2
Zechariah 9:9
Zechariah 11:12
Zechariah 12:10
Malachi 3:1

Prophecy concerning Judah
Genesis 49:10

Prophecy fulfilled
Matthew 4:12-16
Matthew 8:17
Matthew 26:15
Matthew 27:34-35
Matthew 27:57-60
Luke 7:27
Luke 22:37
Luke 23:34
John 12:14-15
John 12:37-38
John 19:33-34

Acts 2:31
Acts 3:22
Acts 8:33-35
Romans 10:16

Joy

Definition:
An emotion of delight, satisfaction, or happiness.

Key Verses:
Psalm 30:11
Romans 15:13

See Also:
Celebration
Peace

After victory
Nehemiah 8:10

At Christ's birth
Luke 2:10

At Christ's return
1 Peter 4:13

At Israel's redemption
Isaiah 44:23

Because of childbirth
1 Samuel 2:1

Because of success
Nehemiah 8:17-18

From Christ
John 15:11

From God
Psalm 4:7
Isaiah 29:19
Jeremiah 31:13

From salvation
Psalm 13:5
Psalm 51:12-13
Habakkuk 3:18

From the Lord's work
Ezra 6:22

From the Scriptures
Psalm 119:24
Jeremiah 15:16

In the Holy Spirit
Acts 13:52
Galatians 5:22

In the kingdom of God
Romans 14:17

In trials
James 1:2-4

Praise out of
Psalm 71:22

Relationship to worship
Psalm 100:1-2

Resulting from worship
Numbers 10:10

To God's faithful servants
Matthew 25:21

Judgment

Definition:
The act or process of forming an opinion based on reasoning; used especially to condemn someone based on a negative opinion.

Key Verses:
Psalm 7:8
Romans 2:3

See Also:
Critical Spirit
Hypocrisy
Legalism
Spiritual Abuse

God's responsibility
James 4:12

Improper judgment
Acts 23:3

Judge fairly
Leviticus 19:15
Deuteronomy 1:16
Deuteronomy 16:18
Matthew 7:1-5
Luke 6:37
Luke 6:41-42

May be despised by others
Exodus 2:14

May result in retaliation
Genesis 19:9

May result in self-condemnation
Romans 2:1

Not according to appearance
John 7:24

Not judge prematurely
1 Corinthians 4:5

Justice

Definition:
The principle of fairness, equity, and conformity to moral rightness.

Key Verses:
Exodus 23:6
Psalm 9:8

See Also:
Government
Injustice
Righteousness

Administered
2 Samuel 1:1-16
2 Kings 14:5-6
Esther 7:1-10
Acts 1:18-20

Blessings for upholding
Psalm 106:3
Proverbs 24:24-25

Brought about by Jesus
Revelation 19:11

Commanded
Leviticus 19:15

Denial of
Proverbs 29:7
Habakkuk 1:4

Effects on a country
Proverbs 29:4

For the oppressed
Psalm 103:6

God loves
Proverbs 22:22-23
Isaiah 61:8

God will honor
Psalm 112:5

Importance of
Matthew 23:23

Of God
2 Samuel 24:12-17
Psalm 7:11
Psalm 98:8-9
Ezekiel 33:10-20
Matthew 12:18-21
Luke 18:7
Acts 10:34-35
Acts 17:31
Romans 2:11
Hebrews 10:30
1 Peter 1:17
Revelation 16:5-7

Of Messiah
Isaiah 9:7

**Partiality
condemned**
Deuteronomy 16:19

**Pray for those who
persecute you**
Matthew 5:44-45

Kindness

Definition:
The quality of being warmhearted, sympathetic, compassionate, or friendly.

Key Verses:
Proverbs 12:25
Proverbs 14:31

See Also:
Blessing
Generosity

**Characteristic of
the righteous**
Matthew 1:19
Colossians 3:12

Commanded
Colossians 3:12-14
2 Timothy 2:24
1 Peter 3:8

**Effects on the
personality**
Proverbs 12:25

From captors
2 Kings 25:27-30

From love
1 Corinthians 13:4

Fruit of the Spirit
Galatians 5:22

Pursuit of
1 Thessalonians 5:15

**Relationship to
forgiveness**
Ephesians 4:32

Reward for
Proverbs 19:17

To enemies
Genesis 50:15-21
2 Kings 6:18-23
Luke 6:30-31

To foreigners
Leviticus 19:34

To one's neighbor
Romans 15:1-5

**To others in
the church**
Romans 12:10-15
Galatians 6:10

**To those who
are in need**
Proverbs 14:21
Proverbs 31:20
Matthew 5:42
Matthew 25:34-36

**To those who
are kind**
Exodus 2:16-21

Kleptomania

Definition:
The recurring inability to resist the impulse to steal, even when one does not need the item or has the means to purchase it.

Key Verses:
Exodus 20:15
Ephesians 4:28

Cannot serve both God and money
Matthew 6:24

Comes from the heart
Matthew 15:19
Mark 7:21

Condemned
Exodus 20:15
Leviticus 19:11
Deuteronomy 5:19
Deuteronomy
25:13-16
Luke 3:12-14
Luke 20:20-25
Romans 13:9-10
Ephesians 4:28

Do not rob God
Malachi 3:8

Folly of
Psalm 62:10
Proverbs 10:2
Jeremiah 17:11

God sees
Proverbs 5:21
Proverbs 15:3

Hated by God
Isaiah 61:8

Leads to poverty
Proverbs 22:16

Needs met in Christ
Philippians 4:19

Repentance from
Exodus 22:3-4
Luke 19:8

Small theft leads to great theft
Luke 16:10-11

Wicked borrow and do not repay
Psalm 37:21

Knowledge

Definition:
To be aware, perceive, or understand through observation, study, or experience.

Key Verses:
Proverbs 9:10
2 Peter 3:18

Laughter

Definition:
The sound produced when one is overjoyed, amused, or tickled; often accompanied by smiles.

Key Verses:
Genesis 21:6
Luke 6:21

As expression of unbelief
Genesis 18:10-15

A time for
Ecclesiastes 3:4

Changes to mourning over sin
Luke 6:25
James 4:9

Does not truly reveal the heart
Proverbs 14:13

Of fools
Ecclesiastes 7:6

Of God
Psalm 2:4
Psalm 37:13

Of the wicked
Job 12:4

Laziness

Definition:
The state or quality of refusing, resisting, or refraining from work, activity, or movement.

Key Verses:
Proverbs 19:15
Hebrews 6:12

Avoidance of
2 Thessalonians
3:7-12

Condemned
Matthew 25:14-30
Romans 12:11
2 Thessalonians 3:10
1 Timothy 5:13
Hebrews 6:11-12

Consequences of
Proverbs 6:10-11
Proverbs 10:4
Proverbs 10:26
Proverbs 12:24
Proverbs 13:4
Proverbs 18:9
Proverbs 20:4
Proverbs 20:13
Proverbs 24:33-34

Excuses for
Proverbs 22:13

Lazy person does not get out of bed
Proverbs 26:14-15

Make the most of the time
Ephesians 5:14-16

Of watchmen
Isaiah 56:10

The example of Paul
1 Thessalonians 2:9

Leadership

Definition:
The quality of being able to guide or direct others.

Key Verses:
Matthew 23:11
Hebrews 13:17

See Also:
Business Ethics
Decision Making
Discipleship
Example

Abuse of
3 John 9-10

Amidst opposition
Numbers 14:1-30

Authority in
Titus 2:15

By service
1 Kings 12:7
Matthew 20:26
Mark 10:42-45
John 13:14
2 Corinthians 8:8-9

By the Lord
Judges 8:22-23

By youth
1 Kings 3:7
1 Timothy 4:12-13

Characteristics of
Titus 1:7-9

Consultation with
1 Chronicles 13:1

Corruption of
Isaiah 1:23

Deception by
Isaiah 9:16

Effects of
Proverbs 29:4

Established and removed by God
2 Chronicles 1:1
Job 12:24
Psalm 21:7
Jeremiah 3:15
Daniel 2:21
Ephesians 2:19-20

Example of
1 Chronicles 29:9
1 Timothy 4:12-16
1 Peter 5:2-3

Gift of
Romans 12:8

Godliness in
1 Samuel 17:32-37
2 Samuel 8:15
Esther 10:3

Humility in
2 Corinthians 4:5

Importance of
Judges 5:2
Judges 8:33-34

Importance of delegation
Deuteronomy
1:12-13

In ministry
Acts 6:1-4

Instability in
Isaiah 3:4

Instructions for
1 Peter 5:2-5

In the church
Ephesians 4:11-12

In the family
Ephesians 5:22-33

Justice in
Deuteronomy 1:17
1 Chronicles 18:14
Nehemiah 5:1-12

Leader must not be a new convert
1 Timothy 3:6

Nobility of
1 Timothy 3:1

Obedience to
Hebrews 13:7-17

Of Christ
Colossians 2:9-10

Of God's people
Psalm 77:20

Of Joshua
Deuteronomy 3:28

People rule over the earth
Genesis 1:26

Qualifications for
1 Timothy 3:1-12

Respect for
1 Samuel 24:1-7

Transition in
Numbers 27:18-23
Deuteronomy 34:9

1 Kings 1:47-48
2 Kings 2:1-18

Wisdom in
1 Kings 3:16-28

Working together
Nehemiah 3:1-32

Learn

Definition:
To gain knowledge or skill by study, observation, or experience.

Key Verses:
Deuteronomy 5:1
Matthew 11:29

See Also:
Discipleship
Parenting

Legalism

Definition:
A religious system emphasizing strict adherence to laws or a code of conduct as a means of earning the approval of God.

Key Verses:
Romans 10:4
Galatians 2:21

See Also:
Grace
Manipulation
Spiritual Abuse

Accept the weak
1 Corinthians 6:12

Cannot save
John 7:19
Romans 7:7-12
Romans 7:14
Romans 9:30-33
Galatians 3:10-14
Galatians 5:3-4
Ephesians 2:8-9
Hebrews 7:18-19
Hebrews 10:1

Condemned
Matthew 15:10-20
Acts 15:1-11
1 Corinthians 10:27-30
Galatians 3:2-5
Colossians 2:20-21

Folly of
Matthew 23:23
Mark 7:7

Freedom from
Galatians 2:11-21
Galatians 3:23-25
Galatians 4:9

Fulfilling the law through faith
Romans 3:31

God sees the heart
Isaiah 29:13

Honoring the Sabbath
Matthew 12:1-12
Mark 3:1-4

The Biblical Counseling Reference Guide

Hypocrisy in
Luke 11:45-46

Hypocrisy of
Mark 7:13

Leads to death
Romans 5:20-21
2 Corinthians 3:6

Of little value
Philippians 3:2-11

Relationship to false teaching
1 Timothy 4:1-4

Results of
Romans 10:3

Righteousness comes from Christ
Galatians 2:20-21
Philippians 3:8-9

Role of the law
1 Timothy 1:8-11

Lending

Definition:
The act or process of allowing the use of something under the condition that it (or its equivalent) will be returned, often with interest.

Key Verses:
Proverbs 22:7
Luke 6:34-35

See Also:
Borrowing

Business Ethics
Generosity
Restitution

Borrower slave to the lender
Proverbs 22:7

Canceling debts
Deuteronomy 15:1

Do not charge interest
Exodus 22:25
Deuteronomy 23:19

Give to the needy
Leviticus 25:35-37
Proverbs 19:17
Matthew 5:42

Lend generously
Psalm 112:5

Lend without expecting a return
Luke 6:34-35

Of the righteous
Psalm 37:26

Liberty

Definition:
Freedom from restraint, restriction, control, bondage, or servitude.

Key Verses:
2 Corinthians 3:17
Galatians 5:13

See Also:
Freedom
Obedience
Oppression

Abuse of
1 Corinthians 8:9
1 Corinthians 10:23-33
1 Peter 2:16

Called to freedom
Galatians 5:13

From sins
Colossians 1:13-14

From slavery to sin
Galatians 4:1-7

From the Mosaic Law
Acts 10:9-16
Romans 7:1-6

In Christ
John 8:36
Romans 8:1-3
Galatians 3:28

In the Spirit
2 Corinthians 3:17

In truth
John 8:31-32

Judged by the law of freedom
James 2:12-13

Limitations on
1 Corinthians 6:12
1 Corinthians 8:7-13

To obey Christ
Psalm 119:45

Romans 6:1-2

Under grace
Romans 6:14

Listen

Definition:
To hear with intent
and consideration.

Key Verses:
Psalm 143:1
James 1:22

See Also:
Attention
Discipleship
Obedience

Loneliness

Definition:
The emotion of sad-
ness or emptiness that
can accompany soli-
tude or isolation.

Key Verses:
Psalm 139:7-8
James 2:23

See Also:
Bereavement
Friendship
Grief
Intimacy
Singleness

Alone but not lonely
Matthew 14:23

**Because of
abandonment**
Job 6:14-15
Job 19:13-14
Job 30:29
Psalm 27:10
Psalm 31:11
Psalm 38:11
Psalm 68:6
Psalm 88:8
Psalm 142:4
John 5:7
2 Timothy 4:16

**Companionship
with God**
Psalm 23:1-3

Danger of
Genesis 2:18

Effects of
Psalm 31:9-12

Forsaken by God
Mark 15:34

God is always present
Deuteronomy 31:8
Joshua 1:5
Psalm 139:7-8

God's grace in
Psalm 25:16

**God's purpose
prevails**
Jonah 2:2-6

Held by God
Psalm 139:9-10

Hope in
Psalm 62:5-6

Importance of friends
Ecclesiastes 4:9-10
1 Thessalonians
2:17-20
Hebrews 10:24-25

In persecution
2 Timothy 4:16-18

In suffering
Job 19:13

Jacob alone with God
Genesis 32:24-30

**Kindness to
the lonely**
Luke 14:12-14

Of Jesus
Matthew 26:56

Prayer in
Psalm 22:1
Psalm 73:25
Psalm 142:4-5
Matthew 26:36-46

**Reasons for crying
will cease**
Revelation 21:4

Satisfaction in
Hebrews 13:5

Someone needs you
2 Timothy 1:3-4

Strength in
Isaiah 41:10

Time for
Ecclesiastes 3:4

Upheld by God's love
Psalm 63:1-8

You matter to others
Romans 14:7
1 Corinthians
12:14-27

Your ministry
2 Corinthians 1:3-4

Lord

Definition:
Master or one who
holds authority; a title
of Jesus indicating
deity.

Key Verses:
Matthew 7:21
Philippians 2:9-11

See Also:
Jesus Christ
Obedience
Submission

Love

Definition:
Unconditional devo-
tion accompanied by
affection and a desire
for the well-being of
someone.

Key Verses:
John 13:34
1 Corinthians 13:13

See Also:
Charity
Compassion
Friendship
God
Intimacy

Marriage
Salvation

Characteristics of
1 Corinthians 13:1-8

Commanded
Leviticus 19:18
Deuteronomy 10:12
Luke 6:31
John 13:34
John 15:12
Colossians 3:12-14
1 Thessalonians
4:9-10
James 2:8
1 Peter 2:17
1 Peter 3:8
1 John 3:11
1 John 3:23
1 John 4:7-21

Discipline from
Revelation 3:19

For enemies
Matthew 5:43-46

For foreigners
Deuteronomy 10:19

For God
Deuteronomy 6:5
Deuteronomy 30:20
1 John 4:20

For one's neighbor
Matthew 7:12
Luke 10:25-37
Galatians 5:14

From a pure heart
1 Peter 1:22

Fruit of the Spirit
Galatians 5:22

**Fulfillment of
the Law**
Romans 13:8-10

Importance of
1 Corinthians 13:1
1 Peter 4:8

Jesus' model of
John 15:13

Joy of
Song of Songs 8:7

**Motivation from
love of Christ**
2 Corinthians
5:14-15

Need for growth
Philippians 1:9

Of God
Psalm 63:3
John 3:16
Ephesians 2:4
Ephesians 3:17-19
1 John 4:8

Prayer for growth in
1 Thessalonians 3:12

Pursue love
Romans 12:9-10

**Relationship
to action**
1 Corinthians 16:14
1 John 2:5
1 John 3:18
2 John 6

Relationship to faith
Galatians 5:6
1 John 4:16

Relationship to the world
1 John 2:15-17

Relationship to truth
1 John 2:9-11

Romantic
Song of Songs 2:5
Song of Songs 8:6

Walking in
Ephesians 5:1-2

Loyalty

Definition:
The quality of being faithful, true, or devoted to something or someone.

Key Verses:
Psalm 12:1
Psalm 18:50

See Also:
Commitment
Endurance
Respect

Is difficult to find
Proverbs 20:6

Judgment for disloyalty
Ezra 7:26

Of friends and family
Proverbs 17:17

Questioned
1 Samuel 29:1-11

Relationship to honesty
Proverbs 27:6

To Christ
Matthew 10:37-39
Luke 9:62
John 14:21-24
John 21:15-17
1 Corinthians 10:21

To family
Ruth 1:14-16

To friends
1 Samuel 14:7
1 Samuel 20:1-4

To God
Genesis 22:1-14
Jeremiah 2:11
Matthew 6:24

To government
2 Samuel 15:19-21
2 Kings 11:1-3
1 Peter 2:13

To leaders
Joshua 1:16-17

Lust

Definition:
An intense desire or craving; used especially in regard to sexual desire.

Key Verses:
Job 31:1
Matthew 5:28

See Also:
Infatuation
Materialism
Sexual Addiction
Sexual Temptation

Avoidance of
Proverbs 6:25
2 Timothy 2:22
James 1:14-15
1 Peter 2:11

Comes from the heart
Matthew 15:19

Condemned
Exodus 20:17
1 Thessalonians 4:3-5
1 John 2:16

Consequences of
Romans 7:5

For idols
Ezekiel 6:9

For recognition
1 Kings 11:1-13

Homosexual lust
Romans 1:24-26

Insatiability of
Ephesians 4:19

Leads to sexual sin
Ezekiel 22:11
Amos 2:7

Overcoming
Job 31:1
Romans 13:14
Galatians 5:16

The Biblical Counseling Reference Guide

Ephesians 4:22
Colossians 3:5

**Relationship
to adultery**
Jeremiah 5:8
Matthew 5:27-28

**Relationship
to marriage**
1 Corinthians
7:36-38

Lying

Definition:
The act or process of
speaking falsehood
with the intent to
deceive.

Key Verses:
Job 27:4
Psalm 141:3

See Also:
Deception
Dishonesty
Slander

**Abhorred by
the righteous**
Job 31:5-6
Psalm 119:163

About friends
Jeremiah 9:3-5

Accept correction
Proverbs 9:7-9

Accountable to God
Romans 14:12
Hebrews 4:13

Avoidance of
Job 27:3-4
Psalm 26:4
Psalm 101:7
Psalm 141:3

Avoid the deceitful
Psalm 101:7

**A well-spoken word
is invaluable**
Proverbs 25:11

**Blessed are the
persecuted**
Matthew 5:11

By Abram
Genesis 12:13

By God's prophets
Jeremiah 27:14-15

By Satan
John 8:44

**Characteristic
of Satan**
John 8:44

**Characteristic of
the ungodly**
Psalm 10:7
Psalm 12:2
Psalm 50:19
Psalm 52:2-8
Proverbs 6:12-14
Colossians 3:9

Comes from the heart
Jeremiah 17:9
Matthew 12:34
Matthew 15:19

Condemned
Exodus 20:16
Exodus 23:1
Leviticus 19:11-12
Deuteronomy 5:20
Psalm 34:13
Psalm 119:29-30
Proverbs 24:28
Micah 6:12
Colossians 3:9

**Confess and abandon
sin to find mercy**
Proverbs 28:13

Consequences of
Genesis 20:1-18
Leviticus 6:1-7
Job 15:6
Psalm 5:6-9
Proverbs 11:3
Proverbs 12:19
Proverbs 19:5
Proverbs 21:6
Proverbs 29:12
Ephesians 4:25
Revelation 21:8

Defiance of the truth
James 3:14

Detestable to God
Proverbs 12:22

From the womb
Psalm 58:3

God desires integrity
Psalm 15:1-2
Proverbs 6:16-19
Proverbs 12:22

God does not lie
Numbers 23:19

Titus 1:2

Harm of
Proverbs 26:28

Impact of
Proverbs 17:4

In a trial
Deuteronomy
19:16-20
Proverbs 19:28

Lying accusations
Mark 14:53-59

Lying spirit
2 Chronicles
18:15-22

Of Abraham
Genesis 12:10-13

Of Jacob
Genesis 27:21-24

Of wicked rulers
Isaiah 28:15

**Please God rather
than men**
Galatians 1:10

Prayer amidst
Psalm 120:2

**Produces short-
lived joy**
Proverbs 20:17

Punishment for
Jeremiah 28:15-17

Rahab's lie
Joshua 2:1-6

Satan's lie
Genesis 3:4-5

Speak the truth
Ephesians 4:25

To neighbor
Psalm 12:2

To the Holy Spirit
Acts 5:1-5

**Truthfulness
commanded**
John 3:21
Ephesians 4:15

Will be punished
Proverbs 19:9
Proverbs 21:28

Magic

Definition:
Rites, charms, or spells
intended to exert
supernatural influence
over natural objects or
processes.

Key Verses:
Exodus 8:18-19
Revelation 21:8

See Also:
Fortune Telling
Occult
Satan, Demons, and
Satanism

Malice

Definition:
The desire to bring

injury or harm to
another.

Key Verses:
Psalm 28:3
1 John 2:9

See Also:
Anger
Evil
Hatred
Revenge

Based on jealousy
Esther 5:10-14

Condemned
Leviticus 19:18
Zechariah 8:17
Romans 1:29-32
Ephesians 4:31
Colossians 3:8

Desire to do evil
Proverbs 4:16

Effects of
Psalm 140:3

God judges hatred
Ezekiel 25:15-17

**Hatred a
characteristic of
the wicked**
1 John 2:9-11
1 John 3:15

Intent on murder
Acts 23:12-14

Protection from
Psalm 28:3

Punishment for
Micah 2:1

Rid oneself of
1 Peter 2:1

Turn the other cheek
Matthew 5:38-41

Manipulation

Definition:
The art of control-
ling or influencing
by indirect, unfair,
or deceptive means,
especially to one's own
advantage.

Key Verses:
Psalm 101:7
Galatians 1:10

See Also:
Codependency
Dependency
Persuasion

Condemned
Proverbs 21:6
Ephesians 4:25-26

Conformed to Christ
Romans 12:1-2

Control your tongue
Proverbs 10:19
Proverbs 12:18
Proverbs 15:4
Proverbs 17:27
Proverbs 26:28

Do good to others
James 1:17

Do not mock
Isaiah 57:4

Encourage each other
1 Thessalonians 5:11
Hebrews 3:13

**Evil comes from
the heart**
Matthew 15:19

Examples of
2 Corinthians 11:20

False accusation
Psalm 35:20

Forgive
Colossians 3:13

Grow to maturity
1 Corinthians 13:11

Guard your heart
Proverbs 4:23

Hypocrisy
Proverbs 26:24

**Keep a clear
conscience**
Acts 24:16

Live by love
1 Corinthians 13:4-5

**Ministers are to
be examples**
1 Peter 5:1-3

Please God not men
1 Thessalonians
2:3-8

Pursue wisdom
Proverbs 14:24

Reap what is sown
Galatians 6:7

**Rebellion and
hypocrisy**
Hosea 7:14

Sexual manipulation
Proverbs 7:21-22

Speak with integrity
Matthew 5:37
James 5:12

Teaching self to lie
Jeremiah 9:5

Trusting the Lord
Galatians 1:10

Verbal attacks
Psalm 64:3-4
Psalm 140:3

Marriage

Definition:
A covenant agreement
between a man and a
woman in which they
are legally and spiritu-
ally united and com-
mitted.

Key Verses:
Matthew 19:4-5
1 Corinthians 7:8-9

See Also:
Adultery
Bigamy
Monogamy
Polygamy
Premarital Counseling

A virtuous wife
Proverbs 31:10-12
Proverbs 31:23
Proverbs 31:25
Proverbs 31:27

Behaviors in
Ephesians 5:33

Between believers
2 Corinthians 6:14

Divorce discouraged
Matthew 5:31-32
Matthew 19:1-12
Mark 10:9
Luke 16:18
1 Corinthians 7:27

Enjoyment of
Proverbs 5:18
Ecclesiastes 9:9

Example of a covenant
Genesis 9:11-17
Genesis 17:2

From the Lord
Genesis 1:28
Genesis 2:18
Genesis 2:24
Proverbs 19:14

Importance of
Proverbs 12:4
Proverbs 18:22

Importance of faithfulness
Proverbs 6:27-35

Joy of
Song of Songs 4:9

Love in
Song of Songs 4:11
Song of Songs 8:7
1 Corinthians 13:4-8

Marriage covenant
Malachi 2:14-15

Reflection of Christ and the church
Ephesians 5:22-33

Relationships in
Ephesians 5:21-25
Colossians 3:19
1 Peter 3:1-2
1 Peter 3:7

Remarriage of widows
1 Corinthians 7:39-40

Sanctity of
Deuteronomy 22:22-29
Matthew 5:32
Hebrews 13:4

Servant attitude
Matthew 20:28
Philippians 2:3-4

Sexuality in
Song of Songs 4:16
Song of Songs 8:2
1 Corinthians 6:19-20
1 Corinthians 7:3-5

Sexual union
1 Corinthians 7:2

To God
Isaiah 54:5
Hosea 2:19
Revelation 19:7
Revelation 21:2

Unity in
Matthew 19:6

Masochism

Definition:
Deviant sexual activity involving pain and humiliation; used colloquially to describe affinity for suffering.

Key Verses:
Romans 13:13
1 Corinthians 6:13

See Also:
Purity
Sexual Addiction
Sexual Integrity

Materialism

Definition:
A value system that places priority on possessions and material well-being rather than on spiritual values.

Key Verses:
Psalm 49:16-17
Proverbs 11:28

See Also:
Prosperity
Success

Avoidance of
Acts 4:32

**Cannot save
from death**
Psalm 49:5-12
Zephaniah 1:18

Can't satisfy
Ecclesiastes 5:10
Micah 6:14
Haggai 1:4-6

Condemned
Deuteronomy 7:25
Matthew 6:19
Mark 8:35-37
1 Timothy 3:2-3
Hebrews 13:5
1 Peter 5:2-3

Cost of
Psalm 37:16-17
Matthew 4:8-9

Dangers of
Judges 8:24-27
Isaiah 2:7-8
Hosea 12:8
Matthew 21:12-13
Mark 4:18-19

Folly of
Job 1:13-21
Proverbs 11:28
Ecclesiastes 5:15
Isaiah 55:1-2
Jeremiah 48:7
Lamentations 4:1
Luke 12:13-21
2 Peter 3:5-13

**God's sovereignty
over wealth**
Job 41:11
Psalm 24:1-2

Of the wicked
Zechariah 9:3

Relationship to love
1 John 3:17

**Represented
by Babylon**
Revelation 18:11-19

Robbing God
Malachi 3:8-10

**Seek God first and
the Lord will provide**
Matthew 6:25-34

**Sharing with the
less fortunate**
Luke 3:11

Sin of
Job 31:24-28

Warning against
Job 36:18-19
Luke 6:24

| Maturity |

Definition:
Physical, mental, or
spiritual wholeness or
completeness.

Key Verses:
Ephesians 4:11-13
Hebrews 5:14

See Also:
Aging
Mentoring
Parenting

Based on suffering
Romans 5:3-4
Hebrews 2:10
James 1:2-4

Commanded
Hebrews 6:1-3
2 Peter 3:18

Description of
Ephesians 4:11-14
Colossians 1:9-12
Hebrews 5:14

Desire for
1 Peter 2:2-3

In love
2 Thessalonians 1:3

In speech
James 3:2

In thinking
1 Corinthians 14:20

Necessity of
1 Corinthians 13:11
Philippians 1:6

Power for attaining
2 Peter 1:3

Prayer for
Ephesians 1:17
Colossians 4:12

**Requirement of
leadership**
1 Timothy 3:6

Role of contentment in
Philippians 4:12

Role of Scripture in
2 Timothy 3:16-17

Through practice
Hebrews 5:11-14

Justice in
Deuteronomy 25:1

Of God
1 Samuel 2:25

Of Messiah
Isaiah 2:4
Micah 4:3

Pain reliever
Mark 15:22-23

Role in health
1 Timothy 5:23

Sick need a doctor
Matthew 9:12

Mediation

Definition:
Intervention for the purpose of reconciliation.

Key Verses:
1 Corinthians 6:5-7
1 Timothy 2:5-6

See Also:
Conflict Resolution
Reconciliation

By Jesus
1 Timothy 2:5
Hebrews 8:6
Hebrews 9:15
Hebrews 12:24

By the law
Galatians 3:20-21

For God's people
Exodus 18:16
1 Corinthians 6:1-5

Impartiality in
Deuteronomy 1:16

Importance of
Proverbs 17:14
Proverbs 18:19

Medicine

Definition:
A drug or other substance that remedies a disease or promotes well-being.

Key Verses:
Jeremiah 8:22
1 Timothy 5:23

See Also:
Disease
Health

First aid
Luke 10:33-34

For recovery
Isaiah 38:21

From leaves
Ezekiel 47:12

Healing in heaven
Revelation 22:1-2

Luke the physician
Colossians 4:14

Ointment for sight
John 9:6-7
Revelation 3:18

Meditation

Definition:
The religious or philosophical discipline of contemplation.

Key Verses:
Joshua 1:8
Psalm 19:14

See Also:
Prayer
Thoughts
Worship

Acceptable
Psalm 19:14

On God
Psalm 48:9
Psalm 63:6

On God's deeds
Psalm 77:10-12
Psalm 143:5
Luke 2:19

On God's Word
Joshua 1:8
Psalm 1:2
Psalm 119:15
Psalm 119:48
Psalm 119:97-100

The Biblical Counseling Reference Guide

Medium

Definition:
Means of communication sometimes in reference to one who supposedly communicates with spirits, the dead, or supernatural beings.

Key Verses:
Leviticus 19:31
Isaiah 8:19

See Also:
Communication
Fortune-Telling
Occult
Satan, Demons, and
   Satanism

Meekness

Definition:
The state or quality of submitting or enduring; maintaining control of one's own strength.

Key Verses:
Psalm 37:11
Matthew 5:5

See Also:
Humility
Pride

Blessing for
   Matthew 5:5

Characteristic of God's servants
   1 Thessalonians
   2:7-8

Commanded
   Galatians 5:22-23
   Galatians 5:26
   Colossians 3:12

In love
   1 Corinthians 13:4-7

Not defending oneself
   Matthew 27:13-14

Not haughty at spiritual success
   Luke 10:17-20

Of Christ
   2 Corinthians 10:1

Protection for
   Zephaniah 2:3

Turns away anger
   Proverbs 15:1

Value in God's eyes
   1 Peter 3:4

Walking with gentleness
   Ephesians 4:1-2

Mental Illness

Definition:
Psychological or emotional malady or disorder distinguished by abnormal or harmful thinking, acting, or feeling.

Key Verses:
Psalm 103:2-3
Romans 12:2

See Also:
Counseling
Disease
Disorder
Health

Alter thought patterns
   Romans 12:2
   Ephesians 4:23
   Titus 3:5

Cope with depression
   Psalm 42:3-6
   Lamentations
   3:19-23

Deal with anxiety
   Psalm 94:19
   Proverbs 12:25
   1 Peter 5:7

Maintain stability and balance
   1 Peter 1:13
   1 Peter 4:7

Move from fear to faith
   Joshua 1:9
   Job 13:15
   Psalm 23:1-6
   Psalm 56:10-11
   Isaiah 41:10

Seek help
   Romans 15:5-6

Galatians 6:2-5
1 Thessalonians 5:11

Mentoring

Definition:
The act or process of guiding or educating.

Key Verses:
2 Timothy 1:13-14
Titus 2:3-5

See Also:
Coaching
Discipleship

Be an example to others
1 Timothy 4:12

Can do nothing without Jesus
John 15:5

Close relationship
Proverbs 18:24

Direction from God
Psalm 119:35-36

Disciple to become like teacher
Luke 6:40

Gentle instruction
2 Timothy 2:24-25

In service
John 13:14-15

In spiritual growth
Matthew 28:19-20
2 Timothy 2:2
3 John 4

Of Jesus with disciples
Luke 6:12-13

Of Paul
1 Corinthians 11:1

Proper treatment of a disciple
1 Thessalonians 2:11-12

To aid in maturity
Hebrews 5:12-14

Value of the Bible
Psalm 119:13-14
2 Timothy 3:16-17

Wisdom in
Ephesians 5:15-16
1 Timothy 3:4

Mercy

Definition:
Kindness and compassion shown to someone in distress.

Key Verses:
Hosea 6:6
Ephesians 2:4-5

See Also:
Generosity
Grace
Justice
Love
Righteousness

Based on confession
Proverbs 28:13

Blessed are the merciful
Matthew 5:7

Commanded
Colossians 3:12-13

David had mercy on Saul
1 Samuel 24:10-17

During trials
Hebrews 4:16

For apostasy
Hosea 14:4

For repentance
Jeremiah 3:12-13

For sinners
Matthew 9:13

From captors
2 Kings 25:27-29

Gift of
Romans 12:8

Honors God
Proverbs 14:31

Importance of
Matthew 23:23

Of God
Exodus 15:13
Exodus 34:6
Numbers 14:13-25
Deuteronomy 4:31
Lamentations 3:31-33
Micah 7:18-19
Nahum 1:3
Luke 6:36

Ephesians 2:1-5
Titus 3:5

On God's people
Psalm 89:30-34

Prayer for
Psalm 109:21

Relationship to judgment
James 2:13

Messiah

Definition:
From the Hebrew word meaning "Anointed One." The Greek translation is "Christ." Used by Christians to describe Jesus of Nazareth.

Key Verses:
Mark 8:29
John 20:31

See Also:
Jesus Christ
Lord
Salvation

Born in Bethlehem
Micah 5:2

Death of
Zechariah 12:10

Immanuel
Isaiah 7:14

Jesus Christ
Mark 14:61-62
Luke 9:20

Luke 23:2
John 1:45
John 20:30-31

Justice of
Isaiah 9:7

Kingdom of
Isaiah 9:1-7
Daniel 7:13-14
Revelation 19:11-16

Miracles performed by
Matthew 11:2-6

Promise of
Psalm 89:3-4
Jeremiah 31:31-34

Redemption through
1 Peter 1:18-20

Suffering of
Isaiah 53:1-12

Midlife Crisis

Definition:
A time of emotional distress in middle age in which one is faced with mortality and may reevaluate one's identity, values, and goals.

Key Verses:
Psalm 90:12
Ecclesiastes 5:18-20

See Also:
Adultery
Purpose in Life

David's mistake during
2 Samuel 11:1-27

God is present in difficult times
Isaiah 43:2

God provides a way to escape temptation
1 Corinthians 10:13

God provides strength
Isaiah 40:31

God's faithfulness
Lamentations 3:22-23

God sustains life
Isaiah 46:4

Leaving first love
Revelation 2:4-5

Live worthy of the Lord
Colossians 1:10

Look to God for hope
Psalm 62:5-8

Number your days and use them well
Psalm 90:12

Prayer of an afflicted person
Psalm 102:11

Reap what is sown
Galatians 6:8-9

Repentance and consequences of
2 Samuel 12:1-23

The will of God
Psalm 40:8
Proverbs 16:9
Ephesians 5:17
Hebrews 10:36

Trust God with the future
Jeremiah 29:11

Trust in God
Psalm 23:1-6

Wisdom comes with age
Job 12:12

Mind

Definition:
Inner reasoning faculties responsible for rational and intellectual reflection and understanding.

Key Verses:
Isaiah 26:3
Philippians 2:5

See Also:
Counseling
Identity
Knowledge

Ministry

Definition:
Christian service.

Key Verses:
Psalm 2:11
2 Corinthians 5:18

See Also:
Compassion
Generosity
Grace
Spiritual Gifts

Authority in
Titus 2:15

Boldness in
2 Corinthians 13:2-3

By example
1 Thessalonians 1:5
1 Thessalonians 2:1-6

Characteristics of
Titus 1:7-9

Comfort in
2 Corinthians 7:5-7

Desire for
Colossians 4:3

Encouraging believers
Acts 14:21-22
Titus 1:9

Errant
Acts 20:30

Faithfulness in
1 Corinthians 4:1-2
2 Timothy 4:1-5

Glorifying God in
Acts 3:12-13
Galatians 1:10

1 Thessalonians 2:4

Guidance in
Acts 16:6-7

Meeting needs of others
Job 4:3-4
Romans 12:13

Of Jesus
Matthew 4:23
Hebrews 8:6

Of preaching
Galatians 2:1-2
Colossians 1:24-29

Of priests
Judges 17:7-13

Passion in
Acts 20:31

Persecution in
2 Corinthians 6:4-10

Perseverance in
1 Corinthians 9:24-27

Prayer in
Ephesians 6:18

Purpose of
2 Corinthians 12:19

Qualifications for
1 Timothy 3:1-7

Refreshment in
Romans 15:31-32

Rejection in
Luke 10:16

The Biblical Counseling Reference Guide

Restore sinning believers
Galatians 6:1-2
Jude 22-23

Reward for
2 Timothy 4:6-8

Role of God in
1 Corinthians 3:5-9

Should not be motivated by money
1 Peter 5:2

Teach the Bible accurately
Acts 18:24-26
2 Timothy 2:15

Miracles

Definition:
Supernatural events that occur contrary to what is normal or expected.

Key Verses:
Psalm 77:14
Mark 13:22

See Also:
Jesus Christ
Healing

As a sign
Isaiah 38:7-8
John 2:11
Acts 13:6-12

For deliverance
Exodus 14:13-22
Daniel 3:28

Of false Christs
Matthew 24:24

Of healing
Isaiah 38:1-6

Of Jesus
Luke 5:4-8
Luke 7:13-16
Luke 7:21-23
Luke 17:12-14
John 11:38-44

Of resurrection
2 Kings 13:21

Of Satan
2 Thessalonians 2:9

Purpose of
Exodus 3:19-20
Matthew 11:23
John 20:30-31
Hebrews 2:4

Sun stands still
Joshua 10:12-13

To preserve life
Jonah 1:17

Mocking

Definition:
The act or process of ridiculing by means of imitation or mimicry.

Key Verses:
2 Corinthians 12:10
1 Peter 3:9

See Also:
Bullying
Insult

Rebuke
Ridicule
Slander

Against biblical truth
Acts 17:32

As cruelty
Nehemiah 4:1-3
Matthew 26:67-68
Matthew 27:27-31

By God
Judges 10:13-14

By the wicked
Isaiah 57:4

Endured by those who suffer
Psalm 22:7
Psalm 69:10-11
Ezekiel 36:3-5

Of children against the elderly
2 Kings 2:23

Of sinners against God
2 Chronicles 30:10
2 Chronicles 36:16
2 Peter 3:3
Jude 18

Result of misunderstanding
Matthew 9:23-24
Acts 2:13

Results in judgment
Proverbs 30:17

Definition:
Unlawful sexual contact.

Key Verses:
Psalm 10:12
Mark 9:42

See Also:
Abuse
Childhood Sexual
Abuse
Incest

**Deliverance
for victims**
Psalm 10:14

Do not take revenge
Romans 12:19

**Forgiveness of
oppressors**
Matthew 6:14-15
Mark 11:25

**God cares for
children**
Psalm 27:10

**God heals
broken lives**
Psalm 30:2

**God is near the
brokenhearted**
Psalm 34:18
Isaiah 61:1-3

**God's compassion
never fails**
Lamentations
3:22-23

**Importance of
forgiveness**
Ephesians 4:32

**Overcome effects
of abuse through
new life**
2 Corinthians 5:17

Patience in
Romans 12:12

**The Lord brings
justice**
Psalm 9:12
Psalm 9:18
Psalm 72:2

**The Lord cares
for victims**
Psalm 10:17
Psalm 22:24

Money

Definition:
An established means
of exchange, including
coins and paper currency.

Key Verses:
Psalm 37:16
1 Timothy 6:10

See Also:
Business Ethics
Finances
Materialism
Poverty
Prosperity

**Attained with
hard work**
Proverbs 13:11

Belongs to the Lord
Haggai 2:8
Malachi 3:8-10

**Cannot buy
God's gift**
Acts 8:18-24

Contentment with
Philippians 4:19
1 Timothy 6:6
Hebrews 13:5

Dangers of
Matthew 13:22
Matthew 19:23-24
Acts 16:16-24
Acts 19:23-28
1 Timothy 6:10

Folly of trusting in
Ezekiel 7:19
Luke 12:13-21

Freedom from
Hebrews 13:5-6

Giving of
Luke 6:38
Luke 21:2-4
2 Corinthians 9:6-11

Greed for
Luke 22:3-6

Honesty with
Matthew 22:16-21
Romans 13:8

Of Abram
Genesis 13:2

Offerings in the wilderness
Numbers 7:13-88

Right to earn money in Lord's service
1 Corinthians 9:9-14

Set aside money for spiritual service
1 Corinthians 16:1-2

Stewardship of
Matthew 25:14-30
Luke 16:10-13

Treasures in heaven
Matthew 6:19-34

Warning against
Matthew 6:24
1 Timothy 3:2-3
1 Timothy 6:17-19
1 Peter 5:2

Monogamy

Definition:
Marriage to only one person at a time.

Key Verses:
Matthew 19:3-6
1 Timothy 3:2

See Also:
Bigamy
Commitment
Marriage
Polygamy

Commanded
Genesis 2:24
Malachi 2:15

Commanded for church leaders
1 Timothy 3:2
1 Timothy 3:12
Titus 1:6

Commanded for leaders
Deuteronomy 17:17

Consequences of polygamy
1 Kings 11:3-4

Mood Disorders

Definition:
Group of diagnosable maladies characterized by varying degrees and lengths of depression, mania, or rapidly changing temperament.

Key Verses:
Psalm 13:2
Jeremiah 17:14

See Also:
Anxiety
Depression
Postpartum
  Depression

Morality

Definition:
Conformity to an ethical system.

Key Verses:
Matthew 22:39
1 Thessalonians 5:4-6

See Also:
Immorality
Integrity

Character of God's servant
1 Timothy 3:1-13

Claim of
Matthew 19:16-22
Mark 10:17-22

Commanded
1 Peter 1:15

Consequences of lying
Genesis 12:10-20
Genesis 20:1-18

Convicted by teaching on morality
Acts 24:24-25

Do not satisfy immoral desires
Romans 13:14

Friends influence
1 Corinthians 15:33

Holy Spirit guides
Galatians 5:22-23

Ministry to the immoral
Mark 2:17

Proper judgment
Matthew 7:1-5

Refusing to lust
Job 31:1

Scripture gives instructions for morality
2 Timothy 3:16-17

Sexual purity
1 Thessalonians 4:3-7

Ten Commandments
Exodus 20:1-17

Mormonism

Definition:
A worldwide religion with errant teaching and practices such as a rigid authoritarian structure, baptism for the dead, and progression toward the status of a deity.

Key Verses:
Isaiah 43:10-11
Revelation 22:18

See Also:
Bible Reliability
Cults
God
Jesus Christ

Authority of God's Word
Isaiah 40:8

Authority of Scripture
2 Timothy 3:16-17

Availability of salvation
Romans 10:1-15

Birth of Jesus
Matthew 1:18-20
Matthew 1:25
Matthew 2:1

Death and judgment
Hebrews 9:27
Revelation 20:15

Deity and humanity of Jesus
John 1:1
John 1:14

Deity of Jesus
John 1:1
John 1:3
1 John 4:1-3
Revelation 22:13

Employ discernment
1 John 4:6

God's goodness
James 1:17

God's love
John 3:16

God's unique authority
Deuteronomy 4:35-36
Deuteronomy 4:39
Psalm 90:2
Isaiah 43:10-11
Isaiah 44:6
Isaiah 45:5

Holy Spirit's work
John 16:13

Integrity of Scripture
Revelation 22:18-19

Jesus' authority
John 1:18
Colossians 1:16
1 Timothy 2:5

Jesus initiates the New Covenant
Hebrews 8:1-13

Ready with an answer
1 Peter 3:15-16

Renewal of creation
Revelation 21:1-27

Salvation by grace
Romans 11:6
Ephesians 2:8-9

Salvation in Jesus
John 1:12-13
Acts 4:12
Acts 16:30-31
Romans 5:1
Romans 8:15-16
2 Corinthians 11:3-4
Galatians 1:8-9
Galatians 3:13
Galatians 3:26
Galatians 4:5-6
Ephesians 1:5
1 Peter 1:3-5
1 John 1:7

Salvation through faith
Romans 4:4-6
Galatians 3:11

The Biblical Counseling Reference Guide

Ephesians 2:8-9

Teaching of Jesus
Matthew 7:13-14
Matthew 12:39
Matthew 13:49-50
Matthew 23:39–
24:51
Matthew 25:41-46

Worship of God
John 4:24

Zeal for God
Romans 10:2

Mother

Definition:
A female parent.

Key Verses:
Proverbs 23:22
1 Timothy 5:1-2

See Also:
Family
Father
Wife

Blessing of
Genesis 24:60
Proverbs 31:28-29

**Children are
from God**
Psalm 113:9
Psalm 127:3

Compassion of
1 Kings 3:16-28

Godliness of
1 Timothy 2:15

1 Timothy 5:9-10

Grief of
2 Samuel 21:8-10

Honor for
Exodus 20:12
Exodus 21:15
Exodus 21:17
Leviticus 19:3
Proverbs 1:8
Proverbs 6:20
Proverbs 23:22
Ephesians 6:2

Importance of
Ruth 4:11

Influence of
Ezekiel 16:44
2 Timothy 1:5

Spiritual
Luke 8:19-21

The first mother
Genesis 3:20

Motivation

Definition:
That which provides
incentive to act.

Key Verses:
Psalm 10:17
Romans 15:4

See Also:
Ambition
Procrastination
Purpose in Life
Time Management

By God's strength
Haggai 2:4

By jealousy
Ecclesiastes 4:4

By love
1 Thessalonians 1:3

By the Holy Spirit
Acts 20:22-24

**Entrusted with
task by God**
1 Corinthians
9:16-18

For doing good
Amos 5:14
James 4:17

For enjoying life
Ecclesiastes 9:10

**For following
the Lord**
Job 1:9-11
Psalm 37:4
Psalm 40:8
Jeremiah 29:10-14
John 21:15-17
Ephesians 6:5-8
Colossians 3:17
Philemon 14

For hard work
1 Thessalonians
2:7-9

For living
1 Thessalonians
4:11-12

For maturity
Philippians 3:12-16

For ministry
1 Corinthians
3:12-13

From Christ
2 Corinthians 5:14

From examples
Hebrews 12:1-2

From God
Revelation 17:17

From hope
1 Peter 1:13

From salvation
Philippians 3:12-13

From the heart
Jeremiah 31:33
Mark 7:20-23

Glorifying God
1 Corinthians 10:31

In prayer
James 4:3

Not from money
Proverbs 23:4-5
1 Timothy 6:9-10

Not primary concern
Philippians 1:15-18

Of a noble person
Isaiah 32:8

Of faith
Hebrews 11:8

Pleasing Christ
Colossians 3:23-24

The Lord weighs
Proverbs 16:2

**Your labor is
not in vain**
1 Corinthians
15:57-58

Mourning

Definition:
The act or process of
expressing deep sorrow
or grief resulting from
death or loss.

Key Verses:
Isaiah 57:18
Romans 12:15

See Also:
Bereavement
Death
Grief
Loneliness
Terminal Illness

After battle
2 Samuel 1:11-12
2 Samuel 19:2

Because of judgment
Amos 8:10
Micah 1:8
Micah 1:16

**Certain mourning
rites forbidden**
Deuteronomy
14:1-2

For brother
Genesis 37:29

For child
Genesis 37:34-35
Exodus 12:30
Matthew 2:18
Mark 5:38-39

For friend
Acts 9:39

For spiritual leader
Deuteronomy 34:8
1 Samuel 25:1

For spouse
Genesis 23:2
2 Samuel 11:26

Professional
Jeremiah 9:17
Mark 5:38

Murder

Definition:
The act of killing
another human being
unjustly. Biblical jus-
tifications for killing
another human being
include self-defense,
accident, war, and
administration of jus-
tice.

Key Verses:
Exodus 20:13
1 John 3:15

See Also:
Assault
Death
Violence

The Biblical Counseling Reference Guide

By the devil
John 8:44

Comes from the heart
Genesis 27:41-45
Matthew 15:19
Mark 7:21
1 John 3:15

Condemned
Exodus 20:13
Deuteronomy 5:17
Matthew 19:18
Romans 13:9
1 Peter 4:15

Conspiracy to commit
2 Samuel 11:14-17
Jeremiah 11:18-19
Micah 7:2
Acts 23:12-22

Disobedience can lead to murder
Genesis 4:1-16

God hates
Genesis 9:5

Hatred equals
Matthew 5:21-26

Of a brother
1 John 3:12

Of Jesus
Mark 14:1

Of the righteous
Matthew 14:1-12

Punishment for
Genesis 9:5-6
Numbers 35:16-34

Proverbs 28:17

Murmuring

Definition:
The act or process of quietly or inaudibly complaining or expressing disapproval.

Key Verses:
1 Corinthians 10:10
1 Peter 4:9

See Also:
Gossip
Grumbling
Slander

Against God
Deuteronomy 9:8
Malachi 3:14
Romans 9:19-20

Against spiritual leaders
Exodus 5:15-21
Exodus 14:11-12
Exodus 15:22-24
Exodus 16:2-3
Exodus 17:3
Numbers 14:2
Numbers 16:1-3
Numbers 20:1-5

Condemned
Philippians 2:14

Result of misunderstanding
John 6:41-43
John 6:52
Jude 10

Results in judgment
Numbers 11:1
Numbers 14:26-37
1 Corinthians 10:10

Nagging

Definition:
To persistently scold, criticize, or find fault

Key Verses:
Judges 16:16
Proverbs 27:15

See Also:
Dysfunctional Family
Verbal and Emotional
  Abuse

Consequences of
1 Samuel 8:5-18

Do everything without complaining
Philippians 2:14

Effectiveness of
Exodus 10:7-11
Luke 18:1-5

Of a wife
Proverbs 19:13
Proverbs 21:9
Proverbs 25:24
Proverbs 27:15

Worn down through
Judges 14:17
Judges 16:16

Narcissism

Definition:
Used to describe a highly conceited or egotistical personality or pattern of behavior.

Key Verses:
Romans 12:3
James 4:10

See Also:
Identity
Pride
Self-Esteem
Self-Exaltation
Selfishness
Self-Worth

Neglect

Definition:
To disregard or leave unattended. Often associated with failing to provide for a child's needs.

Key Verses:
Psalm 25:16
Isaiah 40:1

See Also:
Abandonment
Child Abuse
Resentment
Victimization

Leads to larger problems
Ecclesiastes 10:18

Of doing good
James 4:17

Of Jesus' words
Matthew 7:26

Of justice, mercy, and faith
Matthew 23:23
Luke 11:42

Of ministry duties
Acts 6:2

Of self
Song of Songs 1:6

Of spiritual gifts
1 Timothy 4:14

Punishment for neglect of duties
Luke 12:47

New Age Spirituality

Definition:
Late 20th-century social movement based on Eastern mysticism and characterized by pantheism, hope of global enlightenment, creation of reality through positive thinking, and belief in reincarnation.

Key Verses:
Colossians 2:8
1 John 4:1

See Also:
Cults

Salvation
Spiritual Warfare

Abandoning sound doctrine
2 Timothy 4:3-4

Abandoning the faith
1 Timothy 4:1

Abide in Christ
John 15:5

All glory belongs to God
Romans 11:36

All Scripture is divine
2 Timothy 3:16-17

A person dies once and faces judgment
Hebrews 9:27

Believers will be resurrected
1 Corinthians 15:39-57

Chosen by Christ
Ephesians 1:4-6

Christ has all authority
Matthew 28:18
John 5:22

Christ is supreme
Colossians 1:15-19

Do not seek knowledge from the dead
Leviticus 19:31

False claim to
be a god
  Ezekiel 28:2

Fear the Lord
  Proverbs 3:7-8

God became man
  John 1:1
  John 1:14

God created all
  Jeremiah 27:5

God does not change
  Psalm 102:25-27

God is in control
  Isaiah 45:7
  Isaiah 45:18

God is the Creator
  Isaiah 44:24

God knows all things
  Isaiah 46:10

God offers
forgiveness
  Isaiah 1:18

God's hatred of
magic charms
  Ezekiel 13:20

God will establish an
everlasting kingdom
  Isaiah 9:6-7

God will judge
  Leviticus 20:6

Idolatry in Athens
  Acts 17:16-34

Jesus is God
  John 1:1-3

Jesus reveals
the Father
  John 1:18

Justification is
through faith
in Christ
  Galatians 2:16

Only way to God
is through Jesus
  John 14:6

Peace in Christ
  John 16:33

Peace through Christ
  John 14:27

Resurrection and
judgment will occur
  John 5:28-29

Salvation is
through Jesus
  John 3:16-17

Simple gospel
  1 Corinthians 15:3-6

Store treasure
in heaven
  Matthew 6:19-21

Test the spirits to see
if they are from God
  1 John 4:1

The Lord alone reigns
  Psalm 103:19

There is one God
  Deuteronomy 32:39

The Spirit
reveals truth
  John 16:13

Turn to the Bible
not spiritists
  Isaiah 8:19-20

Warning against
false prophets
  Matthew 7:15
  Matthew 24:4-5

Warning against
false teaching
  Colossians 2:8

Worshipping creation
rather than God
  Romans 1:18-25

Nightmare

Definition:
A disturbing or frightening dream occurring during sleep that often results in anxiety, terror, and loss of sleep.

Key Verses:
Psalm 4:8
Psalm 91:5

See Also:
Anxiety
Fear
Insomnia

Definition:
Compliance or sub-
mission to authority,
rule, or law.

Key Verses:
Romans 6:16
Ephesians 6:1

See Also:
Faith
Purpose in Life
Rebellion

Benefits of
Genesis 22:15-18
Deuteronomy
28:1-14
1 Kings 3:14
2 Kings 21:8
2 Chronicles 15:2
Proverbs 1:33
Proverbs 7:2
Proverbs 19:16
Isaiah 1:19
Isaiah 48:17-18
John 8:51
2 Timothy 2:5

Blessings for
Deuteronomy 5:10
Psalm 112:1
Psalm 119:2
Luke 11:28
Revelation 3:10

Commanded
James 1:22

Desire to obey God
John 4:34

Effects of
Job 36:11

From faith
Romans 1:5
Hebrews 11:7-12
James 2:21

From the heart
Ezekiel 11:19-20
Romans 6:17
Ephesians 6:6

Importance of
Joshua 23:6
1 Samuel 15:7-31
Luke 6:46-49
2 Timothy 2:19

In persecution
Jeremiah 26:1-16

In the wilderness
Numbers 9:23

Of Abraham
Genesis 12:1-4
Genesis 17:23

Of angels
Psalm 103:20

Of Caleb
Numbers 14:24

Of Jesus
Hebrews 5:8-9

Relationship to loving God
John 14:15
John 14:21
1 John 2:3-6
1 John 5:1-3

Relationship to worship
1 Samuel 15:22
Psalm 40:6
Jeremiah 7:22-23

Results in wisdom
Psalm 119:1-16
Psalm 119:100

To God
Exodus 24:7
Joshua 1:7
Joshua 10:40
Joshua 24:14
Ezra 7:10
Luke 2:39
John 12:50
Acts 4:18-20
Acts 5:29
1 John 3:21-22

To government
Romans 13:4-5

To Jesus
Matthew 9:9
John 15:14

To oaths
Jeremiah 35:1-16

To spiritual leaders
Hebrews 13:17

To the words of a prophet
2 Kings 5:13

Understanding leads to
Psalm 119:33-34

Value of
Psalm 119:35-36

Obscenity

Definition:
Language, behavior, or thing that is indecent, crass, lewd, or offensive.

Key Verses:
Ephesians 5:4
Colossians 3:8

See Also:
Blasphemy
Pornography
Verbal and Emotional
   Abuse

Condemned
Job 31:1
Ephesians 5:4

Do not speak evil
Proverbs 4:24
Ephesians 4:29
1 Peter 3:10

Wicked speak evil things
Proverbs 2:12
Proverbs 10:32
Proverbs 15:28
Romans 3:13-14

Obsession

Definition:
A persistent, controlling preoccupation

with an unreasonable idea.

Key Verses:
Ecclesiastes 1:14-15
Philippians 3:13-14

See Also:
Addiction
Codependency
Compulsion
Sexual Addiction

Consequences of sinful obsessions
Romans 7:5
Romans 8:7-8

Danger of
Proverbs 19:2

Self-control encouraged
Proverbs 25:28
Galatians 5:22-23
1 Thessalonians 4:4
1 Thessalonians
   5:6-8
1 Timothy 3:2
Titus 1:8
Titus 2:2
1 Peter 1:13
1 Peter 4:7
1 Peter 5:8

Sinful obsessions condemned
Romans 6:20-21

With God's glory
Numbers 25:11
1 Kings 19:10
2 Kings 10:16

With keeping the law
Galatians 1:14

Obsessive Compulsive Disorder

Definition:
Feelings of anxiety that impair normal life by causing repetitive behaviors in attempt to prevent feared outcomes or events.

Key Verses:
Matthew 6:27
2 Corinthians 10:5

See Also:
Anxiety
Compulsion
Fear
Worry

Occult

Definition:
Knowledge or control of hidden or mysterious powers. Used especially of secret societies claiming to possess this knowledge.

Key Verses:
Isaiah 5:20
Luke 10:18-20

See Also:
Cults
Demons
Satan, Demons, and
   Satanism

Arming yourself
Ephesians 6:10-18

Astrology
Isaiah 47:13-15

Characteristics
Galatians 5:19-21

Consulting the dead
Isaiah 8:19

Deceit of "different" gospel
2 Corinthians 11:3-4

Deceit of humanism
Colossians 2:8

Demonic power
Mark 9:17-18

Demon possession
Matthew 8:28

Destructive talk
Psalm 52:1-3

Disposing of occult items
Acts 19:19

Divination and sorcery forbidden
Deuteronomy 18:10-12

Do not look to objects in the sky for
Jeremiah 10:2

Do not make or worship idols
Exodus 20:4-5

Do not participate in pagan sacrifices
1 Corinthians 10:20-21

Do not seek knowledge from the dead
Leviticus 19:31

Effect of evil spirit
Mark 9:20-21

Effects of repentance
2 Chronicles 33:1-20

Enticement to idolatry
Deuteronomy 13:6-8

Evil deeds confessed
Acts 19:18

False prophets, teachers
2 Peter 2:1-2

Fortune tellers
Ecclesiastes 8:7-8

Freedom from evil spirit
Acts 16:16-18

God forbids sorcery
Leviticus 19:26

God's hatred of magic charms
Ezekiel 13:20

God's judgment on those who practice
Micah 5:12

Revelation 21:8

Healing value of prayer
James 5:16

How the devil operates
1 Peter 5:8

How to avoid evil
1 Thessalonians 5:21-22

In opposition to truth
Isaiah 5:20

Interpreting dreams
Jeremiah 29:8

No peace with idolatrous
2 Kings 9:22

Origin of evil
Revelation 12:8-9

Penalty for sorceress
Exodus 22:18

Process of temptation
James 1:14-15

Prompted by devil
John 13:2

Prophet of the Lord: the test
Deuteronomy 18:20-22

Recognizing Spirit of God
1 John 4:2-3

Renouncing occult
2 Corinthians 4:2

Resist enticement
Deuteronomy 13:8

Sacrifices, sorcery, seances
Deuteronomy 18:10-14

Satan entered Judas
John 13:27

Séance, Saul, and a witch
1 Samuel 28:1-25

Some will follow demonic teachings
1 Timothy 4:1

Source of fear not God
2 Timothy 1:7

Spirit of truth or falsehood
1 John 1:6

Split loyalties
1 Corinthians 10:20-21

Testing the spirits
1 John 4:1-6

Turn to the Bible not spiritists
Isaiah 8:19-20

Value of God's Word
2 Timothy 3:16-17

Walking in darkness
1 John 1:5-7

Worshipping other gods
Deuteronomy 30:17-18

Opposition

Definition:
Hostility, antagonism, or hindrance.

Key Verses:
1 Thessalonians 2:2
Hebrews 12:3

See Also:
Debate
Enemies
Hatred
Persecution
Prejudice

Boldness before
Deuteronomy 20:1
Psalm 3:6
Psalm 27:3
Acts 4:23-26
1 Thessalonians 2:1-2
Hebrews 13:6

By evil people
Psalm 69:4
Acts 17:5

By family
Deuteronomy 2:4-5
Matthew 10:21

By God
Nahum 1:2

By religious leaders
Matthew 27:62-66

By the man of lawlessness
2 Thessalonians 2:4

Deliverance from
Nehemiah 6:16
Jeremiah 17:18
Acts 16:16-40

Do good to opposition
Luke 6:27-31

Expectation of
Matthew 10:16
Philippians 1:29-30
1 Thessalonians 3:4

Faithfulness to God in
Ezekiel 2:6-7

God opposes the proud
James 4:6

God overcomes
2 Samuel 5:17-19
2 Samuel 22:30
Psalm 56:1-7
Jeremiah 1:17-19
2 Corinthians 1:8-11

In ministry
Micah 2:6
2 Timothy 4:14-15

Intimidation tactics
Nehemiah 6:1-9

Overcoming in Christ
Romans 8:31-34

**Overcoming
with good**
Romans 12:21

Rejoicing in
Philippians 1:15-18

Response to
Matthew 5:43-48
Romans 12:14

Results in death
2 Kings 21:23-24

Spiritual
Acts 19:13-16
Ephesians 6:13
1 Thessalonians 2:18
1 Peter 5:8-9

To God's prophets
Revelation 11:3-12

To Jesus
Matthew 21:33-44
Mark 12:13-17

To the church
Galatians 1:13

To the gospel
Matthew 28:11-15
Luke 10:16
Acts 13:45-51
1 Corinthians 16:9

Oppression

Definition:
Cruel or unjust
exercise of power or
authority.

Key Verses:
Isaiah 1:17
Isaiah 53:7

See Also:
Persecution
Spiritual Warfare

By government
1 Kings 12:1-11

By religious leaders
Matthew 23:2-4

By the rich
Ezekiel 22:29
Amos 5:11-12
Amos 8:4-6

Condemned
Exodus 22:21
Exodus 23:9

**God helps the
oppressed**
Psalm 9:9
Psalm 12:5
Psalm 56:1
Psalm 103:6
Psalm 119:134
Isaiah 50:6-7

Insults God
Proverbs 14:31

**Judgment on
the oppressor**
Isaiah 10:1-2
Habakkuk 2:6

Of employees
Deuteronomy
24:14-15

Of Israel
Exodus 3:9

Of slaves
Exodus 5:6-9

Optimism

Definition:
The tendency to antic-
ipate the best outcome
in every situation.

Key Verses:
Psalm 33:20
Proverbs 23:18

See Also:
Encouragement
Hope
Pessimism

Always confident
2 Corinthians 5:6

God's encouragement
2 Thessalonians
2:16-17

**Hope for the
repentant**
Job 11:14-18

In battle
Joshua 1:6
Joshua 1:9
1 Samuel 17:32

In God's work
Philippians 1:3-6

**In spite of
persecution**
1 Thessalonians 1:6

Joy from the Lord
Job 8:21

Of a good report
2 Samuel 18:27

Promise for a future
Psalm 37:37
Jeremiah 29:10-11

Rejoice always
1 Thessalonians 5:16

Trusting in God
Psalm 31:24
Psalm 34:19
Psalm 42:5
Psalm 73:28
Psalm 112:7-8
Psalm 121:1-2
Romans 4:18-22

Orphan

Definition:
A child without parents.

Key Verses:
Psalm 27:10
James 1:27

See Also:
Adoption
Children

Overeating

Definition:
The act or process of ingesting too much food.

Key Verses:
Proverbs 23:1-2
1 Corinthians 10:31

See Also:
Gluttony

Benefits of discipline
Proverbs 15:32

Be self-controlled
Proverbs 25:28

Consider your appetite
Proverbs 23:1-3

Divine enablement
2 Peter 1:3

Do everything for God's glory
Romans 12:1
1 Corinthians 6:19-20
1 Corinthians 10:31

Do good
James 4:17

Do not eat when it will harm others
Romans 14:20

Don't be a slave to
2 Peter 2:19

Eat only what you need
Proverbs 25:16

God's in control
Daniel 1:8-21

God will provide for you
Matthew 6:25

Greed for food
1 Samuel 2:15
Philippians 3:19

Harmful effects of
Proverbs 23:20-21

Honesty before God
Psalm 139:23-24

Live by the Holy Spirit not the flesh
Romans 8:5

Not everything is beneficial
1 Corinthians 6:12

Please God
2 Corinthians 5:9

Seek what is right
Proverbs 25:27

You are God's temple
1 Corinthians 3:16-17

Pain

Definition:
Distress or suffering of the body, mind, or soul.

Key Verses:
Psalm 69:29
Revelation 21:4

See Also:
Abuse
Cry

Evil and Suffering
Hope

Panic

Definition:
Sudden, overwhelming anxiety or terror that inhibits or paralyzes normal, sound judgment.

Key Verses:
Psalm 46:10
John 14:27

See Also:
Anxiety
Fear

Paranoia

Definition:
Mental state characterized by delusional perceptions of conspiracy, suspicion, and mistrust.

Key Verses:
1 Samuel 18:29
Titus 1:15

See Also:
Anxiety
Fear
Insanity
Obsession

Parenting

Definition:
The process of raising, nurturing, and protecting a child.

Key Verses:
Proverbs 23:13
Ephesians 6:4

See Also:
Discipline
Father
Maturity
Mother

Avoid favoritism
   James 2:1

Benefits of discipline
   Proverbs 23:13-14
   Proverbs 29:16-17

Children as a gift
   Psalm 127:3-4

Children blessed
   Psalm 112:1-2

Children grow in wisdom
   Luke 2:52

Depend on God
   Psalm 31:4

Discipline in
   Hebrews 12:9-11

Discipline your children
   Proverbs 13:24

Do not provoke children
   Ephesians 6:4
   Colossians 3:21

Encourage
   1 Thessalonians 2:7-12
   1 Thessalonians 5:11

Example of faith
   2 Timothy 1:5

Example of parent
   2 Timothy 1:4-5

Follow God's Word
   Psalm 111:10

God as parent
   Matthew 7:11
   John 1:12

God disciplines
   Proverbs 3:12

God's love
   Isaiah 49:15

Importance of
   Proverbs 13:24
   Proverbs 17:6
   Proverbs 17:25
   Proverbs 19:18
   Proverbs 22:6
   Proverbs 22:15

Listen
   Proverbs 1:8

Live for God
   1 Thessalonians 4:1

Model of spiritual ministry
1 Thessalonians 2:7
1 Thessalonians 2:11-12

Older women teach
Titus 2:3-4

Parents protect child
Hebrews 11:23

Parents provide for children
2 Corinthians 12:14

Parents' teaching
2 Timothy 3:14-15

Parents to manage household
1 Timothy 3:4

Provide for
1 Timothy 5:8

Repent
Revelations 3:19

Resist hatred
Proverbs 10:12

Result of
Luke 2:40

Role of prayer in
Job 1:5
Matthew 15:28

Seek godly examples
Judges 13:8

Teach God's truth to children
Genesis 18:19
Deuteronomy 6:6-7

Train women to love their children
Titus 2:4-5

Trust God
Jeremiah 17:5

Unconditional love
Luke 15:11-32

Use wisdom
Proverbs 24:3-4

Woman who is blessed
Proverbs 31:27-29

Passive

Definition:
Unable or unwilling to act assertively; enduring without resistance.

Key Verses:
Joshua 1:9
Ephesians 6:10

See Also:
Communication
Conflict Resolution
Confrontation

Passive-Aggressive

Definition:
Attitude or disposition characterized by indirect resistance, consistent obstruction, or lack of cooperation without any overt forceful confrontation or disagreement.

Key Verses:
Proverbs 4:26
1 Corinthians 16:13

See Also:
Communication
Conflict Resolution
Confrontation

Patience

Definition:
The state or quality of being tolerant or able to calmly endure opposition, affliction, or persecution.

Key Verses:
Proverbs 14:29
Ephesians 4:1-2

See Also:
Diligence
Endurance

Commanded
2 Corinthians 6:4-6
Colossians 3:12-13
1 Thessalonians 5:14
2 Timothy 4:2
Titus 2:2

For the Lord
Psalm 37:7
Psalm 37:34
Hebrews 6:12
Hebrews 6:15
Hebrews 10:36

From God
Colossians 1:11

Fruit of the Spirit
Galatians 5:22

Growth in
2 Peter 1:5-6

In hope
Romans 8:25

In suffering
Romans 12:12
2 Corinthians 1:6
James 1:2-4
James 5:7-11
1 Peter 2:19
Revelation 1:9

Of God
Numbers 14:18
Psalm 86:15
Isaiah 7:13
2 Peter 3:9

Of love
1 Corinthians 13:4

**Relationship
to maturity**
Proverbs 14:29
James 1:4

Virtue of
Proverbs 19:11

See Also:
Calm
Joy

**Based on Christ's
resurrection**
John 16:33

**Blessed are the
peacemakers**
Proverbs 12:20
Matthew 5:9

Complacency in
2 Kings 20:17-19

False claims of
Jeremiah 6:14

For doing good
Psalm 34:11-14

From God
Joshua 23:1
Isaiah 2:1-5
Micah 4:3
1 Corinthians 1:3
Galatians 1:3
Philippians 4:7
1 Thessalonians 1:1
2 Thessalonians 1:2

From Jesus
John 14:27

Fruit of the Spirit
Romans 8:6
Galatians 5:22

Greeting from Jesus
Luke 24:36

In the church
Ephesians 2:14-18

**In the kingdom
of God**
Romans 14:17

Pursuit of
Romans 14:19

**Result of
Messiah's rule**
Isaiah 9:1-7

Wisdom brings
Proverbs 20:3

With God
Romans 5:1-11

Pedophile

Definition:
One whose sexual
desires are primarily
directed toward chil-
dren.

Key Verses:
Luke 17:2
1 Corinthians 6:18

See Also:
Childhood Sexual
   Abuse
Pornography

Peace

Definition:
Calm, tranquility,
harmony, or freedom
from war and hostility.

Key Verses:
Psalm 29:11
Psalm 34:14

Perfection

Definition:
The state or quality
of being completely
without fault, flaw, or
defect.

Key Verses:
Psalm 18:30
Hebrews 10:14

See Also:
God
Jesus Christ
Perfectionism

**Cannot come
through the law**
Hebrews 7:11
Hebrews 7:19
Hebrews 10:1

**Comes through
Christ**
Hebrews 10:14

Commanded
Matthew 5:48
2 Corinthians 13:11

Of Christ
Hebrews 2:10
Hebrews 5:9

Of following Christ
Matthew 19:21

Of God
Deuteronomy 32:4
2 Samuel 22:31
Psalm 18:30
2 Corinthians 12:9

Of God's law
Psalm 19:7

Of holiness
2 Corinthians 7:1
2 Corinthians 13:9
Colossians 1:28
Hebrews 11:40

Of the law
James 1:25

**Of unity in
the church**
1 Corinthians 1:10

Perfectionism

Definition:
Thought pattern characterized by insistence upon flawlessness and dissatisfaction with anything less.

Key Verses:
Philippians 3:12
Colossians 1:28

See Also:
Critical Spirit
Perfection

**Christ's power shown
in your weakness**
2 Corinthians 12:9

Everyone sins
Ecclesiastes 7:20

Figurative use
Ezekiel 28:12

**Follow Christ's
example**
Hebrews 12:1-2

Forgiveness in Christ
Romans 8:1-2

Freedom in Christ
Colossians 2:16

**Freedom
through truth**
John 8:32

Fruit of the Spirit
Galatians 5:22-23

God's enablement
2 Peter 1:3-4

God's grace
2 Corinthians 9:8

God's love
Romans 8:38-39

God's protection
Proverbs 3:26

God's work
Ephesians 2:10

Gradual maturity
Luke 10:38-42
Romans 12:2
Ephesians 4:11-13
Philippians 3:12-14
2 Peter 1:5-8

Growth in grace
2 Peter 3:18

Impossibility
Romans 3:23
Romans 7:10
Romans 7:14-25
1 Corinthians 10:12

**Limitations of
human effort**
Galatians 3:3

Live by grace
Galatians 5:4

Live peacefully
2 Corinthians 13:11

Mature love
1 John 4:18

Only God is perfect
Deuteronomy
32:3-4
2 Samuel 22:31

Paul's progressive maturity
Philippians 3:1-14

Progressive growth
Philippians 1:6
Philippians 3:12-14
James 1:4

Recognize your own problems
Matthew 7:3

Rely on God
1 Peter 5:7

Saved by grace not works
Ephesians 2:8-9

Seek approval from God not people
Galatians 1:10

Suffering
James 1:2-4
1 Peter 4:19

Weakness of Paul
2 Corinthians 12:10

Your adequacy is from God
2 Corinthians 3:5

Perform

Definition:
To act, carry out, or fulfill a specific role.

Key Verses:
Philippians 1:6
James 1:4

See Also:
Grace
Spiritual Abuse
Work

Permissive

Definition:
Longsuffering or lacking in firm boundaries.

Key Verses:
Proverbs 12:1
Ephesians 6:4

See Also:
Children
Parenting
Teenagers

Persecution

Definition:
To continually pursue, harass, or afflict.

Key Verses:
Matthew 5:10
John 15:20

See Also:
Oppression
Suffering
Victimization

Because of Christ
John 16:1-4

Benefits of
James 1:2-4

Blessings for
Matthew 5:10
Luke 6:22

Boldness in Christ
Hebrews 13:6

By family
Matthew 10:21

By friends
Psalm 55:12-13

By government
Jeremiah 20:1-2
John 19:1

By Satanic forces
Job 2:4-5
Ephesians 6:16
Revelation 13:5-7
Revelation 17:6

By the wicked
Psalm 11:2
John 15:18-19
1 John 3:13

Certainty of
Matthew 10:16
Mark 8:31-38
Luke 21:12
Philippians 1:29-30
1 Thessalonians
3:2-4
2 Timothy 3:12
Revelation 6:9

Deliverance from
  Jeremiah 17:18
  Acts 16:16-40
  2 Peter 2:7-9

Do not fear
  Matthew 10:28
  Revelation 2:10

Endurance of
  Psalm 56:1
  Romans 5:3-4
  Philippians 3:10-11
  2 Thessalonians
    1:3-4
  James 1:1-12
  Revelation 2:13
  Revelation 14:12

For doing good
  1 Peter 2:19-21
  1 Peter 3:17

For God's sake
  Psalm 69:7
  1 Thessalonians 1:6
  1 Peter 4:12-16
  Revelation 1:9

God's sovereignty in
  Genesis 50:20
  Romans 8:28

Hope during
  Romans 8:18
  Hebrews 10:32-34

In ministry
  2 Corinthians 6:4-10

Joy in
  Acts 5:41

Martyrdom
  Acts 7:54-60

Ministry during
  Acts 8:3-4
  Acts 11:19

Of God's prophets
  Revelation 11:3-12

Of Jesus
  Mark 12:1-12
  Mark 15:29-32
  1 Thessalonians
    2:14-15
  Hebrews 2:10

Of the saints
  Hebrews 11:36-38

Ordained by God
  Revelation 13:10

Overcoming
  Acts 13:45-51

Patience in
  Psalm 119:84-88
  Romans 12:12
  James 5:7-11

Prayer in
  Daniel 3:16-18
  Matthew 5:44

Remember the persecuted
  Colossians 4:18

Response to
  Romans 12:14

Results of
  Philippians 1:14

Perseverance

Definition:
Steadfast determination or persistence.

Key Verses:
John 15:7
James 1:12

See Also:
Integrity
Motivation
Time Management

Against evil
  Ephesians 6:13

A godly character quality
  2 Peter 1:5-6

Of believers
  James 5:11
  Revelation 13:10

Of God's discipline
  Hebrews 12:7

Of hope in the Lord
  1 Thessalonians 1:3

Of persecution
  2 Timothy 3:10-11

Of trials
  Matthew 10:22
  Romans 5:3-4
  2 Thessalonians 1:4
  James 1:2-4
  James 1:12
  Revelation 3:10

Run with
  Hebrews 12:1

Through God's strength
Colossians 1:11

Personality

Definition:
Qualities and characteristics that define a person.

Key Verses:
1 Corinthians 12:4-5
2 Timothy 1:7

See Also:
Character
Identity

Persuasion

Definition:
The act or process of convincing, changing, or influencing through argument, reason, or insistence.

Key Verses:
Proverbs 25:15
1 Corinthians 2:4

See Also:
Communication
Manipulation

In evangelism
Luke 16:31
Acts 19:8
Acts 26:28
Acts 28:24
1 Corinthians 2:4
2 Corinthians 5:11

To commit evil
Proverbs 7:21
Matthew 27:20
Acts 6:11

To grow in Christ
Romans 12:1
Ephesians 4:1

With words of wisdom
Proverbs 25:15

Pessimism

Definition:
The tendency to anticipate the worst outcome in every situation.

Key Verses:
2 Corinthians 4:8
Isaiah 57:10

See Also:
Optimism

From doubting God
Numbers 13:30-31

Losing will to live
1 Kings 19:4

Negative view of a person
1 Kings 22:8

Pessimistic view of life
Job 2:7-9
Job 3:25
Job 9:25
Ecclesiastes 1:2

Result of oppression
Ecclesiastes 4:1-3

Results in judgment
Numbers 14:36-38

Phobia

Definition:
An intense, irrational, and often incapacitating fear of an object or a situation.

Key Verses:
Genesis 15:1
2 Corinthians 7:5

See Also:
Fear

Can be overcome in Christ
Psalm 34:4
Psalm 46:1
Luke 1:37
Romans 8:31
Philippians 4:7
Philippians 4:13
2 Peter 1:3

Cast your cares upon God
1 Peter 5:6-7

Caused by God
Leviticus 26:36
Joshua 2:24

Condemned
Deuteronomy 31:6
Deuteronomy 31:8
Jeremiah 1:6-8
Matthew 10:26-28

Mark 4:35-41
Luke 12:4-12
John 6:20
Philippians 1:27-30
1 Peter 3:14

**Confidence in
the Lord**
Deuteronomy 1:21
Psalm 23:1-4
Psalm 27:1
Psalm 118:6
Proverbs 29:25
Isaiah 41:10

**Courage from
the Lord**
Psalm 27:2-3

Peace in
John 14:27

Relationship to love
1 John 4:18

Trust in the Lord
Psalm 56:3

Physical Abuse

Definition:
To intentionally cause
bodily harm and
injury.

Key Verses:
Psalm 11:5
Romans 13:10

See Also:
Abuse
Hope

Polygamy

Definition:
The state of being
married to two or
more people at the
same time.

Key Verses:
Genesis 2:24
Mark 10:7

See Also:
Bigamy
Marriage
Monogamy

Condemned
Genesis 2:24
Malachi 2:15

Corruption from
1 Kings 11:3-4

Leads to favoritism
2 Chronicles 11:21

Produces rivalry
1 Samuel 1:6

**Prohibited for
church leaders**
1 Timothy 3:2
1 Timothy 3:12
Titus 1:6

Prohibited for leaders
Deuteronomy 17:17

Popularity

Definition:
The state or quality
of being widely liked,

admired, appreciated,
or valued.

Key Verses:
Proverbs 14:20
1 Thessalonians 2:4

See Also:
Influence
Respect

Dangers of desiring
Matthew 7:13-14
Acts 12:1-4
Galatians 1:10

**Gained through
flattery**
2 Samuel 15:1-6

**Gained through
good character**
2 Samuel 3:36

Love of
John 12:42-43

Of the wicked
2 Samuel 15:13-14

**Political
manipulation
to receive**
Acts 24:27

**Rejection by
the wicked**
1 Samuel 10:26-27

**Should not be
based on money**
James 2:1-13

Wrongdoing to gain
Acts 12:1-3

Pornography

Definition:
The depiction of erotic behavior intended to sexually arouse.

Key Verses:
Proverbs 6:25-26
Romans 13:14

See Also:
Lust
Sexual Addiction

Abstinence from sexual immorality
1 Thessalonians 4:1-8

Blamelessness at Christ's coming
1 Thessalonians 5:23-24

Enslaved to what defeats them
2 Peter 2:19

Friendship with world is hostility toward God
James 4:4

God desires integrity
Psalm 51:6

Lust condemned
Matthew 5:27-28

Overcoming through Christ
Job 31:1
Psalm 25:15

Psalm 51:10
Psalm 101:3-4
Psalm 139:23-24
Proverbs 4:23-27
Isaiah 1:16-17
Romans 7:15-25
Romans 8:9
Romans 12:1-2
1 Corinthians 3:16-17
1 Corinthians 6:16-20
1 Corinthians 10:13
1 Corinthians 15:56-57
2 Corinthians 10:3-5
2 Corinthians 12:9
Philippians 4:8-9
Philippians 4:13
Philippians 4:19
Colossians 3:1-5
Hebrews 4:13
James 1:21
James 4:7
2 Peter 1:3

Self-discipline
1 Peter 1:13

Sexual immorality condemned
1 Corinthians 6:12-13
Galatians 5:19-21
Ephesians 5:3-4

Source of temptation
James 1:14-15

Wicked given over to impure life
Ephesians 2:1-3
Ephesians 4:19

Postpartum Depression

Definition:
Debilitating indifference of a mother toward herself and her baby following birth.

Key Verses:
Psalm 42:5
Psalm 127:3

See Also:
Depression
Mother

Post-Traumatic Stress Disorder

Definition:
Intense fear or anxiety along with intrusive, vivid recollections of a horrific event.

Key Verses:
Isaiah 41:10
Isaiah 54:14

See Also:
Anxiety
Stress
Trauma

Poverty

Definition:
Lack of wealth, possessions, or means of support.

Abuse of the poor
Amos 5:11
Amos 8:4-6

Benefits of
Matthew 19:21

Better than lying
Proverbs 19:22

Better than wealth without God
Psalm 37:16-17

Blessing for
Matthew 5:3
Luke 6:20
James 2:5

Compassion toward
Deuteronomy 15:7-8
Deuteronomy 15:11
Proverbs 31:8-9
Jeremiah 39:10
Galatians 2:9-10

Contentment in
2 Corinthians 6:10

Dangers of
Proverbs 30:8-9

Faith in God is true riches
Revelation 2:9
Revelation 3:17-18

From laziness
Proverbs 20:13
1 Timothy 5:8

Giving out of
Luke 21:1-4
2 Corinthians 8:1-3

God defends the poor
Psalm 9:18
Psalm 14:6

Justice for the poor
Isaiah 11:4

Of Christ
2 Corinthians 8:9

Of the saints
Hebrews 11:37-38

Oppression of the poor
Exodus 23:6
Proverbs 22:22-23
Zechariah 7:10

Poor hear good news
Luke 7:22

Praising God in
Job 1:21

Relationship to favoritism
James 2:1-9

Power

Definition:
The ability or capacity to act or accomplish.

Key Verses:
Mark 10:42-45
John 13:3

See Also:
Ambition
Influence

Belongs to God
Psalm 62:11

For the powerless
Isaiah 40:29

From God
2 Timothy 1:7

In weakness
2 Corinthians 12:9

Of Christ
Matthew 28:18
Luke 6:19
Acts 10:38
Philippians 3:10
Colossians 1:17
2 Thessalonians 2:8

Of death
Ecclesiastes 8:8

Of God
Deuteronomy 3:24
Isaiah 48:13
Jeremiah 10:6
Jeremiah 10:12
Jeremiah 32:27
Romans 8:11
Ephesians 1:18-20

Ephesians 6:10
2 Timothy 1:8
1 Peter 1:5

Of Satan
2 Thessalonians 2:9

Of the Holy Spirit
Acts 1:8
Ephesians 3:16
1 Thessalonians 1:5

Of the Word of God
Romans 1:16-17
1 Corinthians 1:18
Hebrews 4:12

Over demons
Matthew 10:1

Spiritual
2 Peter 1:3

To overcome sin
Matthew 19:26

Prayer

Definition:
Communion with God.

Key Verses:
Psalm 102:17
Matthew 21:22

See Also:
Communication
God
Intimacy

Answers to
Genesis 25:21
1 Kings 8:52

Psalm 28:6
Psalm 65:2
Psalm 66:18-19
Psalm 91:14-16
Psalm 116:1-4
Isaiah 30:19
Isaiah 65:24
John 14:13-14
1 Peter 3:7
1 Peter 3:12
1 John 3:21-22
1 John 5:14-15

Before a meal
Mark 14:22-23

Commitment to
Luke 2:36-38

Devotion to
Colossians 4:2

Effects of
Genesis 24:15
1 Samuel 12:18
Daniel 10:12
James 5:17-18

For blessing
Nehemiah 5:19

For boldness
Acts 4:23-26

For deliverance
1 Samuel 7:8
Psalm 34:17
Psalm 145:17-19
Isaiah 37:14-20
Jeremiah 18:18-23

For guidance
Psalm 139:23-24

For healing
Luke 5:12-13

For increased love
1 Thessalonians 3:10-12

For provision
Zechariah 10:1
Mark 11:24
Philippians 4:6-7

For spiritual growth
Colossians 1:9-14
Colossians 4:12

For strength
Nehemiah 6:9

For success in ministry
Matthew 9:37-38
Ephesians 6:19-20
Colossians 4:3-4

For those in prison
Acts 12:5

Hindrances to
Lamentations 3:44
Micah 3:4
Zechariah 7:13

Hypocrisy in
Matthew 6:7

Importance of obedience
Isaiah 1:11-17

In Jesus' name
John 14:13

In persecution
Daniel 6:10

　　　The Biblical Counseling Reference Guide

Intimacy in
Romans 8:15

In times of sorrow
Matthew 26:36-46

In times of stress
Philippians 4:6

Mercy and grace in
Hebrews 4:14-16

Of community
Romans 15:30

Of confession
Psalm 32:5
Proverbs 28:13

Offered to God
Revelation 8:3-4

Of Jacob
Genesis 32:9-12

Of Jesus
John 17:1-26
Hebrews 5:7

Of repentance
2 Chronicles 7:14

Patience in
Hebrews 6:13-15

Persistence in
Psalm 55:17
Psalm 77:2-4
Matthew 7:7-12
Luke 11:5-8
Luke 18:1-8
1 Thessalonians 5:17

Power of
Matthew 21:21-22
James 5:15-18

Preparation for
1 Peter 4:7

Proper motives in
James 4:3

Relationship to faith
James 1:5-7

**Relationship
to fasting**
Nehemiah 1:4

Solitude in
Mark 1:35
Luke 5:16

**Thanking God
for believers**
1 Corinthians 1:4
Philippians 1:3

Toward God
Revelation 15:3-4

Trust in the Lord
Proverbs 3:5-6

Unanswered
Job 30:20
Jeremiah 7:16
Jeremiah 11:14
2 Corinthians
12:7-10

Unity in
Acts 1:14

Without disputing
1 Timothy 2:8

Pregnancy...
Unplanned

Definition:
A pregnancy that is
unexpected, inconve-
nient, or unintended.

Key Verses:
Psalm 139:13-14
Ecclesiastes 11:5

See Also:
Abortion
Adoption
Infanticide
Parenting
Single Parenting

Be humble
1 Peter 5:6-7

**Benefit of a
difficult situation**
Psalm 119:71

Be self-controlled
Titus 2:12

Care for others
Philippians 2:3-4

**Cast your burden
on the Lord**
Psalm 55:22

Child in womb
Hosea 12:3

**Children a gift
from God**
Psalm 127:3-5

Choose life
Deuteronomy
30:19-20

Comfort during
Psalm 103:4-5
Psalm 121:1-8

Created by God
Psalm 119:73
Isaiah 43:7

Do not sin
Psalm 4:4

Encouragement
1 Thessalonians 5:11

Forgiveness from
Psalm 103:2-3
Psalm 103:10-12
2 Corinthians
5:17-18
Ephesians 4:32

Freedom
John 8:36

God cares
Psalm 68:6

**God cares for
the fatherless**
Psalm 10:14
Psalm 27:10
Psalm 68:5-6

God comforts
2 Corinthians 1:3-4

God gives life
Deuteronomy 32:39

God is with you
Deuteronomy 31:8

Isaiah 41:10

God is your husband
Isaiah 54:5-6

God knows all
Psalm 139:1-24

God made all
Isaiah 44:24

God's acceptance
Psalm 27:10

God's control
Ecclesiastes 11:5

God's counsel
Psalm 32:8

God's direction
Psalm 119:105

God sees the heart
1 Samuel 16:7

God's everlasting love
Jeremiah 31:3
Romans 8:38-39

God's guidance
Psalm 25:4-5
Psalm 27:11
Isaiah 58:11

God's love
Psalm 117:2
Psalm 138:8
1 John 4:16

**God's love for
children**
Luke 9:48

**God's plan for the
unborn child**
Psalm 139:13-16
Jeremiah 1:4-5
Jeremiah 29:11

God's presence
Matthew 28:20

God's protection
Isaiah 43:2

God's sovereignty
Ecclesiastes 3:11
Romans 11:33-36

God's way
Proverbs 14:12
Proverbs 16:25

Help during
Proverbs 3:5-6

Jesus gives life
John 1:2-4
John 10:10

Love God in midst of
Deuteronomy 6:5-9

Love one another
John 13:34-35

Obey God
Acts 5:29

Pure heart
Proverbs 21:2-3

Pursue righteousness
2 Timothy 2:22

Refuse sexual sin
1 Corinthians 6:18

The Biblical Counseling Reference Guide

**Responsibility
to provide for**
1 Timothy 5:8

Seek the Lord's will
1 Kings 22:5

Show love
1 John 3:16

Stand firm
Proverbs 1:10

Strength during
Isaiah 40:29-31

Think about
Philippians 4:8

Wisdom a shelter
Proverbs 14:8
Ecclesiastes 7:12

Accept each other
Romans 15:7

**All people are made
in God's image**
Genesis 1:27

Be a good listener
Proverbs 20:5

Be cautious
Proverbs 14:12

Be humble
Proverbs 26:12
Isaiah 5:21
Matthew 7:4

**Be peaceable
to all people**
Titus 3:1-3

**Blessed are the
persecuted**
Matthew 5:11-12

Christ's sacrifice
Mark 10:45

Condemned
Proverbs 28:21
Matthew 7:1
Acts 10:24-28
Acts 11:1-18
2 Corinthians 7:2
Philippians 2:3-4
James 2:1-9
James 3:9-10

Control your words
Ephesians 4:29

Danger of
James 2:4

**Employ
understanding**
Proverbs 11:12

Essential equality
Malachi 2:10
Acts 17:26

2 Corinthians
5:16-19

Examine yourself
Proverbs 27:19

Forgive others
Colossians 3:13

**God does not
show favoritism**
Acts 10:34-35
Acts 15:5-9
Romans 2:11
Galatians 3:28

**God looks at
the heart**
1 Samuel 16:7

**God seeks to
reconcile world
to Himself**
2 Corinthians
5:18-19

God sees all
Proverbs 21:2

**God's grace in
weakness**
2 Corinthians
12:9-10

**Jesus brings peace
to Christians**
Ephesians 2:14

Jesus heals a child
Mark 7:24-30

Jesus heals a servant
Luke 7:1-10

Love others
Matthew 7:12
Galatians 5:14
1 Peter 3:8-9
1 John 2:9-11

New creation
2 Corinthians 5:17

No hidden sin
Psalm 119:23-24

**Persecuting out
of ignorance**
1 Timothy 1:13

Power for overcoming
Romans 12:2
2 Peter 1:3-4

Racial
Luke 10:30-37
John 4:9

Reconciliation from
2 Corinthians
5:18-19

Work for peace
Hebrews 12:14-15

**Zacchaeus's
change of heart**
Luke 19:1-10

Premarital Counseling

Definition:
The process of
advising an engaged
couple with regard to
their marriage plans,
expectations, and
potential problems.

Key Verses:
Proverbs 15:22
2 Corinthians 6:14

See Also:
Counseling
Family
Marriage

**Arranged marriage
in Israel**
1 Samuel 18:17-29

Authority of Christ
Colossians 2:9-10

Be holy
1 Thessalonians
4:3-7

Be humble
Ephesians 4:2

Be submissive
Ephesians 5:21

Be unselfish
Philippians 2:3-4

Blessing of marriage
Proverbs 5:18-19

**Caution in dealing
with angry people**
Proverbs 22:24

Compatibility
Genesis 2:18

Control your tongue
Ephesians 4:29

Divorce prohibited
Malachi 2:16
Mark 10:9

**Do not be
mismatched with
unbelievers**
2 Corinthians
6:14-15

Encourage each other
Hebrews 10:24-25

**Examples of
covenants**
Genesis 17:9
Numbers 30:2

Family discord
Proverbs 19:13

Following Christ
Luke 9:23

Forgiveness in
Ephesians 4:32

Glorify God together
Romans 15:5-6

God judges adulterers
Hebrews 13:4

Healing words
Proverbs 15:4

Honesty in
Ephesians 4:15

Importance to success
Proverbs 15:22

Integrity in
Proverbs 11:3

Love and forgiveness
Proverbs 10:12

Love in
1 Corinthians 13:4-7

The Biblical Counseling Reference Guide

Ephesians 5:33
1 John 3:16

Male and female
Genesis 2:22

Prayer in
James 5:16

Roles in marriage
Ephesians 5:21-33

Sanctity of marriage
Malachi 2:13-14

Sex in marriage
1 Corinthians 7:4

Speak graciously
Colossians 4:6

Stewardship
Luke 16:10

Strength of love
1 Corinthians 13:8

Submit to the Spirit
Galatians 5:16-18

Trust in the Lord
Proverbs 3:5-6

Unity in
Genesis 2:24
Amos 3:3
Romans 12:18
Philippians 2:1-2

Unity of marriage
Malachi 2:15

**Warning against
sexual immorality**
Ephesians 5:3-4

Wisdom in
Ephesians 5:15

Pride

Definition:
Excessive estimation of
one's abilities, worth,
or accomplishments;
conceit.

Key Verses:
James 3:13
James 4:6

See Also:
Arrogance
Humility
Identity
Inferiority

Avoidance of
Proverbs 8:13
Proverbs 27:2

Be wise
Proverbs 12:15

Comes from the heart
Mark 7:20-23

Condemned
Matthew 18:1-10
Matthew 20:20-23
Matthew 23:12
Luke 9:46-48
Romans 3:27
Romans 12:3
Romans 12:16
1 Corinthians 4:7
1 Corinthians 13:4
Galatians 5:26
Philippians 2:3-4

Consequences of
Psalm 52:7
Proverbs 11:2
Proverbs 13:10
Proverbs 16:18
Proverbs 18:11-12
Proverbs 29:23
Zephaniah 2:9-10
Luke 18:9-14
Acts 12:19-23

Creates loss
1 Corinthians
3:11-15

Discipline for
Proverbs 3:11-12

Fear God
Proverbs 9:10

Folly of
Isaiah 10:12-16
Romans 1:22

**Forbidden in
ministry**
Luke 10:17-20

From materialism
Hosea 12:8

**God knows
your heart**
Psalm 138:23-24

God's response to
1 Samuel 2:1-3
2 Samuel 22:28
Psalm 138:6
Proverbs 16:5
Isaiah 13:11
Isaiah 14:13-15
Daniel 4:37

Daniel 5:20-23
Amos 6:13-14
Zephaniah 2:15
James 4:6
1 Peter 5:5-6
Revelation 18:7-8

Ignorance in
2 Corinthians 10:12

In endurance
2 Thessalonians 1:4

In human wisdom
1 Corinthians 3:18
1 Corinthians 8:1-3

In riches
Jeremiah 48:7
Revelation 3:17-18

In the gospel
Romans 15:17

In the Lord
Psalm 34:2
Jeremiah 9:23-24
1 Corinthians
1:26-31
Philippians 3:7

In weaknesses
2 Corinthians 11:30

**New believers
vulnerable to pride**
1 Timothy 3:6

Of unbelievers
1 Timothy 6:3-5

Over sin
1 Corinthians 5:1-2

Produces rebellion
Romans 10:3

Revealed to God
Psalm 139:23-24

Scoffers have pride
Proverbs 21:24

Warning against
Mark 12:38-39

Pride and Humility

Definition:
Antonyms denoting
attitudes of self-
exaltation or self-
interest and lowly
mindset and concern
for others, respectively.

Key Verses:
Proverbs 16:18
James 4:6

See Also:
Character
Discipleship
Humility
Pride
Virtue

Procrastination

Definition:
The act or process of
needlessly deferring,
postponing, or delay-
ing.

Key Verses:
Proverbs 10:4
Ephesians 5:15-16

See Also:
Failure
Integrity
Manipulation
Motivation
Perfectionism
Time Management

Abide in Christ
John 15:5-8

Accept correction
Proverbs 15:32

Accepted by God
Ephesians 1:11

Accept instruction
Proverbs 9:9

Arriving too late
Matthew 25:1-13

Be diligent
Proverbs 13:4
Proverbs 14:23
Proverbs 18:9
Proverbs 21:5
Proverbs 24:30-31
Proverbs 28:19

Be disciplined
1 Corinthians 9:24

Be humble
1 Peter 5:6-7

Be self-controlled
Proverbs 19:2

Confidence in God
Proverbs 3:25-26

Control your words
Proverbs 15:23

**Delayed hope
is depressing**
  Proverbs 13:12

Do good
  James 4:17

Encourage each other
  Hebrews 10:24-25

Eternal life
  John 14:1-7

Following Christ
  Matthew 16:24-26

Folly of
  Proverbs 15:19
  Proverbs 27:1
  Luke 16:19-31

Freedom
  Galatians 5:1

God is on time
  Habakkuk 2:3

God's blessing
  Psalm 62:12

God's control
  James 4:13-14

God's favor
  2 Corinthians 6:2

God's gifts
  Romans 12:6-8
  2 Peter 1:3-4

God's grace
  2 Corinthians 9:8

God's guidance
  Psalm 16:11
  Isaiah 58:11

God's love
  Jeremiah 31:3
  John 3:16-17
  Romans 8:38-39

God's peace
  Isaiah 26:3

God's plans
  Jeremiah 29:11

God's purpose
  Romans 8:28

God's salvation
  Psalm 34:4

God's work
  Ephesians 2:10

**Guidance from
the Spirit**
  John 14:16-17

Importance of vows
  Ecclesiastes 5:4-5

**In hearing
spiritual matters**
  Acts 24:25

In obeying the Lord
  Joshua 18:3
  2 Chronicles 24:5

Jesus waits
  John 11:1-6

Leads to poverty
  Proverbs 6:9-11
  Proverbs 20:4
  Proverbs 21:25
  Proverbs 24:32-34

Live out faith
  Philippians 2:12-13

Move forward
  Isaiah 43:18-19
  Philippians 3:12-14

**Now is the time
for salvation**
  2 Corinthians 6:2

Obey God
  Psalm 119:60

Offering excuses
  Luke 9:59-62
  Luke 14:16-21

Peace from God
  Philippians 4:6-7

**Persecution
and peace**
  John 16:33

Persevere
  Hebrews 10:36

**Persuaded to
procrastinate**
  Judges 19:1-10

Please God
  Psalm 19:14

Prayers of Samuel
  1 Samuel 12:23

Propriety
  Ecclesiastes 8:5-6

Unbelief of Israel
  Numbers 13:31–
    14:3

Use time wisely
  Ephesians 5:15-17

Wisdom encouraged
Luke 14:28-30
Hebrews 6:11-12

Work for peace
Romans 14:19

Profanity

Definition:
Speech characterized
by blasphemy, cursing,
and coarse language.

Key Verses:
Leviticus 22:32
Colossians 3:8

See Also:
Communication
Holiness
Purity

Projection

Definition:
Identifying one's own
ideas, feelings, or atti-
tudes with someone
else.

Key Verses:
Psalm 139:23
Proverbs 4:26

See Also:
Conflict Resolution
Confrontation
Identity

Prophecy

Definition:
Inspired explanation
and prediction of the
future.

Key Verses:
Deuteronomy 18:22
2 Peter 1:20-21

See Also:
Bible Reliability
Jesus Christ

Prosperity

Definition:
The state or quality of
thriving, succeeding,
or flourishing; used
especially of wealth.

Key Verses:
Deuteronomy 8:17-18
Psalm 39:6

See Also:
Finances
Materialism
Money
Prosperity Gospel

Prosperity Gospel

Definition:
Faulty, twisted teach-
ing that Christians
should always be
healthy and wealthy.

Key Verses:
Matthew 7:15
Philippians 4:12

See Also:
Disease
Evil and Suffering
Wealth

Ask of God
Matthew 7:7
Mark 11:24
John 15:5-7
John 16:24

Avoidance of greed
Luke 12:15

Believer's suffering
Romans 8:18
2 Corinthians 4:17

**Blessings for
obedience**
Job 36:11
Job 42:12
Daniel 4:27

**Blessings for
repentance**
Deuteronomy
30:1-3

Christ's suffering
1 Peter 2:24

Confidence in God
1 Corinthians 1:31
1 John 5:14

Dangers of wealth
Deuteronomy 32:15
Proverbs 30:8-9
Isaiah 2:7-8
Matthew 6:24
Luke 16:13
Luke 18:25

James 5:3

Delusion in wealth
Proverbs 18:11

Emptiness of wealth
1 Timothy 6:17

Folly of riches
Psalm 49:16-20
Isaiah 55:1-3
Jeremiah 48:7

Future healing
Ezekiel 47:12

Giving and generosity
Luke 21:2-3
Acts 2:45
Acts 4:32
1 Corinthians 16:2
2 Corinthians 9:5-8

God oversees all
Ecclesiastes 2:26
Isaiah 43:20-21
Isaiah 45:3

God's grace in suffering
2 Corinthians 12:9

Hezekiah's illness
Isaiah 38:1

Human arrogance
James 4:13-15

Illness for God's glory
John 11:4

Importance of contentment
Philippians 4:12-13

1 Timothy 6:6-10
Hebrews 13:5

Meditate on the Word for success
Joshua 1:8

Of the wicked
Job 24:24
Psalm 37:35-36
Psalm 73:12
Jeremiah 12:1-3

Paul's suffering
2 Corinthians 12:7

Poverty of Christ
Matthew 8:20

Prosperity and health are gifts from God
Genesis 39:2
Deuteronomy 28:8
1 Chronicles 29:11-12
2 Chronicles 26:5
Psalm 23:1
Proverbs 28:25
Ezekiel 16:13-14
Ezekiel 36:11
Joel 3:1-2

Prosperity's connection with hard work
Proverbs 12:11

Reputation more important than wealth
Proverbs 22:1

Responsibility of stewardship
Luke 16:10

Robbing God
Malachi 3:8

Seek the kingdom of God
Matthew 6:33
1 Timothy 6:17-19

Spiritual riches in Christ
Philippians 3:7-8
Colossians 1:27

Spiritual wealth
Revelation 3:17-18

Suffering and perseverance
James 1:12

Suffering of believers
Mark 10:29-30
Romans 8:17
Hebrews 10:34
Hebrews 11:36-37
James 1:2
1 Peter 4:12-13
1 Peter 4:19
Revelation 2:9

Suffering of Christ
Hebrews 12:2

Suffering of Lazarus
Luke 16:19-21

Unique authority of Christ
Matthew 28:18
Revelation 1:18

Unique authority of Christ and apostles
Matthew 10:1

Value of heavenly treasure
Matthew 6:19-21

Protection

Definition:
That which guards or keeps safe from harm, exposure, or danger.

Key Verses:
Psalm 32:7
2 Thessalonians 3:3

See Also:
Safety

By angels
Isaiah 37:36
Hebrews 1:14

By the Lord
Genesis 21:9-21
Numbers 10:35
Psalm 11:1
Psalm 32:7
Psalm 138:7
Isaiah 43:1-2
Jeremiah 26:13-15
Daniel 3:22-27
Daniel 6:13-24
Zechariah 2:3-5
Matthew 2:12-15
Matthew 10:28-30
John 7:30
Acts 23:12-24
1 Peter 1:5
Revelation 6:15-17

From the evil one
John 17:15
Ephesians 6:16
1 John 5:18-19

From unwise sources
Isaiah 31:1

From wild animals
Ezekiel 34:25

Providence

Definition:
Theological term describing God's activity in creating, sustaining, and controlling the universe.

Key Verses:
Job 10:12
Psalm 31:15

See Also:
Decision Making
God
Submission

God brings the wind and thunder
Psalm 135:6-7
Jeremiah 10:13

God changes the seasons
Daniel 2:21

God creates all things
Jeremiah 27:5

God gives life
Job 14:5
Acts 17:25-27

God plans for the unborn
Psalm 139:16

God plans to preserve life
Genesis 50:20

God provides for His creation
Job 5:10
Psalm 65:9-10
Psalm 104:14
Psalm 147:8-9
Matthew 6:26
Matthew 10:29-31
Acts 14:17

God rules all nations
Genesis 45:8
Job 12:23-24
Psalm 22:27-28
Daniel 4:17

God works in all circumstances
Romans 8:28

Prudence

Definition:
The ability to use reason to make wise decisions.

Key Verses:
Proverbs 8:5
Proverbs 13:16

See Also:
Decision Making
Tact
Wisdom

The Biblical Counseling Reference Guide

Gain discernment
Proverbs 8:5

In seeing danger
Proverbs 27:12

In speech
Daniel 2:14
Amos 5:13

Of a manager
Genesis 39:4-10
Luke 12:42

Of considering one's ways
Proverbs 14:8
Proverbs 14:18

Of consulting many counselors
Proverbs 24:6

Prudent wife is from the Lord
Proverbs 19:14

Take measures to keep from sin
Psalm 39:1
Psalm 139:23-24

Psychotic

Definition:
Related to a mental illness or psychosis.

Key Verses:
Psalm 23:1-2
1 Peter 4:7

See Also:
Counseling

Health
Mental Illness

Puberty

Definition:
The period of time when one is first capable of sexual reproduction, characterized by dramatic physical changes.

Key Verses:
Luke 2:52
1 Timothy 4:12

See Also:
Adolescence
Teenagers

Immaturity of youths
2 Kings 2:23-24
Proverbs 7:7

Of Jesus
Luke 2:40
Luke 2:52

Serving God in youth
1 Samuel 3:19
1 Samuel 17:33
Ecclesiastes 12:1
2 Timothy 2:22

Vigor of youth
Job 20:11

Wisdom of youths
Ecclesiastes 4:13

Punishment

Definition:
Injury or penalty inflicted upon someone for breaking a rule, law, or code in order to prevent further violations.

Key Verses:
Isaiah 13:11
Hebrews 12:6

See Also:
Correction
Justice

By God
Isaiah 65:6-7

Delay of
Ecclesiastes 8:11

Eternal
Revelation 20:10

For disobedience
2 Samuel 13:23-29
Psalm 89:30-34
Acts 5:1-11

For incompetence
Acts 12:18-19

For injustice
Jeremiah 17:10

For murder
Genesis 9:5-6
Numbers 35:16-21

For rebellion
Numbers 16:31-33
Judges 8:16

For the unrighteous
2 Samuel 24:13-14
Matthew 25:41
Revelation 14:11

God punishes less than is deserved
Ezra 9:13
Psalm 103:8-10

God's punishment delayed
1 Kings 21:29

Purity

Definition:
The state or quality of being unmixed, unpolluted, or undefiled; innocence.

Key Verses:
Psalm 73:1
Matthew 5:8

See Also:
Holiness
Innocence
Virtue

Based on hope
2 Corinthians 7:1

Be holy for God is holy
1 Peter 1:13-16

Blessing for
Psalm 18:20-21
Matthew 5:8

Commanded
1 Corinthians 6:13-16
Ephesians 5:1-3
1 Timothy 6:14
1 Peter 1:15-16
1 Peter 1:22

Focus on
Philippians 4:8

From God
Psalm 51:7

In response to salvation
Titus 2:11-14

Prayer for forgiveness
Psalm 51:10

Relationship to worship
Psalm 24:3-4
James 4:8

Sexual
1 Thessalonians 4:3-7

Walk by Spirit to live in purity
Galatians 5:16

Purpose in Life

Definition:
The end to which one is striving in life; one's reason or motivation for living.

Key Verses:
Ecclesiastes 4:8
Ephesians 1:4-6

See Also:
Discipline
Faith
Maturity

Accountability for
2 Corinthians 5:9-10

Build love of God in your family
Deuteronomy 6:5-7

Changed
Acts 9:1-15

Christlikeness
Romans 8:28-29
2 Corinthians 5:17
Galatians 6:14
Ephesians 4:22-24
Philippians 3:13-14
Colossians 3:23

Christ's
Mark 10:45
John 3:16-17
John 17:1-4

Determined by God
Jeremiah 1:5
John 15:16
Ephesians 1:4-5

Enabled by God
Jeremiah 1:9-10

Enabled by the Spirit
Romans 15:13

Enjoy life and glorify God
Psalm 37:4
Proverbs 14:26
Ecclesiastes 11:9

Ecclesiastes 12:13-14
Isaiah 43:7
Jeremiah 29:11
Matthew 6:33
1 Corinthians 10:31
2 Corinthians 3:18
Ephesians 1:11-12
Ephesians 5:15-17

Enter the narrow gate to salvation
Matthew 7:13-14

Eternal perspective
Ecclesiastes 3:11

Fullness in Christ
Colossians 2:9-10

Futility of worldly pleasure
Ecclesiastes 2:11
Ecclesiastes 4:4
2 Corinthians 4:18

God vindicates
Psalm 57:2
Psalm 138:8

God will reward
Psalm 62:12

Guidance from God
Psalm 32:8
Proverbs 19:21
Proverbs 20:24
Philippians 4:6-7

Honorable make honorable plans
Isaiah 32:8

Honor parents
Exodus 20:12

Including relationships
Ephesians 5:22-27

Known by God
Luke 12:6-7

Love enemies
Matthew 5:44

Love one another
John 15:12

Rule as God's representative
Genesis 1:26-27

Suffering with Christ
Romans 8:17

To do good works
Ephesians 2:10

To glorify Christ
Philippians 1:21

To grow in relation to Christ
Philippians 3:8-11

Unique to glorify God
1 Peter 4:10-11

Work out progressively
Philippians 2:12-13

Quarrel

Definition:
An intense verbal dispute or altercation.

Key Verses:
Proverbs 26:17
James 4:1-2

See Also:
Argue
Disagreement
Sibling Rivalry
Strife

Angry man causes quarrels
Proverbs 15:18

Condemned
Philippians 4:2

Consequences of
Genesis 4:8
Genesis 21:10
Proverbs 17:19
Proverbs 18:6
Proverbs 18:19
Proverbs 26:21

Consider your actions carefully
Proverbs 25:8

Honorable to resolve a quarrel
Proverbs 20:3

Instructions about religious quarrels
2 Timothy 2:14

Peacemakers have joy
Proverbs 12:20

Settle quarrels quickly
Matthew 5:25

Rage

Definition:
Violent anger characterized by loss of self-control.

Key Verses:
Proverbs 16:32
Isaiah 41:11

See Also:
Anger
Fury
Wrath

Against God is futile
Psalm 2:1-6

Avoidance of
Psalm 37:8
Proverbs 15:1

Condemned
James 1:19

Control of
Ephesians 4:26-27

Folly of
Proverbs 29:22

Harmful effects of
Matthew 5:22

In response to domestic violence
2 Samuel 13:20-22

In response to refusal to cooperate
Esther 1:12

Of leaders
Proverbs 16:14

Proverbs 20:2
Daniel 2:12

Rape

Definition:
Forced sexual intercourse by means of violence, threat, or deception.

Key Verses:
Psalm 34:18
Psalm 103:6

See Also:
Abuse
Alcohol and Drug Abuse
Childhood Sexual Abuse
Incest
Spiritual Abuse

Accept instruction
Proverbs 23:12

Beware of hypocrisy
Proverbs 26:24-25

Christ reconciles
Colossians 1:22

Comfort in
Psalm 23:4
Psalm 34:18
Jeremiah 31:3
2 Corinthians 1:3-4

Confront the guilty
Proverbs 24:24

Consider your ways
Proverbs 14:8

Control your tongue
Proverbs 12:18

Develop relationship with Christ
Philippians 3:7-9

Do not trust the untrustworthy
John 2:24

Employ good judgment
Proverbs 3:21-23

Enablement through Christ
Philippians 4:13

Fear described
Psalm 55:4-7

Forget the past
Isaiah 43:18-19

Forgiveness in
Matthew 6:14-15
Colossians 3:13

From tribe of Benjamin
Judges 19:25

God executes justice
Ezekiel 45:9

God gives strength
Isaiah 40:28-31

God has good plans
Jeremiah 29:11

God heals
Jeremiah 17:14

The Biblical Counseling Reference Guide

God heals wounds
Psalm 147:3

God hears you
1 John 5:14-15

God is in control
Romans 8:28

God is with you
Isaiah 43:2

God knows you
Isaiah 49:1-2

God will execute justice
Psalm 37:1-40

Guard eyes
Job 31:1

Help in
Proverbs 18:24

In Sodom
Genesis 19:1-10

Joy will return
Psalm 30:5

Love your spouse
Colossians 3:19

Pursue justice
Ecclesiastes 8:11
Acts 25:10-11

Pursue knowledge
Proverbs 18:15

Pursue peace
Proverbs 12:20

Severe consequences for perpetrator
Deuteronomy 22:25-26

Sex in marriage
1 Corinthians 7:4

Strength in
Psalm 118:6
Psalm 119:28
Psalm 119:50
Proverbs 29:25
2 Corinthians 4:8-9

Suffering of Christ
1 Peter 2:21

Support one another
Galatians 6:2

The Lord hears you
Psalm 22:24

The Lord is with you
Deuteronomy 31:8
Isaiah 54:5

The prudent take refuge
Proverbs 22:3

The strong oppress the weak
Psalm 10:9

The wicked described
Psalm 36:1-4

Trust God
Psalm 56:3

Trust in the Lord
Psalm 37:7
Proverbs 3:5-6

Isaiah 26:3

Trust the Shepherd
Psalm 23:1-6

Truth creates freedom
John 8:32

Vengeance condemned
Romans 12:19

Wisdom brings safety
Proverbs 28:26

You will forget your suffering
Job 11:15-16

Rationalization

Definition:
To present a reasonable argument or to create a contrived justification for inappropriate behavior.

Key Verses:
1 Chronicles 29:17
2 Corinthians 1:12

See Also:
Avoidance
Excuses

Rebellion

Definition:
The act or process of defying, resisting, or opposing authority.

Accountability for
Proverbs 10:9
Hebrews 4:13

A family characteristic
2 Kings 21:21

Against God
Isaiah 14:12-14
Ezekiel 28:13-18
Nahum 1:9
Romans 1:18-32
Romans 9:20
Colossians 1:21
Revelation 16:10-11

Anger opposes righteousness
James 1:20

Avoidance of
Exodus 19:5-6
Proverbs 13:3
Proverbs 21:23

By the dragon
Revelation 12:3-4

Condemned
Proverbs 3:7
Ephesians 4:29
Hebrews 3:15

Consequences of
Numbers 14:41-45
1 Samuel 15:23
Proverbs 11:3
Proverbs 14:12
Romans 13:1-2

Depravity
Psalm 51:5

Do not associate with rebels
2 Thessalonians 3:14-15

Folly of
Proverbs 12:15
Proverbs 15:32
Proverbs 28:13-14
Proverbs 29:11

Forgiveness from
Psalm 25:7
Psalm 32:1

Forgive one another
Colossians 3:13

From the heart
Zechariah 7:11-12

Godly separation
Colossians 3:8

God values brokenness
Psalm 51:17

God will correct
Hebrews 12:5-7
Hebrews 12:11

Law is meant for rebellious people
1 Timothy 1:9

Moral law
Romans 2:14-15

Of Israel
Isaiah 30:9

Of Korah
Numbers 16:1-4

Of youth
Luke 15:11-32

Pharisees condemned
Mathew 23:23-26

Return from
James 5:19-20

Universality of
Isaiah 53:6
Romans 3:23

Rebuke

Definition:
To confront with a stern, strict reprimand, reproof, or censure.

Do not abandon instruction
Proverbs 4:2

**Do not rebuke
the elderly**
1 Timothy 5:1

For sinful behavior
1 Samuel 13:13
2 Thessalonians
3:14-15

**Leading to
repentance**
2 Corinthians 7:8-9

Leads to retaliation
Acts 7:51-60

Michael and the devil
Jude 9

Of Christians
Titus 1:13

Of Peter
Mark 8:31-33

Of unbelief
Mark 16:14

**Public rebuke
of leaders**
Acts 23:1-5
1 Timothy 5:20

Value of
Proverbs 25:12
Proverbs 27:5-6

Reconciliation

Definition:
The act, process, or
result of harmonizing
or restoring a friend-
ship.

Key Verses:
Romans 5:10
2 Corinthians 5:19

See Also:
Communication
Conflict Resolution
Forgiveness
Mediation
Salvation

Abigail's appeal
1 Samuel 25:2-42

Accountable to God
Romans 14:12

Avoid bitterness
Acts 8:22-23
Hebrews 12:15

Be a peacemaker
Matthew 5:9

Be humble
Ephesians 4:2
2 Timothy 2:24-25

Commanded
Proverbs 6:2-3
Matthew 6:14-15
Luke 12:58
Romans 12:17-21
Ephesians 4:32
Philippians 4:2-3
Colossians 3:13

**Confession and
forgiveness**
1 John 1:8-9

**Consider others as
more important**
Philippians 2:2-4

David appeased
1 Samuel 25:35

Difficulty of
Proverbs 18:19

Forgiveness
Psalm 32:5

For sinning believers
Matthew 18:15-18

**God working
for good**
Romans 8:28

**Hard-hearted fall
into trouble**
Proverbs 28:14

**Identification
with Christ**
Galatians 2:20
Colossians 3:1-3

In Christ
1 Timothy 2:5

In the church
1 Corinthians 1:10
1 Corinthians 6:1-7
Ephesians 2:14-18
Ephesians 3:6

Make amends
Proverbs 14:9

Mediation
Job 33:23-28

Message of
2 Corinthians
5:18-20

Of Jacob and Esau
Genesis 33:1-20

Of Joseph
Genesis 37:1-36
Genesis 39:1–45:15
Genesis 50:15-21

Peace from Christ
John 14:27
Colossians 3:15

Relationship to worship
Matthew 5:23-24

Resist bitterness
Hebrews 12:15

Results in blessing
1 Peter 3:9

Speak what builds up others
Ephesians 4:29

Stubborness leading to destruction
Proverbs 29:1

Through Christ
Romans 5:1
Romans 5:10
2 Corinthians 5:17-20
Colossians 1:19-22

To those who hate you
Matthew 5:44
Luke 6:27-28

Redeem

Definition:
To clear from obligation or debt, to buy back or free.

Key Verses:
Psalm 107:2
Ephesians 1:7

See Also:
Debt
Salvation

Regret

Definition:
A feeling of sorrow, disappointment, or distress following loss.

Key Verses:
Isaiah 53:3
2 Corinthians 7:10

See Also:
Grief
Guilt
Sorrow

Of God
Genesis 6:6

Over betraying Christ
Matthew 27:3

Over consequences of sin
Numbers 12:11
Proverbs 5:11-14

Over foolish decision
Judges 11:30-40
Daniel 6:13-18

Over rejecting Christ
Revelation 1:7

Over sinful past
Psalm 103:12
Ezekiel 16:63

Reincarnation

Definition:
The notion of rebirth into other forms or human bodies following death.

Key Verses:
Psalm 6:5
Hebrews 9:27

See Also:
New Age Spirituality
Resurrection

Rejection

Definition:
The condition of being or feeling refused, discarded, or cast off.

Key Verses:
Deuteronomy 31:8
Luke 6:22-23

See Also:
Acceptance
Alienation
Hostility

Acceptance by God
Psalm 27:10
Psalm 66:20
Psalm 94:14
Isaiah 42:16
Isaiah 54:10
Luke 12:6-7

The Biblical Counseling Reference Guide

Romans 5:1
Revelation 3:20

Because of sin
Isaiah 59:2

Be content
Hebrews 13:5-6

Benefits of
Psalm 119:71

By friends and family
Judges 11:1-10
Job 19:19
Psalm 31:11-13
Isaiah 53:3
John 1:11

By God
Isaiah 65:12
Amos 5:22
Amos 8:10
Matthew 27:46

Develops character
Romans 5:3-5

Enablement through Christ
Philippians 4:13

Encourage one another
Hebrews 3:13

Example of Christ
1 Peter 2:20-23

For doing God's will
Jeremiah 26:1-16

Forgive one another
Ephesians 4:31-32
Colossians 3:13

God's compassion never ends
Lamentations 3:19-23

God's control
Psalm 139:1-18

God's provision
Isaiah 58:11

God's standards
Genesis 3:1-6

In families
Genesis 37:2-29

In ministry
Jeremiah 36:1-26
1 Thessalonians 2:1-2

No condemnation in Christ
Romans 8:1

Nothing can separate from God
Romans 8:28-39

Of Christ
Matthew 9:10-12
Matthew 10:32-36
Matthew 21:33-44
Mark 8:31
Luke 10:16
Luke 13:31-34
John 7:25-31
John 12:27
John 12:37-40
John 12:48-49
Acts 18:5-6
Romans 9:33
1 Peter 2:8

1 Peter 4:17

Of Christians
Luke 6:22
Luke 6:35
John 15:19-25
John 16:33

Of God
Jeremiah 2:27
Matthew 23:37
Romans 10:21

Of immoral Christians
1 Corinthians 5:9-13

Of sin
2 Corinthians 6:17

Of the truth
2 Timothy 4:3-4

Of wisdom
Proverbs 1:24-27
Jeremiah 32:33
Jeremiah 44:15-19

Overcome with love
Matthew 5:44

Perseverance
2 Corinthians 4:8-9

Possible blessing
Matthew 5:10

Prayer in
Psalm 22:1

Rejoice in suffering
1 Peter 4:12-14

Submission to Christ
2 Corinthians 10:5

Relationship

Definition:
The condition of being closely associated. Used especially of that which exists between people associated through blood, marriage, or friendship.

Key Verses:
Romans 12:10
1 Peter 1:22

See Also:
Friendship
Intimacy
Reconciliation

Avoid evil companions
Psalm 1:1
Proverbs 13:20
Proverbs 24:1
2 Thessalonians 3:14

Benefit of
Ecclesiastes 4:9-10

Desire for
1 John 1:3

Effects of money on
Proverbs 19:7

Fellowship offered
Galatians 2:9

Forsaken by friends
Psalm 55:13-14
2 Timothy 4:9-10

Holiness in
2 Corinthians 1:12

Loyalty to family
Genesis 14:14
Leviticus 25:25
1 Timothy 5:8

With the godly
Psalm 119:63

Religious

Definition:
Acts of devotion or firmly held beliefs according to a tradition of faith.

Key Verses:
Matthew 23:29
James 1:27

See Also:
Belief
Faith

Remarriage

Definition:
The act of marrying again.

Key Verses:
1 Corinthians 7:39
1 Timothy 5:14

See Also:
Blended Family
Divorce
Marriage

After death of spouse
Genesis 25:1
Romans 7:1-3

A response to human desire
1 Timothy 5:11

Condemned
Deuteronomy 24:1-4

Good not to remarry
1 Corinthians 7:8-9

Provides security
Ruth 3:1

To perpetuate family name
Ruth 4:10

Remember

Definition:
To keep or bring back to memory; to recall.

Key Verses:
Ecclesiastes 12:1
2 Timothy 2:8

See Also:
Blessing
Providence
Thankfulness

An aid to obedience
Deuteronomy 7:17-19
Deuteronomy 9:7

Failure to
Genesis 40:23

God remembers His people
Genesis 8:1

Exodus 6:5
Leviticus 26:42

God's deliverance
Exodus 13:3
Deuteronomy 5:15

Mnemonic device
Numbers 15:38-40
Deuteronomy 16:3

Of God
Exodus 32:13

Previous blessings
Numbers 11:5
Psalm 77:11-12

The afflicted
Genesis 40:14

Repentance

Definition:
A contemplated change in mind, heart, and action based on conviction of sin.

Key Verses:
Luke 5:32
Acts 2:38

See Also:
Confess
Contrite
Forgiveness
Reconciliation

Based on God's kindness
Romans 2:4

Commanded
Zechariah 1:4

Matthew 3:2
Matthew 4:17
Acts 17:30
James 4:9

Confession of sin
Psalm 32:5

Effects of
Leviticus 26:40-42
Deuteronomy 30:1-10
2 Chronicles 7:14
Nehemiah 1:9
Proverbs 28:13
Jeremiah 4:1-2
Malachi 3:7

For the forgiveness of sins
Jeremiah 31:19
Ezekiel 20:43
Hosea 12:6
Hosea 14:1-2
Joel 2:12-17
Luke 3:3

From extortion
Luke 19:8

From grief
2 Corinthians 7:9-10

From idolatry
1 Samuel 7:3
1 Thessalonians 1:9

From paganism
Acts 19:18-19

Fruit consistent with
Matthew 3:8

God judges after lack of repentance
Amos 4:6-11

God's desire for
2 Peter 3:9

Importance of
Luke 13:3

In order to live
Ezekiel 18:32
Ezekiel 33:10-11

In reaction to God's Word
2 Kings 22:11
Jonah 3:3-6

Joy in heaven over
Luke 15:10

Limitation of
1 Samuel 15:13-35

Of God
Exodus 32:14
Jonah 3:10

Of Pharaoh
Exodus 9:27

Prayer and weeping
Ezra 10:1

Refusal of
Isaiah 22:12-13
Jeremiah 6:16
Revelation 9:20-21

Reward for
Jeremiah 25:5

Time for
Revelation 2:21

With mourning
Joel 2:12

Repercussion

Definition:
The result, whether intentional or accidental, of a prior action.

Key Verses:
Proverbs 22:3
Hebrews 12:10-11

See Also:
Consequences
Parenting

Repression

Definition:
To stifle or suppress, often in the context of a negative memory or impulsive desire.

Key Verses:
Isaiah 54:4
John 16:21

See Also:
Abuse
Counseling
Identity

Reproof

Definition:
Speech expressing blame, disapproval, or fault.

Key Verses:
Proverbs 6:23
Jeremiah 10:24

See Also:
Consequences
Judgment
Rebuke

By God
Job 42:7

By leadership
2 Timothy 4:1-2
Titus 2:15

Commanded
Leviticus 19:17

Expose wickedness
Ephesians 5:11

False accusation
1 Samuel 17:26-30

For pride
Daniel 5:22-23

For rejecting God
Proverbs 1:29-31

Importance of heeding
Proverbs 12:1
Proverbs 13:18
Proverbs 17:10
Proverbs 25:12
Proverbs 27:5-6
Proverbs 28:23

Importance to wisdom
Proverbs 15:31
Ecclesiastes 7:5

In love
Ephesians 4:15

Leading to good sense
Proverbs 15:32

Of evil spirits
Mark 1:23-26

Of sinning believers
Matthew 18:15
Luke 17:3

Reputation

Definition:
Public esteem, value, or approval.

Key Verses:
Proverbs 22:1
Ecclesiastes 7:1

See Also:
Character
Influence
Respect

Among friends and relatives
Luke 4:22-24

Benefits of a good reputation
Genesis 6:9
Proverbs 22:1
Proverbs 27:11
Daniel 6:4-5
Acts 17:11
Acts 22:12
2 Corinthians 8:18-24

The Biblical Counseling Reference Guide

1 Thessalonians
4:11-12
2 Thessalonians 1:4
3 John 3-6
3 John 12

**Consequences of
a bad reputation**
2 Samuel 20:1
Acts 9:26

**Do not praise
yourself**
Proverbs 27:2

Do not seek glory
Proverbs 25:27

For godliness
Daniel 6:1-3
Daniel 10:11

For loyalty
1 Samuel 29:6-9

For wisdom
Daniel 5:10-12

Live honorably
1 Peter 2:12

Of Abraham
Genesis 21:22

Of Jesus
Luke 2:52
1 Peter 2:21-23

**Restoring a bad
reputation**
Galatians 1:23-24

With unbelievers
1 Samuel 29:3

Resentment

Definition:
Feeling of indignation,
ill will, annoyance, or
bitterness.

Key Verses:
Hebrews 12:15
James 3:14

See Also:
Anger
Forgiveness

By a spouse
2 Samuel 6:14-16

Of God
Isaiah 45:9

Of leaders
1 Samuel 30:3-6

Of others
Job 5:2

Of siblings
Genesis 37:3-11
Luke 15:28-30

**Of those who
show mercy**
Luke 13:14-17
Luke 15:1-7

Respect

Definition:
To hold in esteem,
honor, or high opin-
ion.

Key Verses:
Romans 13:7
1 Peter 2:17

See Also:
Disrespect
Honor
Importance

Disrespect of elders
Job 19:18

Do not seek
Luke 14:10

For a godly woman
Proverbs 31:31

For elders
Leviticus 19:32
Job 32:4-6
1 Peter 5:5

For God's law
Nehemiah 8:5
2 Timothy 2:15

For husbands
Ephesians 5:33

For leaders
1 Samuel 24:1-7
Romans 13:1
1 Thessalonians
5:12-13
1 Timothy 5:17

For ministers
Philippians 2:29

For others
1 Timothy 5:1-2
1 Peter 2:17

For parents
Exodus 20:12
Exodus 21:15
Leviticus 19:3
Proverbs 1:8
Proverbs 6:20
Proverbs 23:22
Ephesians 6:1-2
Colossians 3:20

For rulers
Deuteronomy 17:12
Acts 23:5

Responsibility

Definition:
The state or quality of being liable or answerable.

Key Verses:
Luke 12:48
Jude 3

See Also:
Accountability
Blame
Work

Before others
1 Corinthians 8:9-13

Delegated
Acts 6:1-4

Faithfulness required
1 Corinthians 4:1-2

For belief
John 3:18-19

For one's actions
Exodus 15:26

Deuteronomy 24:16
Jeremiah 31:30
Ezekiel 18:20
Galatians 6:5
James 1:13-15
James 4:17

For teaching truth
James 3:1

For words
Matthew 12:36

Importance of
Matthew 25:14-30

In ministry
Romans 1:14-17

Shirking
Genesis 3:12-13
Genesis 16:5
Jonah 1:1-3
Matthew 27:24

To God
Romans 14:12

To help others
Galatians 6:1-2

Toward family
1 Timothy 5:3-8

To warn others
Ezekiel 3:17-19

To weaker brothers
Romans 15:1

Toward sinning believers
1 Corinthians 5:1-8

Rest

Definition:
The state of freedom from anxiety, disturbance, or activity.

Key Verses:
Genesis 2:2
Matthew 11:29

See Also:
Calm
Peace
Weariness

After a journey
John 4:6

For Christian workers
Mark 6:30-32

For God's people
Hebrews 4:9

Lack of
Lamentations 5:5
Hebrews 3:16-19

Of God
Genesis 2:1-3

Offered
Matthew 11:28-30

On the Sabbath
Exodus 23:12
Exodus 34:21

Restitution

Definition:
The act or process of

compensating, restoring, or repairing.

Key Verses:
Exodus 22:14
1 Timothy 5:4

See Also:
Consequences
Forgiveness
Guilt
Honesty

Laws of
Exodus 21:33-36
Exodus 22:1-15
Leviticus 6:1-6
Leviticus 24:18

Making
Numbers 5:5-7
Nehemiah 5:9-12
Proverbs 6:31
Luke 19:8

Restoration

Definition:
The act or process of returning or bringing back to original condition or state.

Key Verses:
Psalm 51:12
Galatians 6:1

See Also:
Forgiveness

Because of repentance
Amos 9:11-15

By God
Job 42:10
Jeremiah 33:23-26
Micah 7:19-20

By Jesus
Revelation 21:1

Of joy
Psalm 51:12

Of sinners
James 5:19-20

Refused
1 Samuel 15:24-26

Resurrection

Definition:
The act of coming back to life from the dead.

Key Verses:
John 11:25
Romans 6:5

See Also:
Death
Heaven
Hell
Jesus Christ
Salvation

At the Lord's return
1 Thessalonians 4:13-17

By the Holy Spirit
Romans 8:11

Denial of
Matthew 28:11-15

Description of
Revelation 20:4-6

For those who believe
John 5:25

God will raise believers
Acts 26:8
Romans 6:5
1 Corinthians 6:14

Hope of
Job 19:25-26
Daniel 12:13
Luke 24:13-35
Acts 1:3
1 Corinthians 15:4-5
2 Corinthians 5:1-2
Philippians 3:20-21
Revelation 1:17-18

In Christ
1 Thessalonians 4:16

Incorruption in
1 Corinthians 15:42

Necessity of
1 Corinthians 15:12-21

Of Abraham, Isaac, and Jacob
Mark 12:26-27

Of Christ
Matthew 28:1-10
Mark 14:28
Luke 24:12
John 2:19-21
Romans 1:4
Romans 6:9-10
Ephesians 1:18-20

Colossians 1:18
1 Peter 1:21

Of God's prophets
Revelation 11:3-12

Of the dead
1 Corinthians
15:50-52

**Power of God
shown in**
2 Corinthians 13:4
Ephesians 1:19-20

**To life and to
judgment**
John 5:29

Revenge

Definition:
Retaliation as
satisfaction for
wrongdoing or
attempt to get even.

Key Verses:
Luke 6:28
Romans 12:19

See Also:
Anger
Conflict Resolution
Forgiveness
Resentment

By the Lord
Deuteronomy 32:43
Psalm 94:1
Proverbs 20:22
Jeremiah 51:49
Lamentations
3:55-66

2 Thessalonians 1:6
2 Timothy 4:14
Revelation 6:9-11
Revelation 16:5-7
Revelation 18:6

Christ did not seek
1 Peter 2:23

Condemned
Leviticus 19:18
Proverbs 24:29
Matthew 5:38-42
Luke 9:54-55
Romans 12:17-21
1 Thessalonians 5:15
1 Peter 3:9

For relative's death
2 Samuel 3:27

**For sexual abuse
and murder**
Judges 20:1-48

For wickedness
2 Samuel 13:28

**For wrongs
committed**
Judges 15:3-5
Judges 15:10-11

**God judges those
who take revenge**
Ezekiel 25:12-13

**Love does not
take revenge**
1 Corinthians 13:4-5

Love for enemies
Luke 6:27-38

**Right attitude
toward enemies**
Acts 7:60

Reward

Definition:
Recompense given in
return for service or
good deed done.

Key Verses:
1 Corinthians 3:8
Hebrews 11:6

See Also:
Accomplishment
Success
Work

For confidence
Hebrews 10:35

For discipline
1 Corinthians
9:24-27

For doing good
Isaiah 3:10-11
2 Corinthians 5:10

For faithfulness
Ruth 2:7-12
1 Samuel 2:18-21
1 Corinthians
3:12-14

For following Christ
Matthew 16:24-27
Mark 10:28-31
Romans 2:7
Romans 2:10

For hard work
2 Timothy 2:6

For honesty
Deuteronomy 25:15

For honoring parents
Exodus 20:12
Ephesians 6:1-3

For obedience
Genesis 14:22–15:1
Genesis 22:15-18
Leviticus 25:18-19
Deuteronomy 4:40
Deuteronomy 6:3
Deuteronomy
11:13-29

For perseverance
Matthew 5:10-12
2 Timothy 2:11-13
2 Timothy 4:6-8
Hebrews 6:10
James 1:12
Revelation 3:21

For serving God
Isaiah 65:13-14
1 Corinthians 3:5-9

From Christ
Revelation 22:12

From God
Isaiah 49:4
Ephesians 6:8
Colossians 3:23-24
Hebrews 11:6

Refused
Daniel 5:17

Warning against losing
2 John 8

Ridicule

Definition:
To mock, laugh at, or make fun of.

Key Verses:
Proverbs 22:10
Matthew 5:11

See Also:
Backbiting
Bullying
Insult
Mocking
Slander

Against the righteous
Nehemiah 4:1-2
Job 12:4
Job 30:1
Psalm 69:10-11
Jeremiah 17:15

At God's work
Acts 2:1-13

By God
Psalm 2:4

Judgment for
Proverbs 30:17

On those judged by God
Jeremiah 48:39
Lamentations 2:15
Micah 2:4

Out of ignorance
Matthew 9:23-24
Luke 8:49-53

Righteousness

Definition:
The character of being morally right, straight, fair, or pure.

Key Verses:
2 Corinthians 5:21
Philippians 3:8-9

See Also:
Forgiveness
Intimacy
Salvation

As Christ
1 John 3:7

Benefits of
Psalm 1:1-3

Blessing for
Psalm 18:20-21

Breastplate of
Ephesians 6:14

Demonstration of
Ezekiel 18:5-9

Example of
Genesis 6:9
Job 1:1
Galatians 3:6

From faith
Romans 1:16-17
Romans 10:9-10

**From obeying
the Scriptures**
Psalm 119:1-16

**Not gained by
human works**
Romans 3:21-22
Galatians 2:16

Of God
Daniel 9:14
Matthew 6:33

Of religious leaders
Matthew 5:20

Persecution for
Matthew 5:10

Prayer for forgiveness
Psalm 51:10

Pursuit of
1 Timothy 6:11

**Relationship
to prayer**
James 5:16
1 Peter 3:12

**The Lord evaluates
motives**
Proverbs 21:2

Through Christ
2 Corinthians 5:21
Philippians 1:9-11

Through faith
Genesis 15:6
Philippians 3:9
James 2:23

Will shine
Matthew 13:43

Robbery

Definition:
The act of taking
property by means of
fraud, force, or threat.

Key Verses:
Leviticus 19:13
Isaiah 61:8

See Also:
Assault
Cheating
Stealing
Violence

Condemned
Exodus 20:15
Leviticus 19:11
Leviticus 19:13
Deuteronomy 5:19
Luke 3:12-14
Ephesians 4:28

God protects from
Ezra 8:31

Hated by God
Isaiah 61:8

Of the needy
Ezekiel 22:29
Amos 8:4

Penalty for
Exodus 22:2-3

Sadism

Definition:
Finding pleasure or
gratification through

painful, demeaning
actions.

Key Verses:
Ephesians 5:3
Colossians 3:5

See Also:
Sexual Addiction
Sexual Integrity

Sadness

Definition:
Mental distress,
anguish, or sorrow
caused by loss, misfor-
tune, or injury.

Key Verses:
Psalm 42:11
Ecclesiastes 7:3

See Also:
Depression
Grief

Safety

Definition:
The state of being free
from the risk of harm,
injury, or loss.

Key Verses:
Proverbs 18:10
1 John 5:18

See Also:
Danger
Providence
Security

Flee for
Jeremiah 48:28

For God's people
Isaiah 32:18

For the righteous
Psalm 91:9-10
Proverbs 1:33
Proverbs 3:23
Proverbs 12:21

From wild animals
Isaiah 35:8-10

None for the wicked
Jeremiah 6:22-25

Precautions for
Deuteronomy 22:8

Protected by God
Deuteronomy 33:29
Psalm 23:4
Psalm 121:3
Isaiah 43:2
Daniel 6:20-23
Acts 27:22-25
1 Peter 1:5

**Protection for
the helpless**
Ruth 2:8-9

Salvation

Definition:
Preservation from
destruction, failure, or
evil. Used especially of
protection from God's
judgment on sin by
means of faith in Jesus
Christ.

Key Verses:
John 3:16-17
Romans 5:9

See Also:
Dependency
Faith
Heaven
Hell
Jesus Christ

A gift
Romans 6:23

Assurance of
1 John 5:13

Available to everyone
Isaiah 55:1
Acts 10:43
Revelation 22:17

**Based on belief
in Jesus**
John 1:12
John 3:16-18
Acts 16:31
Romans 4:5
Romans 10:9-13
2 Timothy 3:15
1 John 5:11-13

**Based on
Christ's work**
Romans 5:9
2 Corinthians 5:21
1 Peter 1:18-19

**By grace
through faith**
Romans 3:23-24
Romans 11:6
Ephesians 2:4-5

Ephesians 2:8-9
Titus 2:11

Day of
2 Corinthians 6:2

For sinners
Matthew 9:12-13
Mark 2:17
1 Timothy 1:15

From evil deeds
1 Corinthians 6:9-11

From the Law's curse
Galatians 3:13

From the Lord
Exodus 15:2
Psalm 27:1
Isaiah 12:2
Isaiah 43:25
Jeremiah 17:14
Joel 2:32
Jonah 2:9

**Give up serving self
to follow Jesus**
Matthew 16:24-26

God's desire for
Ezekiel 33:11
2 Peter 3:9

Helmet of
Isaiah 59:17
Ephesians 6:17

Indwelling Spirit
Romans 8:9-11
Romans 8:15-16
1 John 3:24

**Jesus always
able to save**
Hebrews 7:25

**Miraculous works
do not save**
Matthew 7:21-23

No condemnation
Romans 8:1-2

Only through Christ
John 14:6
Acts 4:12
2 Corinthians
5:18-19
Galatians 2:16
Colossians 1:13-14
1 Thessalonians 5:9
1 Timothy 1:15
1 Timothy 2:5-6
Hebrews 5:7-10
Hebrews 7:25
Hebrews 9:8-15
1 John 2:2-6
1 John 4:9-10

Peace with God
Romans 5:1
Romans 5:5-11

Power of the gospel
Romans 1:16-17

Provides forgiveness
Isaiah 1:18

**Provides
indwelling Spirit**
Ezekiel 36:26-27

**Relation to new
creation**
2 Corinthians 5:17

Requires new birth
John 3:1-8

Results
Galatians 5:22-23
James 2:17
1 John 2:29
1 John 3:6
1 John 5:18

**Results in
persecution**
John 15:18-20

Results in works
Ephesians 2:10
Philippians 2:12-13

Security in God's love
Proverbs 29:25
Romans 8:38-39

Through Christ
John 5:24

**Through enablement
from the Father**
John 6:65

**Through faith
in Christ**
Galatians 2:16

Yearning for
Romans 8:23-24

Same-Sex Attraction

Definition:
To be physically and
sexually drawn to
members of one's own
sex.

Key Verses:
Romans 1:26-27
1 Corinthians 6:9-10

See Also:
Homosexuality

Sanctity of Life

Definition:
The principle that
human life is sacred or
holy because it comes
from God and bears
God's image.

Key Verses:
Psalm 139:13-14
Jeremiah 1:5

See Also:
Abortion
Euthanasia
Pregnancy…
Unplanned

Satan, Demons,
and Satanism

Definition:
Satan is the accuser of
Christians and enemy
of God; demons are
the fallen angels who
support him; and
satanism describes the
devotion of people to
Satan.

Key Verses:
2 Corinthians 2:10-11
1 Peter 5:8

See Also:
Demons
Occult
Spiritual Warfare

Savior

Definition:
The one who rescues or brings salvation; a title for Jesus.

Key Verses:
Isaiah 45:21
1 John 4:14

See Also:
Jesus Christ
Salvation

Security

Definition:
Safety; freedom from danger, injury, or anxiety.

Key Verses:
Psalm 7:9
Hebrews 6:19

See Also:
Eternal Security
Protection
Safety

Based on God's protection
1 Peter 1:3-4

Cannot be found in money
Proverbs 23:4-5

Complacency in
2 Kings 20:19

Dangers of seeking
Mark 4:19

False
Jeremiah 48:7
Jeremiah 49:4

From the Lord
Psalm 18:1-2
Psalm 20:7
Psalm 27:5
Psalm 32:7
Psalm 91:4
Ezekiel 34:25
Luke 12:33
2 Timothy 1:12

God's judgment destroys security
Ezekiel 39:6

In Christ
Isaiah 28:16
Hebrews 7:22
Jude 24

In spiritual warfare
Ephesians 6:13

Of the righteous
Proverbs 18:10

Seduction

Definition:
The act or process of corrupting, turning

away, or leading astray, especially into sexual immorality.

Key Verses:
1 Corinthians 6:18
James 1:13-14

See Also:
Divorce
Lust
Sexual Addiction
Temptation

By a wicked ruler
2 Kings 21:9

By flattering words
Proverbs 7:21

Refused
Genesis 39:6-10

Retaliation for failed seduction
Genesis 39:12-20

Seductive women
Isaiah 3:16-17

Warning against
Ecclesiastes 7:26

Warning against spiritual deception
Mark 13:22
Acts 20:30
1 Timothy 4:1
2 Timothy 3:6
1 John 2:26

Self-Centered

Definition:
To demonstrate concern only for individual and private interests and needs; self-absorbed.

Key Verses:
Acts 20:35
Philippians 2:3-4

See Also:
Pride
Selfishness

Self-Condemnation

Definition:
The act or process of making or declaring oneself guilty.

Key Verses:
John 5:24
Romans 8:1

See Also:
Guilt
Shame

**Acceptance
of personal
responsibility**
2 Samuel 24:17

**By abusing the
Lord's supper**
1 Corinthians 11:29

By approving of sin
Romans 14:22

By judging others
Romans 2:1

By rebellion
Romans 13:2

By sinning
1 Timothy 5:12
Titus 3:10-11

Freedom from
Romans 8:1-2
1 Corinthians 4:3

Judged by own words
Job 9:20

**Wicked trapped
in own trap**
Job 5:13

Self-Control

Definition:
Governance or restraint of one's emotions, desires, or actions.

Key Verses:
Proverbs 16:32
2 Peter 1:5-7

See Also:
Dependency
Discipline

**Character quality
of church leader**
1 Timothy 3:2
Titus 2:2

**Fruit of the
Holy Spirit**
Galatians 5:22-23

**Increase in
self-control**
2 Peter 1:5-7

Of anger
Proverbs 16:32
Proverbs 29:11
James 1:19-20

Offer yourself to God
Romans 6:12-13

Of speech
Psalm 39:1-2
Proverbs 13:3
James 1:26
James 3:2

Self-Denial

Definition:
Restraint or limitation of one's comfort, pleasure, or satisfaction.

Key Verses:
Matthew 16:24
Philippians 2:8

See Also:
Discipline
Humility
Pride

**Abstinence from
fleshly desires**
Romans 13:14
Galatians 5:24
Ephesians 4:22-24
Colossians 3:5

Titus 2:12
1 Peter 2:11

Abstinence from sexual activity
1 Samuel 21:4-5

Avoid overeating
Proverbs 23:20

Blessing for
Luke 18:29-30

Following Christ
Matthew 10:37-39
Matthew 16:24-25
Matthew 19:21
Mark 8:34-35
Mark 10:28
Luke 5:11
Luke 9:23-24
Luke 14:26-27
Luke 14:33
Philippians 3:8

For God's will
1 Peter 4:2

Personal discipline in
1 Corinthians 9:27

Seeking good for others
1 Corinthians 10:24

Self-Esteem

Definition:
Pride, satisfaction, or respect for oneself.

Key Verses:
Romans 12:3
Philippians 2:3

See Also:
Identity
Inferiority
Self-Worth

Acceptance of others
Romans 15:7

Created by God
Romans 9:20-21

Do not compare
2 Corinthians 10:12

Faithfulness of God
Psalm 27:10

God looks at the heart
1 Samuel 16:7

God's workmanship in Christ
Ephesians 2:10

Known by God
Psalm 139:15-16
Jeremiah 1:5
Luke 12:6-7

Love of God
Jeremiah 31:3
Romans 5:8
1 John 3:1

Made in God's image
Genesis 1:27

Value in God's eyes
Matthew 6:26

Self-Exaltation

Definition:
The act of elevating, lifting up, honoring, or praising oneself.

Key Verses:
Matthew 23:12
1 Corinthians 4:7

See Also:
Arrogance
Boasting
Pride

Boast in the Lord
2 Corinthians 10:17-18

Choosing the best seats
Luke 14:7-10

Exalting self over God
2 Thessalonians 2:4

Folly of
Proverbs 25:6
Proverbs 30:32

Humiliation for
Matthew 23:12
Luke 18:14

Judgment on
Ezekiel 29:15

Over a hurting friend
Job 19:5

Prayer against
Psalm 35:26
Psalm 38:16

Self-Image

Definition:
The sum of a person's ideas concerning themselves.

Key Verses:
Luke 12:6-7
Acts 17:29

See Also:
Identity
Self-Worth

Self-Injury

Definition:
To intentionally harm one's own body.

Key Verses:
1 Chronicles 4:10
Psalm 91:9-10

See Also:
Abuse
Anger
Anorexia and Bulimia
Depression
Self-Worth
Shame

Selfishness

Definition:
The state or quality of being exclusively concerned with oneself without regard to others.

Key Verses:
Psalm 119:36
Romans 2:8

See Also:
Greed
Self-Pity

Care for others
Ezekiel 34:2
1 Corinthians 10:24
Galatians 6:2
Philippians 2:3-4

Desire for position
Mark 10:35-40
Luke 14:7-10

Give to the needy
Matthew 5:42
Luke 12:33

Godless do not help the needy
Isaiah 32:6
Matthew 25:43-44

Leads to fighting
James 4:1-2

Live for Christ
2 Corinthians 5:15

Neglecting God
Haggai 1:1-4
Philippians 2:21

Problem of
Proverbs 18:1

Ungodly will be lovers of self
2 Timothy 3:2

Self-Pity

Definition:
Derogatory term used of extensive sorrow regarding one's pain or misfortune.

Key Verses:
1 Kings 19:3-4
Jonah 4:8-11

See Also:
Selfishness

Desire for death
1 Kings 19:4

Result of comparison to others
Psalm 37:1-2
Psalm 73:12-14

Result of despair
Jeremiah 20:7-8
Jeremiah 20:14-15

Result of insecurity
1 Samuel 22:6-8

Result of pride
Numbers 16:12-14

Result of suffering
Job 6:2-3
Job 7:13-16
Job 19:13-21

Result of wrong priorities
Luke 10:38-42

Self-Righteousness

Definition:
Quality of vindicating one's own conduct according to one's own standard. Also used of a demeaning attitude accompanying the quality.

Key Verses:
Matthew 5:20
Romans 3:21

See Also:
Arrogance
Pride

Consequences of seeking
Romans 10:3

Folly of
Galatians 2:21
Philippians 3:4-7

Hypocrisy in
Matthew 23:13-15
Matthew 23:27
Luke 11:39
Luke 16:15

Pride in
Luke 18:11-14

True source of righteousness
2 Corinthians 5:21
Galatians 3:6
Philippians 3:9

Self-Worth

Definition:
Perception of one's own value or significance.

Key Verses:
Psalm 8:4-5
Matthew 6:26

See Also:
Identity
Inferiority
Self-Esteem

Be unselfish
Philippians 2:3-4

Chosen by God
Deuteronomy 7:6
John 15:16
Ephesians 1:4
Ephesians 1:11

Created by God
Psalm 139:13-14
Romans 9:20-21
Revelation 4:11

Do not compare
2 Corinthians 10:12

God is the Creator
Exodus 4:11
Isaiah 44:2
Isaiah 66:2

God's child
John 1:12
1 John 3:2

God's interest in you
Psalm 33:13
Psalm 34:18

Psalm 139:1-24
Jeremiah 1:5
Jeremiah 29:11
Matthew 6:26
Luke 12:6-7

God's work
Ezekiel 36:26
Ephesians 2:10
Philippians 1:6
Philippians 2:13

In relation to others
Philippians 2:3-4

Love of God
Jeremiah 31:3
Romans 5:8
1 John 3:1

Made in God's image
Genesis 1:27

The incarnation
Galatians 4:4

Separation

Definition:
To move away or divide from another.

Key Verses:
Proverbs 22:24-25
1 Corinthians 15:33

See Also:
Conflict Resolution
Divorce

Sex

Definition:
Sexual intercourse.

Key Verses:
Proverbs 5:18
Hebrews 13:4

See Also:
Marriage
Sexual Addiction
Sexual Integrity
Temptation

Abuse of
Genesis 19:5
Judges 19:22

Adultery condemned
Exodus 20:14
Leviticus 18:20

Bestiality condemned
Exodus 22:19

Enjoyment of
Proverbs 5:18

Incest condemned
Leviticus 18:6

Only within marriage
Proverbs 5:15-20
Hebrews 13:4

Responsibility within marriage
1 Corinthians 7:1-5

Sexual immorality condemned
Romans 13:13
1 Corinthians 6:16-18

Sex Trafficking

Definition:
The business of buying and selling people for the purpose of sex.

Key Verses:
Leviticus 19:29
1 Corinthians 6:16

See Also:
Immorality
Sexual Addiction
Sexual Integrity

Sexual Addiction

Definition:
Compulsive dependence upon sex.

Key Verses:
Galatians 5:16
1 Thessalonians 5:8

See Also:
Alcohol and Drug Abuse
Codependency
Lust
Temptation

Abstinence from sexual immorality
Exodus 20:14
1 Thessalonians 4:1-8

Bestiality forbidden
Deuteronomy 27:21

Blamelessness at Christ's coming
1 Thessalonians 5:23-24

Brings punishment
Jeremiah 6:15
Ezekiel 16:58

Enslaved to corruption
2 Peter 2:19

Homosexuality condemned
Leviticus 18:22

Lust condemned
Job 31:1
Matthew 5:27-28
James 1:14-15

Overcoming through the Lord
1 Corinthians 3:16-17
1 Corinthians 6:16-20
Colossians 3:1-5
James 1:21

Punishment for
Hebrews 13:4

Sexual immorality condemned
1 Corinthians 6:12-13
Galatians 5:19-21
Ephesians 5:3-4

Victory over
Ephesians 4:22-24

The Biblical Counseling Reference Guide

Wicked given over to impure life
Ephesians 2:1-3
Ephesians 4:19

Will reap what you sow
Galatians 6:7-8

Sexual Integrity

Definition:
To live by the highest standards of sexual morality.

Key Verses:
Proverbs 10:9
Ephesians 5:3

See Also:
Lust
Purity
Sex
Sexual Addiction
Temptation

Abstain from immorality
Genesis 39:11-12
Proverbs 6:25
Romans 13:13
1 Thessalonians 4:3

Adultery condemned
Exodus 20:14

Avoid lust
Exodus 20:17
Proverbs 11:6
Matthew 5:28

Avoid temptation
2 Peter 2:18

Be pure
Matthew 5:8
1 Timothy 5:22
Titus 2:11-12
Hebrews 10:22
James 4:8
1 Peter 1:22

Be self-controlled
Proverbs 25:28

Case study of Samson
Judges 14:1
Judges 14:3
Judges 16:1
Judges 16:4-5
Judges 16:15
Judges 16:20-21

Commitment to integrity
Job 27:5

Control the eyes
Job 31:1

Degradation of impurity
Romans 1:24

Effects of failure
2 Samuel 11:2-27
2 Samuel 13:1-29
Proverbs 5:3-4
Proverbs 6:27-29
Proverbs 6:32
Proverbs 10:9
Proverbs 14:12
Galatians 6:7-8

Example of Balaam
2 Peter 2:13-15

Example of Joseph
Genesis 39:1-12

Foolishness and immorality
Romans 1:22-25

God owns your body
1 Corinthians 6:13

Guard your heart
Proverbs 4:23

Immorality comes from the heart
Mark 7:21

Joseph's integrity
Genesis 39:6
Genesis 39:9

Judgment for immorality
1 Corinthians 10:8
Hebrews 13:4

Maintain a clear conscience
Acts 24:16

Marriage
Isaiah 62:5
Mark 10:7

Overcoming in Christ
Colossians 3:5-10

Overcoming sin through the Scriptures
Psalm 119:11

Pursue righteousness
2 Timothy 2:22

Relationship of immorality to alcohol
Genesis 19:30-38

Resist temptation
Proverbs 5:3-10
Proverbs 7:10-21
Ecclesiastes 7:26

Seared conscience
Proverbs 30:20

Sexual immorality condemned
1 Corinthians 5:11
1 Corinthians 6:9-10
1 Corinthians 6:15-20
Galatians 5:19
Ephesians 5:3
1 Thessalonians 4:7

Sin brings pain
Proverbs 6:27-35

Temptation
James 1:13-14

Transformation of character
2 Corinthians 7:1

Unity in marriage
Genesis 1:28
Genesis 2:24-25

Shame

Definition:
A painful emotion of disgrace caused by a strong sense of guilt.

Key Verses:
Psalm 34:4-5
Romans 10:11

See Also:
Guilt
Inferiority
Self-Worth

At nakedness
Genesis 3:7
Genesis 3:10

Because of guilt
Ezra 9:5-9
Ezekiel 16:63

Because of idolatry
Isaiah 45:16

Because of persecution
Psalm 69:7

Because of sin
Micah 3:7

Dead body displayed in shame
1 Samuel 31:8-10

Effects of
Psalm 44:15

In pride
Proverbs 11:2

Lack of
Genesis 2:25
Jeremiah 6:15

Not ashamed of being a Christian
1 Peter 4:16

Revealed by Christ
Revelation 16:15

Sibling Rivalry

Definition:
Competitive spirit between children in a family.

Key Verses:
Genesis 27:40-41
Psalm 50:20

See Also:
Children
Child Training
Parenting
Teenagers

Significance

Definition:
Important; to be worthwhile and valuable.

Key Verses:
Isaiah 43:1
1 Peter 2:9

See Also:
Love
Security
Self-Worth

Sin

Definition:
That which falls short of or is in opposition to God or His will.

The Biblical Counseling Reference Guide

Condemned
Romans 6:11-14
Galatians 5:19-21

Confession of
Psalm 32:5
Matthew 3:6
James 5:16
1 John 1:9

Consequences of
1 Samuel 15:23
Job 4:8
Proverbs 12:21
Ezekiel 18:4

Correction of
Matthew 18:15

Death in
Ephesians 2:1

Disobedience
Genesis 3:1-19

Effects of
Psalm 31:10
Proverbs 5:22
Isaiah 59:2
Romans 6:23
1 Corinthians 11:30
James 1:15
1 John 5:16

Everyone is sinful
Romans 3:10-11
Romans 3:23
1 John 1:8
1 John 1:10

Exposing
John 3:20

Forgiveness from
Psalm 19:12
Psalm 32:1
Matthew 26:28
2 Corinthians 5:21
Ephesians 1:7
1 Timothy 1:12-14
Hebrews 10:17
1 John 1:7

Freedom from
Romans 6:7

God's knowledge of
Job 34:21-22
Psalm 44:20-21
Hosea 7:2

**Grieving the
Holy Spirit**
Ephesians 4:30

Idolatry
Leviticus 26:1
1 Kings 16:31
Colossians 3:5

Judgment on
Lamentations 1:14
Amos 1:13-15
Romans 1:18-32
Revelation 21:8

Lawbreaking
James 2:10

1 John 3:4

Life of
Ephesians 2:1-3

**Lying to the
Holy Spirit**
Acts 5:3

Of omission
James 4:17

Overcoming
Psalm 119:11
Romans 7:18-25

**Overpowers
the evil man**
Proverbs 29:6

**Publicly rebuke
sinning leaders**
1 Timothy 5:20

**Relationship
to the devil**
1 John 3:8

**Resisting the
Holy Spirit**
Acts 7:51

Restoration from
Galatians 6:1

Slavery to
John 8:34

Unrighteousness
1 John 5:17

**Wickedness of
the heart**
Jeremiah 17:9

Singleness

Definition:
The state or quality of being unmarried.

Key Verses:
1 Corinthians 7:7
2 Peter 1:3

See Also:
Purpose in Life

An opportune time for marriage
1 Corinthians 7:36

Benefits of
1 Corinthians 7:32-35

Creation of Eve
Genesis 2:18

Creation of man and his dominion
Genesis 1:27-29

Creation of marriage
Genesis 2:24

Do not be yoked together with an unbeliever
2 Corinthians 6:14-15

Example of
Ruth 1:20-21
Ruth 4:16-17
Acts 21:8-9

Freedom in
1 Corinthians 7:32

It is good for a man not to marry
1 Corinthians 7:1
1 Corinthians 7:8-9

Marriage means divided interests
1 Corinthians 7:33-34

One flesh in marriage
Mark 10:6-9

Remain as you are
1 Corinthians 7:26-29

Separation as a cause
1 Corinthians 7:10-11

Serving the Lord in
1 Corinthians 7:34-35

Some have renounced marriage
Matthew 19:11-12

Two are better than one
Ecclesiastes 4:9-10

Widows staying single
1 Corinthians 7:8
1 Corinthians 7:39-40

Single Parenting

Definition:
Management of a family without a marriage partner.

Key Verses:
Esther 2:7
Psalm 10:14

See Also:
Parenting

Children of God
1 John 3:1

Discipline in
Proverbs 19:18
Proverbs 22:6

Help in
Psalm 10:14
Psalm 68:5

Honor father and mother
Exodus 20:12

Provide for family
1 Timothy 5:8

Seek wisdom
Proverbs 24:3

Slander

Definition:
To spread a false report in order to injure a person's reputation.

Key Verses:
Leviticus 19:16
James 4:11

See Also:
Gossip

Against the righteous
Luke 7:33-34
Acts 14:2

By the ungodly
Romans 1:29-32

Condemned
Exodus 23:1
Psalm 101:5
Ephesians 4:31
1 Timothy 3:11
Titus 3:1-2
1 Peter 3:10

Deliverance from
Job 5:21

Effects of
Psalm 140:3
Proverbs 11:9

Folly of
Proverbs 10:18

Prayer amidst
Psalm 109:1-3

Responsibility for
Matthew 12:36

Sobriety

Definition:
Seriousness; the state of abstaining from alcohol.

Key Verses:
Proverbs 23:29-30
Proverbs 31:4

See Also:
Alcohol and Drug
  Abuse
Temptation

Commanded
1 Thessalonians
  5:5-7

Not addicted to wine
1 Timothy 3:2-3
Titus 1:7
Titus 2:2-3

Practicing abstinence
Proverbs 31:4-5
Jeremiah 35:1-6

Sensible living
Titus 2:12

Sorcery

Definition:
Rites, charms, or spells intended to exert supernatural influence over natural objects or processes.

Key Verses:
Deuteronomy 18:14
Acts 19:19

See Also:
Magic
Occult
Satan, Demons, and
  Satanism

Sorrow

Definition:
Mental distress, anguish, or sadness caused by loss, misfortune, or injury.

Key Verses:
Psalm 90:10
Isaiah 60:20

See Also:
Bereavement
Death
Grief
Sympathy

Because of abandoning the Lord
Jeremiah 3:21

Because of a rebuke
2 Corinthians 2:1-4

Because of giving judgment
Psalm 80:5
Jeremiah 48:33
Lamentations 1:1-2
Lamentations 2:11
Amos 8:1-3
Revelation 16:10-11

Because of illness
Philippians 2:27-28

Because of sin
Nehemiah 8:9-12
Malachi 2:13
James 4:8-9

Benefits of
2 Corinthians 7:11

Blessings in
Matthew 5:4
Luke 6:21

By Christ's enemies
Revelation 1:7

Death of a loved one
Genesis 50:10
2 Samuel 12:16-23
2 Samuel 18:33
Acts 8:2

Effects of
Psalm 6:6
Psalm 31:9-10

God's comfort during
Exodus 3:7-9
Psalm 34:18
2 Corinthians 1:3-4

Hope in
1 Thessalonians
4:13-18

Joy in
Psalm 30:5
2 Corinthians 6:10

Leading to repentance
2 Corinthians 7:9

Mourning with those who mourn
Proverbs 25:20
Romans 12:15

Over missing family
1 Samuel 30:3-4

Over religious leader
1 Samuel 25:1

Prayer in
Psalm 13:2
Matthew 26:36-46

Will cease
Isaiah 25:8
Isaiah 35:10
Isaiah 65:19
John 16:20
Revelation 7:17
Revelation 21:4

Soul

Definition:
The immaterial portion of a human being including the intellect, will, and emotions.

Key Verses:
Deuteronomy 6:5
Ecclesiastes 12:7

See Also:
Eternal Life
Identity

Soul Sleep

Definition:
The errant teaching that human souls exist in an unconscious, inactive state following death until the general resurrection.

Key Verses:
2 Samuel 12:23
2 Corinthians 5:8

See Also:
Death

Eternal Life
Resurrection

Sovereignty of God

Definition:
The teaching that God is the all-powerful ruler over all things.

Key Verses:
Isaiah 64:8
1 Timothy 1:17

See Also:
Decision Making
God
Providence

Spiritism

Definition:
Beliefs and practices associated with communicating with the dead.

Key Verses:
Deuteronomy 18:9-10
Isaiah 8:19

See Also:
Occult
Satan, Demons, and Satanism

Spiritual Abuse

Definition:
Mistreatment by an authority concerning spiritual matters.

The Biblical Counseling Reference Guide

Spiritual Blindness

Definition:
Unable to discern spiritual reality or truth due to separation from God.

Spiritual Gifts

Definition:
Grace flowing from the indwelling Holy Spirit to the believer to provide empowerment to serve and minister to others.

Key Verses:
Romans 12:6-8
1 Corinthians 12:4-6

See Also:
Discipleship
Holy Spirit
Ministry

Spiritual Warfare

Definition:
The ongoing conflict between a believer and the world, the flesh, and Satan.

Key Verses:
Ephesians 6:13-18
1 John 4:4

See Also:
Occult
Satan, Demons, and Satanism

Activity of Satan
Job 1:7
Job 1:12
Job 2:7
Ezekiel 28:17
2 Corinthians 4:4
Ephesians 2:2
1 Peter 5:8
1 John 3:8

Acts of the sinful nature
Galatians 5:19-21

All are born into sin
Psalm 51:5

Consulting a medium
1 Chronicles 10:13-14

Do not engage in occult practices
Deuteronomy 18:9-13

Do not love the world
James 4:4
1 John 2:15-16

Doom of Satan and his followers
Matthew 25:41
Revelation 20:7-15

Escape corruption
2 Peter 1:4

Evil originates in the heart
Matthew 15:18-19
Mark 7:21-23

Flesh and Spirit
Galatians 5:17

Freedom from sin
Romans 6:6-7

God does forgive and considers the heart
1 Kings 8:39

God does not tempt
James 1:13-14

God protects from evil
Job 1:10

Not fought as world fights
2 Corinthians 10:3-4

Nothing good in the sin nature
Romans 7:18-25

Prayer and demon possession
Mark 9:29

Renounce secret ways
2 Corinthians 4:2

Rescued from the dominion of darkness
Colossians 1:13

Role of anger
Ephesians 4:26-27

Satan sifts believers as wheat
Luke 22:31-32

Sinful nature crucified
Galatians 5:24

The body is the temple of the Holy Spirit
1 Corinthians 6:19-20

Victory in
Psalm 119:11
John 16:33
Romans 7:21-25
2 Corinthians 10:4-5
Ephesians 6:10-18
James 4:7
1 John 5:4-5

The Biblical Counseling Reference Guide

Revelation 12:11

Spouse Abuse

Definition:
Systematic or sporadic violence directed toward one's mate.

Key Verses:
Proverbs 22:24
Ephesians 5:25

See Also:
Verbal and Emotional
   Abuse
Wife Abuse

Avoid the angry
   Proverbs 22:24

Condemned
   Psalm 11:5

Control anger
   Ephesians 4:26-27

Control words
   James 3:9-10

Deliverance in God
   2 Samuel 22:3
   Psalm 4:8
   Psalm 13:1-6
   Psalm 56:3
   Psalm 140:1

**Do not commit
adultery**
   Hebrews 13:4

**Essential equality
of sexes**
   Galatians 3:28

Execute justice
   Jeremiah 22:3
   Ezekiel 8:17-18

Failure of justice
   Ecclesiastes 8:11

Fidelity
   Malachi 2:16

**Folly of
uncontrollable anger**
   Proverbs 19:19

God hears prayer
   Psalm 10:17-18

Guard against anger
   Proverbs 29:22

**Judgment on
the abuser**
   Psalm 10:15
   Psalm 11:5
   2 Thessalonians 1:6

Love for wife
   Ephesians 5:28-29
   1 Peter 3:7

Marriage relationship
   Ephesians 5:21-33
   Colossians 3:18-19
   1 Peter 3:1-2

**Punishment
of violence**
   Genesis 6:13

**Responsibilities
of minister**
   Titus 1:7

Treacherous violence
   Proverbs 13:2

Violence
   Psalm 58:2

Wicked speech
   Psalm 10:7

Stealing

Definition:
The act or process of taking without right or permission that which belongs to another.

Key Verses:
Deuteronomy 5:19
Ephesians 4:28

See Also:
Business Ethics
Ethics and Integrity
Kleptomania

Be faithful
   1 Corinthians 4:2

Comes from the heart
   Matthew 15:19
   Mark 7:21

Condemned
   Exodus 20:15
   Exodus 23:4
   Leviticus 19:11
   Deuteronomy 5:19
   Deuteronomy
      25:13-16
   Luke 3:12-14
   Romans 13:9-10
   Ephesians 4:28

Do not rob God
   Malachi 3:8

Folly of
Psalm 62:10
Jeremiah 17:11

Food gained by fraud
Proverbs 20:17

Fortune that's fleeting
Proverbs 21:6

Hated by God
Isaiah 61:8

Make restitution
Exodus 22:2-4

Repentance from
Luke 19:8

Small theft leads to great theft
Luke 16:10

Wicked borrow and do not repay
Psalm 37:21

Steward

Definition:
A trustee, guardian, or overseer who manages the property or finances of another.

Key Verses:
Luke 16:10-11
1 Corinthians 4:2

See Also:
Materialism
Prosperity
Trust

Faithfulness required
1 Corinthians 4:1-2

Importance of
Matthew 25:14-30

In evangelism
1 Peter 3:15
Jude 3

In ministry
Luke 12:47-48
Acts 6:1-4
Romans 1:14-17

Of God
Romans 14:12

Of the tabernacle
1 Chronicles 9:22-23

Relief from Jesus
Matthew 11:28-30

Stress

Definition:
Pressure or strain. Used especially of forces that cause physical, mental, or emotional strain.

Key Verses:
Psalm 116:7
Philippians 4:6-7

See Also:
Chronic Illness
Grief
Work
Workaholism

Be still
Psalm 46:10

Caused by overworking
Exodus 18:17-27

Courage in
2 Corinthians 4:8-10

Dangers of
Ecclesiastes 4:6

From chastening
Job 33:19-20

From disobedience
Jonah 1:4-12

Hope in
Lamentations 3:19-33
Luke 8:22-25
Luke 12:22-34
2 Corinthians 4:8-9

Integrity during
Job 23:10

Of Jesus
Matthew 26:38-39
Mark 14:36
Luke 22:44

Over a sinful act
Genesis 42:21

Overcoming
2 Corinthians 11:22-31
Philippians 4:6

Prayer in
Psalm 18:6
Psalm 55:16-18

Psalm 116:1-4
Mark 14:33-36
Luke 22:41-42

Recovery from
2 Corinthians 4:16

Rest from
Proverbs 14:30
Isaiah 40:30-31
Matthew 11:28-30

Worry in
Philippians 4:6-7

Strife

Definition:
Hostility, contention, or bitter conflict.

Key Verses:
Proverbs 17:1
Proverbs 26:21

See Also:
Disagreement
Quarrel

Avoidance of
Philippians 2:14

Because of jealousy
1 Samuel 1:1-7

Blessed are the peacemakers
Matthew 5:9

Caused by gossip
Proverbs 16:28

Condemned
Genesis 13:8
Proverbs 6:16-19

Proverbs 26:17
1 Corinthians 1:10
2 Corinthians 12:20
Galatians 5:26
1 Timothy 2:8
2 Timothy 2:24

Effects of
Matthew 12:25
Galatians 5:15

Importance of ending
Proverbs 17:14
Proverbs 20:3
Romans 14:19

In leadership
Acts 15:36-40

In the family
Genesis 25:22-23
Proverbs 19:13
Proverbs 21:19
Proverbs 25:24
Proverbs 27:15
Ephesians 6:4
Colossians 3:19

Stronghold

Definition:
A fortification or place of dominance and security.

Key Verses:
Psalm 27:1
2 Corinthians 10:4

See Also:
Spiritual Warfare
Temptation

Strong-Willed

Definition:
Description of one who consistently asserts their own desires.

Key Verses:
Ephesians 5:21
Philippians 2:3-4

See Also:
Children
Child Training
Parenting
Personality

Submission

Definition:
The act or process of voluntarily yielding to power or authority.

Key Verses:
James 3:17
James 4:7

See Also:
Dependency
Rebellion

Authority of Christ
Matthew 28:18

Example of Christ
Ephesians 5:2

God's authority
Proverbs 21:1
Isaiah 54:5

In marriage
1 Corinthians 11:3
Ephesians 5:21-23
1 Peter 3:1, 5-7

In relationships
Ephesians 6:5
Colossians 3:22-23
1 Peter 2:14-21

Mutual
Ephesians 5:21

Of Christ
John 8:28
John 13:12-17
Philippians 2:5-8

Of Messiah
Isaiah 53:1-7

Of Sarah
Genesis 12:10-20
Genesis 20:1-10

**Submission of
the Spirit**
John 16:13

Submit to discipline
Proverbs 15:5

To Christ
Romans 1:5

To elders
1 Peter 5:5

To God
Deuteronomy 4:40
Deuteronomy 28:1
Psalm 139:23-24
Isaiah 64:8
Mark 14:36
Luke 22:42

Acts 5:29
James 4:7
1 Peter 2:23

To human authorities
Deuteronomy 5:27
1 Samuel 14:24-28
Romans 13:1-4
1 Timothy 2:1-2
Titus 3:1
Hebrews 13:17
1 Peter 2:13-15

To husband
Ephesians 5:22-24
Colossians 3:18
1 Peter 3:1

To one another
Ephesians 5:21
Philippians 2:3

To parents
Proverbs 23:22
Colossians 3:20

To wife
Ephesians 5:25

Substance Abuse

Definition:
Use of drugs or medications without a prescription or for recreation.

Key Verses:
1 Corinthians 10:31
Ephesians 5:18

See Also:
Alcohol and Drug
Abuse

Codependency
Habits

Success

Definition:
Completion of a purpose, goal, or intention.

Key Verses:
Genesis 39:23
Philippians 3:7

See Also:
Dependency
Failure
Purpose in Life
Significance

Abundant life
John 10:10

**Because of
faithfulness to God**
2 Chronicles 26:5

Because of hard work
Proverbs 10:4
Proverbs 12:11
Proverbs 13:11
Proverbs 14:23
Proverbs 28:19

Because of obedience
Deuteronomy 29:9
Job 36:11
Daniel 4:27

**Because of pursuing
righteousness**
1 Chronicles 22:13
Proverbs 21:21

Matthew 6:32-33
Galatians 6:9

Because of seeking the Lord
Psalm 1:3
Proverbs 16:3
Jeremiah 17:7-8

Because of the Holy Spirit
Zechariah 4:6
Romans 15:18-19

Because of wisdom
Proverbs 3:1-4

Comes from humility
Proverbs 22:4

Definition of
Philippians 3:7-14

From God
Genesis 39:2-5
Deuteronomy 8:18
Nehemiah 2:20
Nehemiah 6:16
1 Corinthians 3:6-8

Futility of
Ecclesiastes 2:4-11
Luke 12:13-21

God's control
Psalm 75:7

In ministry
Luke 10:17-20
1 Thessalonians 1:8-10
1 Thessalonians 2:17-19

Of Messiah
Isaiah 48:15

Peter's failure
Matthew 16:21-22
Matthew 26:69-75
Mark 14:68
Mark 14:71
Luke 22:56-62

Pursue Christ
Philippians 3:8

Results are unpredictable
Ecclesiastes 8:14
Ecclesiastes 9:11

Spiritual
John 15:4-5
Acts 3:6
Acts 3:12
Acts 3:16

Through counsel
Proverbs 15:22

Through service
Matthew 20:25-28

Through suffering
Matthew 5:1-12

Suffering

Definition:
The state or process of feeling intense pain, loss, or estrangement.

Key Verses:
Romans 5:3-4
Romans 8:17

See Also:
Evil
Pain
Trials

Benefits of
Psalm 119:71
Romans 5:3-4
Philippians 3:10-11

Cannot separate from Christ
Romans 8:35-39

Certainty of
Philippians 1:29-30
1 Thessalonians 3:4
1 Peter 4:12-16

Description of
Job 33:19-21

Endurance of
1 Peter 2:19

For doing good
1 Peter 3:14-17

For Jesus
Acts 9:15-16

For spiritual growth
Isaiah 48:10

For the kingdom
2 Thessalonians 1:4-6

God's sovereignty in
1 Samuel 18:10
1 Kings 22:23
Job 2:10
Daniel 4:34-35
Amos 3:6

Hope in
Job 19:25-26
Job 36:15
Psalm 119:71
Romans 8:18
2 Corinthians
4:17-18

Integrity in
Job 23:10

Loss of appetite in
Job 3:24

**Not due to
personal sin**
John 9:1-3

Of Christ
Matthew 16:21
Matthew 17:12
John 10:15
John 19:28-30
1 Corinthians 15:3
Ephesians 5:25
Hebrews 2:10
Hebrews 2:18
Hebrews 5:8
1 Peter 2:21

Of the righteous
Psalm 73:14

Patience in
Romans 12:12

Perspective in
2 Corinthians
4:16-18

Praising God in
Job 1:20-22

Prayer in
Psalm 22:1

Purpose of
Proverbs 17:3
2 Corinthians 4:10
1 John 3:16

Rejoicing in
Habakkuk 3:17-18
Acts 5:41
Colossians 1:24
James 5:13

Relationship to sin
1 Peter 4:1

Relationship with sin
Isaiah 1:5-6

Relief in
Psalm 55:22
Jeremiah 15:11-15
Matthew 11:28-30
2 Corinthians 1:5
2 Corinthians 12:9
1 Peter 5:10

Response to
Matthew 5:38-39

Righteousness in
Job 1:20-22
Job 27:5

Safety with the Lord
Psalm 34:17-19

Sorrow in
Job 3:1-26

Support in
1 Peter 5:7

Will cease
Revelation 21:4

Suicide Prevention

Definition:
To prevent someone
else from deliberately
ending their own life.

Key Verses:
Psalm 62:5-6
John 10:10

See Also:
Depression
Hope
Hopelessness

Against murder
Deuteronomy 5:17

Assisted suicide
Judges 9:54

Body belongs to God
1 Corinthians
6:19-20

Choose life
Deuteronomy 30:19

**Defense against
suicide**
Psalm 27:1-14

Futility of suicide
Ecclesiastes 9:4-6

**People are God's
creation**
Psalm 139:16

Regretting one's birth
Jeremiah 20:14-18

The Biblical Counseling Reference Guide

Root of death
Genesis 2:16-17

Suicide because of guilt
Matthew 27:3-5
Acts 1:18

Suicide of Ahithophel
2 Samuel 17:23

Suicide of Saul
1 Samuel 31:4

Suicide of Saul's armor-bearer
1 Samuel 31:5

Suicide of Zimri
1 Kings 16:18-19

Superstition

Definition:
Naïve or ignorant beliefs and practices disconnected from critical reflection.

Key Verses:
Isaiah 2:6
1 Timothy 4:7

See Also:
Ignorance
Occult

Suppression

Definition:
To stifle or repress, often in the context of a negative memory or impulsive desire.

Key Verses:
Psalm 32:3
Daniel 7:28

See Also:
Abuse
Counseling
Identity

Sympathy

Definition:
The act of sharing in or identifying with the pain or distress of another.

Key Verses:
Hebrews 4:15
Hebrews 10:34

See Also:
Bereavement
Brokenhearted
Grief
Kindness
Sorrow

Commanded
Luke 6:36
1 Peter 3:8

For Babylon
Revelation 18:10

For others
Leviticus 19:18
Galatians 6:2
James 2:8

For the needy
Isaiah 58:7
Luke 10:30-37

Hebrews 13:3

Lack of
Job 12:5
Psalm 69:20

Of Christ
Hebrews 4:15

Of God
Psalm 78:39
Psalm 103:13
Isaiah 63:9

Tact

Definition:
Keen perception of appropriate or fitting responses to potentially offensive, divisive, or hostile situations.

Key Verses:
Proverbs 13:3
Matthew 10:16

See Also:
Conflict Resolution
Discernment
Peace

Benefits of
Proverbs 25:11

Characteristics of
James 3:17-18

Commanded
Matthew 10:16

Gift from the Lord
Isaiah 50:4

In speech
Proverbs 15:1
Proverbs 25:15
Ecclesiastes 3:7
Ephesians 4:15
Colossians 4:6
James 1:19-20

Of Joseph
Genesis 41:33-46

Responding with tact
Daniel 2:14

Toward the ignorant
Hebrews 5:2

Wise use of questions
Matthew 21:23-27

Teenagers

Definition:
People generally
between the ages of
thirteen and nineteen.

Key Verses:
Proverbs 3:11-12
2 Timothy 2:22

See Also:
Adolescence
Children
Family
Parenting
Youth

**As an example
to others**
1 Timothy 4:12

Benefits of discipline
Proverbs 19:18

Proverbs 29:17
Ecclesiastes 8:11
Hebrews 12:11

**Do not stir up anger
in your teens**
Ephesians 6:4
Colossians 3:21

Effects on parents
Proverbs 17:25

Example of Josiah
2 Kings 23:25

Example of Uzziah
2 Chronicles 26:3-5

**Gain prudence
and discretion**
Proverbs 1:4

**God disciplines
those He loves**
Proverbs 3:11-12
Hebrews 12:6

God is a Father
2 Corinthians
6:17-18

God's plan for
2 Chronicles 34:1-5
Psalm 119:9

Honor for parents
Proverbs 4:1
Proverbs 13:1
Proverbs 20:20

Honor vows
Numbers 30:2-4

**Importance of
teaching**
Deuteronomy 6:6-7
Proverbs 3:1-2
Proverbs 22:6

Instructions for
Titus 2:6-8

Pursue purity
2 Timothy 2:22

Stay on the right path
Proverbs 23:19

Temptation

Definition:
The act or process of
provoking, inciting, or
leading to do wrong.

Key Verses:
1 Corinthians 10:13
Hebrews 2:18

See Also:
Discipline
Impulse
Obedience

Battle in the mind
2 Corinthians 10:4-5

Be self-controlled
1 Peter 5:8

By Satan
2 Corinthians 2:11
Ephesians 4:27
1 Thessalonians 3:5

Control your tongue
Proverbs 10:19

The Biblical Counseling Reference Guide

Dangers of
Genesis 4:7
Joshua 7:19-21
Matthew 5:27-30

Delivered from
Proverbs 11:6

Depravity
2 Peter 2:19

Eating the forbidden fruit
Genesis 3:1-6

Effects of
Proverbs 6:27-29
Proverbs 14:12
James 1:2-4

From lust
James 4:1

From money
Deuteronomy 7:25
1 Timothy 6:9-10

From the flesh
Galatians 5:17

God does not tempt anyone with evil
James 1:13-14

Jesus' sympathy with
Hebrews 2:17-18
Hebrews 4:15

Of David
2 Samuel 11:1-13

Of Jesus
Matthew 4:1-10
Luke 4:1-13

Overcoming
Job 31:1
Psalm 119:11
Proverbs 1:10
Proverbs 2:10-12
Proverbs 4:23
Jeremiah 35:1-16
John 15:5
Romans 6:6-7
Romans 8:29
Romans 8:37
Romans 12:2
Romans 12:21
1 Corinthians 10:13
2 Corinthians 12:9
Ephesians 6:11-13
Titus 2:11-12
1 Peter 5:8-9

Prayer in
Matthew 26:41
Luke 11:4
Luke 22:40

Purpose of
1 Peter 1:6-7

Rescue from
2 Peter 2:7-9
Jude 24

Resistance of
Psalm 119:101
Hebrews 12:1

Sexual
Genesis 19:1-29
1 Corinthians 7:5
1 Thessalonians 4:3-7

Source of
1 John 2:15-17

Submit to God
James 4:6-7

To apostatize
Job 2:9-10

Warning against
Deuteronomy 11:16
Mark 14:38
Galatians 6:1
2 Peter 3:17

Terminal Illness

Definition:
A disease with the prognosis of impending death and no known cure.

Key Verses:
Psalm 23:4
Psalm 139:16

See Also:
Chronic Illness
Euthanasia
Grief
Healing
Suffering

Assurance of eternal life
Psalm 73:24

Comfort in
Psalm 23:4
Psalm 119:50

Correction of affliction
Psalm 119:67
Psalm 119:71

Death comes for all
2 Samuel 22:5
Psalm 55:4-5
Isaiah 38:10

Death of Jesus
Matthew 27:46-50

Death of Lazarus
John 11:14

Destiny of the unrighteous
Matthew 13:40-42
Matthew 25:41

Future home
Revelation 21:1-27

God's new creation
Ezekiel 47:12
Revelation 22:1-2

God's power over
Luke 18:35-43

Hope in
Romans 8:18
1 Corinthians 2:9
1 Corinthians 15:54
2 Corinthians
4:16–5:5
Philippians 1:21
Revelation 21:4

Inevitability of death
Ecclesiastes 3:1-2
Hebrews 9:27

Jesus' power over death
Luke 7:11-15
Luke 8:49-55
John 11:38-44

Life from God
2 Kings 20:1-6

Maintain a healthy attitude
Proverbs 18:14

Ownership of God
Romans 14:8

Passing of life
1 Peter 1:24-25

Paul's suffering
2 Corinthians 12:7

Preparation for death
Hebrews 11:22

Satan's attacks
Job 2:3-10

Sickness because of sin
1 Corinthians
11:27-30

Terror

Definition:
Intense fear.

Key Verses:
Psalm 91:4-5
Jeremiah 8:15

See Also:
Fear

Thankfulness

Definition:
The state, quality, or expression of gratitude.

Key Verses:
Psalm 7:17
Colossians 2:6-7

See Also:
Gratitude
Prayer
Remember

Commanded
Colossians 3:15-17

For believers
Ephesians 1:15-16
Philippians 1:3

For everything
Ephesians 5:20
1 Thessalonians 5:18

Relationship to worship
1 Chronicles 23:30
Psalm 95:2
Psalm 100:4
Psalm 116:17
Psalm 136:1-26

Thoughts

Definition:
Critical reflection upon; thinking or reasoning.

Key Verses:
Psalm 19:14
Philippians 4:8

See Also:
Counseling
Temptation

Examples of evil
Genesis 6:5
Matthew 15:19

Importance of
Colossians 3:1-2
Hebrews 3:1

Influenced by God
Psalm 139:23-24
Romans 12:2

Of God
Psalm 92:5
Psalm 139:17-18
Isaiah 55:9

To be wisely directed
2 Corinthians 10:5
Philippians 4:8

Time Management

Definition:
Appropriate allocation of time to multiple projects so that the most important are accomplished satisfactorily.

Key Verses:
Ecclesiastes 11:6
Ephesians 5:15-16

See Also:
Integrity
Motivation
Procrastination

Brevity of life
Job 7:6
Job 10:5
Job 16:22

Psalm 39:5
Psalm 89:47
Psalm 90:10
1 Corinthians 7:29
Ephesians 5:15-17
Colossians 4:5

Brings profit
Proverbs 13:4
Proverbs 14:23
Proverbs 21:5

Give thought to steps
Proverbs 14:15

Have faith and patience
Hebrews 6:12

Importance of
Psalm 90:12
Ecclesiastes 3:1
Ecclesiastes 8:5-6
Mark 13:35
James 4:14

Laziness related to destruction
Proverbs 18:9

Work enthusiastically for the Lord
2 Chronicles 15:7
Colossians 3:23-24

Tithing

Definition:
The practice of giving or donating one-tenth of wealth or income.

Key Verses:
Malachi 3:8
Hebrews 7:2

See Also:
Finances

Tradition

Definition:
Custom, practice, or teaching handed down orally from one generation to the next; used especially of Christian teaching not recorded in the Bible.

Key Verses:
Mark 7:6-8
1 John 2:24

See Also:
Family
Legalism
Remember

Biblical
2 Thessalonians 3:6

Developing
Genesis 32:32
Judges 11:39-40

Keeping
Mark 7:3

Of pagans
Deuteronomy 18:9

Preferred over God's command
Matthew 15:2-3

Reject godless
1 Timothy 4:7

Religious
Colossians 2:8

Zeal for
Galatians 1:14

Definition:
To direct or teach
another.

Key Verses:
1 Corinthians 9:25-27
1 Timothy 4:8

See Also:
Child Training
Coaching
Discipleship
Instruction
Mentoring

Transform

Definition:
To change completely.

Key Verses:
Romans 12:2
2 Corinthians 3:18

See Also:
Change
Repentance
Salvation

Transsexual

Definition:
A person with a physi-
ological desire to be
the opposite sex.

Key Verses:
Genesis 1:27
Isaiah 45:9

See Also:
Bisexual
Homosexuality
Transvestite

**Fearfully and
wonderfully made**
Psalm 139:14-16

**Gender comes
from God**
Genesis 1:27
Genesis 5:2
Matthew 19:4
Mark 10:6

Transvestite

Definition:
Someone who
expresses their sexual-
ity by adopting the
dress, appearance, and
mannerisms of the
opposite sex.

Key Verses:
Deuteronomy 22:5
Isaiah 29:16

See Also:
Cross-Dressing

Homosexuality
Transsexual

Condemned
Deuteronomy 22:5

**Fearfully and
wonderfully made**
Psalm 139:14-16

**Gender comes
from God**
Genesis 1:27
Genesis 5:2
Matthew 19:4
Mark 10:6

Trauma

Definition:
A physical, psycho-
logical, or emotional
wound.

Key Verses:
Psalm 109:22
Lamentations 3:19-20

See Also:
Anxiety
Evil and Suffering

Trials

Definition:
Tests of faith, patience,
or endurance by
means of suffering or
temptation.

Key Verses:
Isaiah 43:2
James 1:2-3

See Also:
Adversity
Suffering

As discipline
Amos 4:6

Because of pride
2 Chronicles 25:19

Belief in God during
Psalm 57:1
John 14:1

Benefits of
Genesis 50:20
Psalm 119:67
Psalm 119:71
Romans 5:3-4
Romans 8:28-29
Hebrews 12:11
James 1:1-12
1 Peter 2:19-21

Bitterness and joy
Proverbs 14:10

Blessings of
Matthew 5:10

Bring joy
Psalm 126:5

Certainty of
Job 5:7
Job 14:1
Philippians 1:29
2 Timothy 3:12
1 Peter 4:12-13
1 Peter 5:9

Comfort in
Psalm 34:18
Isaiah 43:2

2 Corinthians 1:3-5

**Create longing
for God**
Psalm 42:1-6

Deliverance from
Job 36:15
2 Peter 2:9

Evangelism in
Acts 8:3-4
Philippians 1:12

Faith in
Job 2:10

For the wicked
Psalm 14:4-5

Help in
Galatians 6:2

Importance of family
Proverbs 17:17

In ministry
2 Corinthians 6:4-12

Of Christ
1 Peter 2:21-23

Patience in
Romans 12:12

Peace from Jesus
John 14:27

Perseverance through
Micah 7:8
James 1:12

Perspective in
2 Corinthians 4:17

Prayer in
Psalm 10:17

Psalm 22:24
Psalm 46:1
Psalm 50:15
Psalm 69:1
Psalm 120:1
Isaiah 37:14-20

Produces character
Romans 5:3-4

Protection in
Psalm 34:17-19
Psalm 138:7
Proverbs 11:8
Nahum 1:7
Revelation 3:10

Purpose of
John 9:3
Hebrews 12:7
1 Peter 1:6-7

Rejoice in
Romans 5:3-5

Relationship to sin
1 Peter 4:1

Rescue from
Job 5:19

Security in Christ
Romans 8:38-39

Strength in
2 Corinthians
12:9-10

Support in
1 Peter 5:10

Sympathy of Jesus
Hebrews 4:15

**To complete
God's purposes**
Jonah 2:10

Victory in Christ
Romans 8:35-39

Trinity

Definition:
God, who exists in a relationship of self-giving love between the three co-equal, co-eternal persons of Father, Son, and Holy Spirit.

Key Verses:
Matthew 28:19
1 Peter 1:1-2

See Also:
God
Holy Spirit
Jesus Christ

Trust

Definition:
Belief, confidence, or assurance placed in the intentions and integrity of another.

Key Verses:
Psalm 20:7
John 14:1

See Also:
Faith
Intimacy
Obedience

Brings peace
Isaiah 26:3

During hard times
Habakkuk 3:17-18

God cares for you
1 Peter 5:7

In people
Jeremiah 17:5

In the Lord
2 Kings 18:5
2 Chronicles 20:20
Psalm 28:7
Micah 7:5-7

Unbelieving Mate

Definition:
A spouse who does not believe in the death and resurrection of Jesus Christ.

Key Verses:
2 Corinthians 6:14-15
1 Peter 3:1-2

See Also:
Marriage
Premarital Counseling
Salvation

Be wise
Proverbs 14:1

Evangelism to
Matthew 5:14-16
1 Corinthians
2:14-15
2 Corinthians 4:3-4

Faithfulness to
1 Corinthians
7:12-16

God's desire for
2 Peter 3:9

Hope in
Ecclesiastes 4:9-10

**Judgment for
unbelieving**
Ephesians 4:18

Love for
Ephesians 5:2
Ephesians 5:21-23
1 Peter 3:1-2
1 Peter 3:7

**Marriage is a
divine union**
Genesis 2:24

Peace with
Romans 14:19

Power for witnessing
Acts 1:8

Purity in marriage
Ezra 10:2

Purity of marriage
1 Corinthians 7:27
2 Corinthians
6:14-15

Shared image of God
Genesis 1:27

Unity

Definition:
Agreement, harmony,

or concord between parts of a whole.

Key Verses:
Psalm 133:1
Ephesians 4:3-5

See Also:
Friendship
Peace

Commanded
Ephesians 4:3
Philippians 1:27
Philippians 2:2
1 Peter 3:8

Desire for
Genesis 13:8

In actions
Amos 3:3

In church
1 Corinthians 1:10-17

In diversity
1 Corinthians 12:12

In possessions
Acts 4:32

In prayer
Acts 1:14

In the church
John 13:34-35
John 17:11

In the Spirit
Ephesians 2:22

In worship
Zephaniah 3:9

Romans 15:6

Pursuit of
Romans 14:19
Ephesians 4:11-13
Philippians 4:1-3

Racial
Ephesians 2:14

Unpardonable Sin

Definition:
Denying and rejecting the saving work of God by blasphemously attributing God's actions to Satan.

Key Verses:
Mark 3:28-30
1 John 2:1-2

See Also:
Forgiveness
Guilt

Unwanted Pregnancy

Definition:
A pregnancy that is inconvenient or undesirable for the mother.

Key Verses:
Ecclesiastes 11:5
Romans 8:28

See Also:
Pregnancy...
Unplanned

Vanity

Definition:
Excessive pride in passing qualities such as one's appearance or accomplishments.

Key Verses:
Ecclesiastes 2:11
Romans 12:16

See Also:
Conceit
Humility
Pride
Self-Exaltation

Boast in the Lord
1 Corinthians 1:31

Claiming to be a great person
Acts 8:9

Condemned
Luke 11:43
Philippians 2:3

Desire for homage
Esther 3:5
Esther 5:9
3 John 9-10

Effects of
2 Chronicles 32:24-26

Folly of
Proverbs 12:9
1 Corinthians 4:7

God's judgment on
Isaiah 3:16-17
Acts 12:21-23

Ignorance in
2 Corinthians 10:12

In knowledge
1 Corinthians 8:1-3

In leadership
2 Chronicles 26:16

In wealth
Ezekiel 28:4-5
Hosea 12:8

Of scoffers
Proverbs 21:24

The Lord sees
Psalm 138:6

Vengeance

Definition:
The act of retaliating or inflicting punishment as retribution.

Key Verses:
Isaiah 34:8
Romans 12:17

See Also:
Anger
Injustice
Revenge
Strife

Belongs to God
Deuteronomy 32:35
Romans 12:19
Hebrews 10:30

For murder
Genesis 4:15

For self-protection
Esther 8:13

For the righteous
Deuteronomy 32:43
1 Samuel 24:12
Psalm 18:47

On the wicked
Jeremiah 46:10
Micah 5:15
2 Thessalonians 1:8

Verbal and Emotional Abuse

Definition:
Systematic affliction or mistreatment through harmful speech or actions.

Key Verses:
Luke 4:18-19
Romans 13:10

See Also:
Abuse
Anger
Communication

Against evil attitudes
Ephesians 4:31

Be joyful
Proverbs 15:13
Proverbs 17:22

Be patient
Proverbs 13:12
Ecclesiastes 7:8

Be self-controlled
Titus 2:11-12

Blessings from
Matthew 5:11-12

Consider others better than yourself
Philippians 2:3-4

Control anger
Proverbs 29:22
Ecclesiastes 7:9
Ephesians 4:26

Control words
Ecclesiastes 9:17
Proverbs 10:19
Proverbs 15:1
Proverbs 16:21
Proverbs 17:27
Ephesians 4:29

Deception
Psalm 5:9
Psalm 35:20
Psalm 52:2-4
Psalm 55:21

Do not seek revenge
Romans 12:17-18

Do right
James 4:17

Effect of
Proverbs 18:14
Isaiah 21:4

Forgive others
Matthew 6:14-15

Fruit of Spirit
Galatians 5:22-23

God can give relief from suffering
Jeremiah 17:14

The Biblical Counseling Reference Guide

Intrinsic value
Luke 12:6-7

Power of words
Proverbs 12:18
Proverbs 18:21

Producing hatred and fights
Galatians 5:15

Rebuke is more helpful than flattery
Proverbs 28:23

Reconciliation
Matthew 5:23-24
Matthew 18:15

Recovery from
Psalm 30:11
Psalm 34:18
Psalm 147:3
Jeremiah 17:14

Respect others
1 Peter 2:17

Root of pride
Psalm 59:12

Speak gently
Proverbs 15:4

Speak truth
Proverbs 12:17
Ephesians 4:25

Speak with integrity
James 5:12

The fear of people is a trap
Proverbs 29:25

Works of flesh
Galatians 5:19-21

Victimization

Definition:
Unjust affliction, injury, adverse treatment, trickery, destruction, or sacrifice.

Key Verses:
Psalm 22:24
Jeremiah 31:13

See Also:
Abuse
Freedom

Against bitterness
Hebrews 12:15

Against revenge
Leviticus 19:18
Deuteronomy 32:35

Brings blessing
Luke 6:22

Christ's mission
Luke 4:18

Comfort for
Psalm 10:14
Psalm 34:18
Proverbs 15:3
2 Corinthians 1:3-4

Condemned
Psalm 10:8

Confidence in God
Proverbs 3:26

Control anger
Ephesians 4:26-27

Control words
Proverbs 12:18

Deliverance from
Psalm 34:4

Endurance of
1 Peter 2:19-21

Future healing
Revelation 21:4

God's care
Genesis 16:13
Psalm 10:14
Matthew 6:26

God's deliverance
Exodus 6:6-9

God's justice
Psalm 10:1-18
Isaiah 58:6

Intrinsic value
Luke 12:6-7

Joy in suffering
Jeremiah 31:13
James 1:2-4

Love enemies
Matthew 5:44
Luke 6:35

Love overcoming fear
1 John 4:18

Move forward
1 Corinthians 9:24
Philippians 3:12-13
Hebrews 5:12
Hebrews 6:1

Hebrews 12:1

Of Christ
Isaiah 53:5-6
1 Peter 2:23

Of Hagar and Ishmael
Genesis 16:1-7
Genesis 21:14-16

Of Israel
Exodus 1:10
Exodus 2:23
Exodus 5:22-23
Lamentations 4:2

Of Naomi
Ruth 1:19-21

Of Tamar
2 Samuel 13:1-20

Overcoming
Psalm 72:14
John 16:33
Romans 8:37-39

Persecution
John 15:20

Prayer in
Psalm 6:2
Psalm 119:86

Rape
2 Samuel 13:11-14

Trust God
Psalm 62:7-8
Psalm 68:19-20
Psalm 91:1-16
Proverbs 29:25
Isaiah 41:10
Isaiah 41:13

Violence

Definition:
An act of aggression, abuse, or physical force.

Key Verses:
Isaiah 60:18
Jeremiah 22:3

See Also:
Evil
Hatred
Suffering

Against God's people
Galatians 1:13

Avoidance of
Psalm 17:4
Psalm 140:1-2

By God's people
Isaiah 59:6
Ezekiel 8:17
Hosea 4:2

By the unrighteous
Psalm 73:6
Proverbs 4:17

By the wealthy
Micah 6:12

God judges
Genesis 6:13

Virtue

Definition:
Quality or behavior that conforms to a code of morality, correctness, or ethics.

Key Verses:
Proverbs 21:8
James 1:21

See Also:
Character
Holiness
Innocence
Purity

Benefits of
Nehemiah 13:13
Psalm 41:12
Proverbs 10:9
Proverbs 11:3
Daniel 6:4

Commanded
Philippians 4:8

Difficulty finding
Jeremiah 5:1

God desires
1 Chronicles 29:17

Hold on to
Proverbs 3:3

Importance of
1 Peter 3:1-2

Righteous live with integrity
Proverbs 20:7

Value of
Proverbs 19:1

Voyeurism

Definition:
Seeking sexual excitement through covert

observation of nudity or sexual activity.

Key Verses:
Ephesians 5:3
2 Timothy 2:22

See Also:
Purity
Sex
Sexual Addiction
Sexual Integrity

Vulnerability

Definition:
The state or quality of being open to attack or damage; used especially of openness and honesty in relationships.

Key Verses:
Psalm 139:23-24
James 5:16

See Also:
Communication
Friendship
Intimacy

God's protection in
Psalm 5:11
Psalm 32:7
Psalm 37:28
John 17:15
Acts 18:9-10

Jesus' compassion in
Matthew 9:36

Prayer in
Psalm 10:12
Psalm 69:29
Psalm 140:1-4

To the attacks of the wicked
Psalm 10:9
Psalm 109:1-3
Proverbs 28:15

Weakness

Definition:
The state or quality of lacking strength, vigor, ability, or defense.

Key Verses:
Romans 8:26
2 Corinthians 13:4

See Also:
Character
Disease
Health

Because of God's judgment
Jeremiah 51:30

Benefits of
Deuteronomy 7:7

Boasting in
2 Corinthians 11:30

Christ's sympathy with
Hebrews 4:15

Dependence upon God in
2 Chronicles 14:11

2 Chronicles 20:12
Isaiah 40:29-31
Hebrews 11:32-34

Grace in
2 Corinthians 12:9

In ministry
2 Corinthians 4:7

In prayer
Matthew 26:36-40

In the church
1 Corinthians 12:22

Of human priests
Hebrews 7:28

Of the flesh
Matthew 26:41
Mark 14:38

Of the godless
Job 8:14

Of the strong
Amos 2:14

Power in
Isaiah 40:29
John 15:5
1 Corinthians 1:27
2 Corinthians 12:9-10
2 Corinthians 13:4

Respect weakness in others
Romans 14:1

Spiritual
1 Corinthians 3:2
1 Corinthians 3:5

Wealth

Definition:
Abundance of money or possessions; riches, affluence.

Key Verses:
Luke 6:24
James 1:10

See Also:
Greed
Prosperity Gospel
Reward

Belongs to the Lord
2 Samuel 8:9-12
Haggai 2:8

Benefits of
Ecclesiastes 7:12

Blessed are the poor
Luke 6:20

Comes from humility
Proverbs 22:4

Dangers of
Deuteronomy 8:13-14
Deuteronomy 31:20
Deuteronomy 32:15
Job 31:24-28
1 Timothy 6:9-10
Revelation 3:15-18

Faithfulness with
Luke 16:11

Faith in God is true riches
Proverbs 16:8
2 Corinthians 6:10

1 Timothy 6:6-8
1 Peter 1:7
Revelation 2:9

Folly of trusting in
Psalm 39:6
Psalm 49:5-12
Psalm 49:16-20
Proverbs 23:4-5
Ecclesiastes 2:4-11
Ecclesiastes 5:10
Jeremiah 17:11
Jeremiah 49:4
James 1:10
1 Peter 1:18-19

Freedom from
Matthew 19:16-30

From God
Deuteronomy 6:10-12
Deuteronomy 8:18
1 Samuel 2:7
Ecclesiastes 5:19

From hard work
Proverbs 13:11

Generosity with
Romans 15:26-27
2 Corinthians 9:11

Greed condemned
Psalm 62:10
Proverbs 28:22

Honoring the Lord with
Proverbs 3:9-10

Importance of humility with wealth
1 Timothy 6:17-19

Judgment for abuse of
Amos 5:11

Less valuable than wisdom
Psalm 119:14
Proverbs 16:16

Needs met in Christ
Philippians 4:19

Of Solomon
2 Chronicles 9:13-16

Pride in
Ezekiel 27:1-36

Responsibility with
Luke 12:48

Taxes to obtain
2 Kings 23:35

Use for noble purposes
Matthew 27:57-61

Warning against
Matthew 6:19-21

Weariness

Definition:
The state or quality of being exhausted, fatigued, or unable to continue.

Key Verses:
Isaiah 40:28-31
Jeremiah 31:25

See Also:
Stress

The Biblical Counseling Reference Guide

Weakness
Work

Attacking while enemy is weary
  2 Samuel 17:1-2

Danger from
  2 Samuel 21:15

From a journey
  John 4:6

From the sun
  Jonah 4:8

Getting rich
  Proverbs 23:4

God gives strength
  Psalm 6:2-3

Leads to accidents
  Acts 20:7-9

Of doing good
  Galatians 6:9

Of God
  Malachi 2:17

Rest in
  Isaiah 28:11-12
  Matthew 11:28-30
  Mark 6:30-31
  2 Corinthians 7:5-7

Strength in
  Isaiah 40:29-31
  Jeremiah 31:25

Wickedness

Definition:
Extreme evil, malice, or injustice.

Key Verses:
Psalm 1:1
Romans 6:19

See Also:
Evil
Sin
Worldly

By leaders
  2 Kings 8:16-19
  Micah 7:3

Compulsion for
  Proverbs 4:16

Judgment on
  Psalm 37:12-13
  Jeremiah 22:13-19
  Amos 2:6-16

No peace for
  Isaiah 57:20-21

Widowhood

Definition:
The time period between the death of a spouse and either remarriage or death.

Key Verses:
Isaiah 66:13
James 1:27

See Also:
Bereavement
Death

Loneliness
Singleness

Comfort in
  Isaiah 54:4-5
  2 Corinthians 1:3-5

Death of Sarah
  Genesis 23:2

Example to others
  Luke 21:1-4
  Titus 2:1-5

Free to remarry
  1 Corinthians 7:39

God's comfort
  Psalm 34:18

God's protection in
  Psalm 68:5
  Isaiah 43:2

Grief and joy
  John 16:20

Grief over anticipated death
  Matthew 17:23

Joy will return
  Psalm 30:5

Lord's compassion and faithfulness
  Lamentations 3:19-25

Ministry to
  James 1:27

Mourning
  Genesis 50:10
  John 11:31

John 11:34-36

Opportunity to serve
1 Kings 17:9
Luke 2:36-37
1 Corinthians
7:32-35

**Precious in the
Lord's sight**
Psalm 116:15

Rest in Christ
Matthew 11:28-29

Sorrow over death
Psalm 116:3

Suffering and glory
Romans 8:18

Support of family
Ruth 2:17-18
Ruth 2:22

Time for mourning
Ecclesiastes 3:4

Wife

Definition:
A married woman.

Key Verses:
Proverbs 12:4
Proverbs 18:22

See Also:
Mother
Parenting
Submission
Unbelieving Mate

A blessing from God
Psalm 18:22

Psalm 128:3

**A helper
corresponding
to man**
Genesis 2:18

Effect on husband
Proverbs 12:4

Foolish advice from
Job 2:9-10

Godly qualities of
Proverbs 31:10-31

**Lack of respect
for husband**
2 Samuel 6:20

Respect for husband
Ephesians 5:22
Ephesians 5:33
Colossians 3:18
1 Peter 3:1

Ungodly influence of
1 Kings 21:1-16
2 Chronicles 21:6

Unity to husband
Genesis 2:24
1 Corinthians 7:10

Warning of
Matthew 27:19

Wisdom of
Proverbs 14:1

Wife Abuse

Definition:
The physical, sexual,
emotional, or verbal

mistreatment of one's
wife.

Key Verses:
Psalm 140:1
Colossians 3:19

See Also:
Spouse Abuse
Verbal and Emotional
    Abuse

Will of God

Definition:
The desire, choice, and
determination of God.

Key Verses:
Romans 8:27
1 John 2:17

See Also:
Decision Making
God
Purpose in Life

Wisdom

Definition:
The ability to make
good decisions or dis-
cern right from wrong.

Key Verses:
Proverbs 1:7
1 Corinthians 1:21

See Also:
Aging
Ignorance
Knowledge
Maturity

Benefits of
Proverbs 2:12
Proverbs 4:6
Proverbs 10:13
Proverbs 28:26

From God
Proverbs 2:6
Ephesians 1:17
James 1:5

From humility
Proverbs 11:2

From the fear of God
Proverbs 1:7
Proverbs 9:10
Proverbs 15:33

Of God
Romans 11:33
1 Corinthians
1:17-25

Of the world
1 Corinthians 3:19

Results of
James 3:13

Value of
Proverbs 8:11
Proverbs 16:16

Witchcraft

Definition:
The practice of sorcery, magic, or communication with spirits and demons.

Key Verses:
Micah 5:12
Galatians 5:19-20

See Also:
Occult
Satan, Demons, and
Satanism

Withdrawal

Definition:
To remove oneself; also a reference to the painful results of discontinuing the use of certain addictive drugs or alcohol.

Key Verses:
Proverbs 23:33
Luke 5:16

See Also:
Depression
Suicide Prevention

Witnessing

Definition:
Sincere and solemn declaration of the truth, used especially of sharing the good news of Jesus Christ.

Key Verses:
Matthew 28:19-20
Acts 1:8

See Also:
Evangelism
Gospel
Holy Spirit
Salvation

Women

Definition:
Female adults.

Key Verses:
Proverbs 31:30
1 Timothy 3:11

See Also:
Mother
Widowhood
Wife

Abuse of
Judges 19:1-30

Beauty can't save
Jeremiah 6:2

Caring for God's servants
2 Kings 4:8

Created in God's image
Genesis 1:27

Deception of
2 Corinthians 11:3
2 Timothy 3:6

Dress in proper clothing
1 Timothy 2:9-10

Employment of
Nehemiah 3:12

Equality in the Lord
Genesis 2:21-23
Galatians 3:28

Importance of
Ruth 4:11

In ministry
Acts 21:8-9

Instructions for
Titus 2:3-5

Ministry to
Acts 16:13
Acts 17:12

Submission to husband
Ephesians 5:22-24
Colossians 3:18
1 Timothy 2:11-12

Treat with honor
1 Timothy 3:11
1 Peter 3:7

True beauty
1 Peter 3:3-4

Wicked
1 Kings 19:1-2

Wisdom of
1 Samuel 25:1-35

Witnesses of the crucifixion
Matthew 27:55-56

Work

Definition:
Physical or mental energy used for a purpose.

Key Verses:
Colossians 3:24
2 Thessalonians 3:10

See Also:
Business Ethics

Employment
Finances
Money
Purpose in Life
Workaholism

Abuse in
Exodus 1:11-14
Exodus 5:6-18

Brings profit
Proverbs 14:23

Commanded
1 Thessalonians 4:11-12

Devotion to God's work
Nehemiah 5:16
John 9:4
1 Corinthians 3:8-9
Philippians 1:22

Devotion to good works
Ephesians 2:10
Philippians 2:12-13
Titus 3:8

Importance of
2 Thessalonians 3:6-15

Laziness condemned
1 Thessalonians 5:14

Of the law
Galatians 3:2-5

Relief from Jesus
Matthew 11:28-30

Repayment for
Romans 2:5-6
Revelation 22:12

Reputation for good works
Acts 10:4
1 Timothy 5:9-10
1 Timothy 6:18-19

Responsibility for
Ezekiel 18:24-27
1 Timothy 5:7-8

Setting an example through
2 Thessalonians 3:9

Success is from the Lord
Isaiah 28:23-29

Trusting in
Jeremiah 48:7

Workaholism

Definition:
The state or quality of being compulsively addicted to working.

Key Verses:
Ecclesiastes 2:21-22
Ecclesiastes 8:15

See Also:
Addiction
Materialism
Prosperity
Success
Time Management

Be diligent
1 Thessalonians
4:11-12
2 Thessalonians 3:10

Be self-controlled
1 Corinthians 6:12

Be unselfish
Philippians 2:3-4

Careful planning
Luke 14:28-30

Condemned
Luke 10:38-42

Effects of
Proverbs 21:5
Ecclesiastes 2:20
Ecclesiastes 2:23

Enjoy God's gifts
Ecclesiastes 2:24
Ecclesiastes 8:15

Folly of
Ecclesiastes 5:10
1 Timothy 6:9

Glorify God
Psalm 127:1-2
Matthew 6:33
Galatians 1:10
Colossians 3:17

God is still working
John 5:17

God oversees all
Psalm 90:17

God owns all
Psalm 24:1

Importance of rest
Exodus 35:2
Psalm 127:2

Role of work
Genesis 2:15

**Skilled workers
are honored**
Proverbs 22:29

Worldly

Definition:
Conformity to the
values and activities of
this world rather than
to Christ.

Key Verses:
Titus 2:12
1 John 2:15

See Also:
Envy and Jealousy
Greed
Lust
Materialism

**Avoidance of
worldliness**
2 Corinthians
6:14-18
2 Timothy 2:4
Titus 2:11-12
1 Peter 2:11

**Cannot love both
God and money**
Luke 16:13

Dangers of being
James 4:4

Effects of being
Luke 8:14
Romans 8:5-8

**Loving praise
from people
more than God**
John 12:43

Overcoming
Galatians 2:20
Galatians 5:16
Colossians 3:2-3
Hebrews 11:24-25

Reason for
2 Timothy 4:10

**Warning against
being**
Matthew 6:24

**Worldliness
condemned**
Matthew 5:13-16
Matthew 11:20
Romans 12:1-2
Ephesians 2:1-2
1 Peter 4:3-5
1 John 2:15-17

Worry

Definition:
To be anxious, trou-
bled, or distressed.

Key Verses:
Matthew 6:27-30
1 Peter 5:7

See Also:
Faith
Trust

About punishment
1 Kings 1:50-53
Romans 8:1-2

About the past
Isaiah 43:18

Absence of peace
Job 3:26

Banish anxiety
Ecclesiastes 11:10

Be content
1 Timothy 6:6-9

Beset by fear
Psalm 55:5

Cast cares on God
Psalm 55:22
Psalm 61:2

Comfort from God
Psalm 23:1-3
Psalm 34:4
Psalm 94:19
Psalm 127:2
Isaiah 26:3
Matthew 7:9-11
Luke 8:22-25
1 Peter 5:6-7

Condemned
Matthew 6:34
Luke 12:22-34
John 14:27
Philippians 4:6

Continual fear
Deuteronomy 28:66-67

Dangers of
Matthew 13:22

Mark 4:18-19

Do not fret
Psalm 37:7-8

Effects of
Proverbs 12:25
Luke 21:34

Folly of
Matthew 6:25-32

God's goodness in meeting our needs
Luke 11:11-13

Importance of contentment
Philippians 4:11-13

Joy and pleasure
Psalm 16:11

Martha's anxiety over meal preparation
Luke 10:40

Nebuchadnezzar troubled by dreams
Daniel 2:1-3

No need to fear
Psalm 27:1

Over work
Ecclesiastes 2:23

Pharaoh's mind troubled
Genesis 41:8

Prayer in
Psalm 25:17
Psalm 62:8
Philippians 4:6-7

Protection by the Lord
Psalm 18:2
Psalm 91:2-7

Rest in God's goodness
Psalm 116:7

Terror and trembling
Job 21:6

The Lord blesses with peace
Psalm 29:11

Worship

Definition:
The expression of thanks, adoration, or reverence toward God.

Key Verses:
Psalm 95:6
John 4:23-24

See Also:
God
Idolatry
Prayer

Abuse of
1 Corinthians 11:17-32

By Abram
Genesis 12:8
Genesis 13:3-4

By angels
Isaiah 6:1-3
Revelation 7:11-12

By Jacob
Genesis 35:3

Commitment to
Luke 2:36-37

For edification
1 Corinthians 14:26

For provision
Psalm 63:5

Humility in
Luke 7:36-39
Luke 18:9-14

Hypocrisy in
Matthew 6:7
Mark 7:6-7

Importance of obedience
1 Samuel 15:22
Psalm 51:15-17
Isaiah 1:11-17
Amos 5:22
Romans 12:1
Colossians 2:23

In heaven
Revelation 4:10-11
Revelation 5:14
Revelation 19:6-8

In response to success
Nehemiah 8:1-6

In spirit and truth
John 4:20-24

Judgment for improper worship
Numbers 16:35

Not to be directed toward angels
Colossians 2:18
Revelation 19:10

Of creation
Romans 1:25

Of God
Psalm 29:2
Revelation 14:7
Revelation 15:2-4

Of God alone
Exodus 20:3-5
Deuteronomy 5:7
Matthew 4:10
Revelation 22:8-9

Of idols
Numbers 25:1-2
Judges 18:30-31
2 Kings 17:33
Daniel 3:1-6
1 Corinthians 12:2

Orderliness of
1 Corinthians 14:40

Pagan
Exodus 32:6

Passion for
Psalm 84:1-2

Relationship to holiness
Leviticus 10:8-10
Psalm 24:3-4
James 4:8

Relationship to service
Luke 10:38-42

Sincerity in
Isaiah 29:13

Unacceptable
Malachi 1:10

With gladness
2 Chronicles 29:28
Psalm 100:2

With incense
Exodus 30:34-38

Wrath

Definition:
Vengeful anger, rage, fury, or indignation.

Key Verses:
Psalm 7:11
Psalm 37:8

See Also:
Anger
Fury
Judgment
Rage
Resentment

Against God
Job 15:12-13
Isaiah 8:21

Against the righteous
Matthew 2:16

Condemned
Genesis 4:3-8
Proverbs 16:32
Proverbs 19:19
Proverbs 22:24-25
Ecclesiastes 7:9
Amos 1:11

Matthew 5:21-24
Romans 12:19
Galatians 5:19-20
Titus 1:7
James 1:19-20

**Fear the wrath
of angry men**
Judges 18:25

Folly of
Proverbs 14:17
Proverbs 14:29
Proverbs 25:28
Proverbs 29:11

**In response to
sinful actions**
1 Samuel 20:32-34

Of God
Exodus 4:14
2 Samuel 24:1
1 Kings 22:53
2 Kings 13:3
2 Kings 17:11
2 Kings 22:13
1 Chronicles 13:10
Psalm 2:10-12
Psalm 30:5
Psalm 86:15
Psalm 145:8
Isaiah 13:9
Isaiah 48:9
Isaiah 57:17
Jeremiah 4:4
Jeremiah 10:10
Ezekiel 5:13
Hosea 12:14
Hosea 14:4
Joel 2:13
Zechariah 1:12-15
Hebrews 3:10-11

**Of God against
the wicked**
Numbers 11:1
Numbers 12:9
Job 40:11
Romans 1:18
Romans 2:8
Revelation 6:16-17

**Of God at
disobedience**
Joshua 7:1
Ephesians 5:6

Of God at idolatry
Exodus 32:8-10
Numbers 25:3-4
Deuteronomy 9:20
Joshua 23:16
Judges 2:11-13
1 Kings 14:15
2 Kings 23:19
2 Chronicles 28:25

Overcoming
Psalm 37:8
Proverbs 15:1
Proverbs 17:27
Proverbs 21:14
Proverbs 29:8
Ephesians 4:31
Colossians 3:8

Righteous anger
Matthew 21:12-13

Youth

Definition:
The state or quality
of lacking age, experi-
ence, or wisdom.

Key Verses:
Ecclesiastes 12:1
1 Timothy 4:12

See Also:
Adolescence
Family
Immaturity
Teenagers

**Courage from
the Lord**
1 Samuel 17:32-37

Death in
Isaiah 38:10-20

Despised
1 Samuel 17:42
1 Timothy 4:12

Godliness in
Ecclesiastes 12:1

**Growing in favor
with God and men**
1 Samuel 2:26
Luke 2:52

Impressiveness in
1 Samuel 9:2

In leadership
2 Kings 14:21-22
2 Kings 21:1
2 Chronicles 17:1-4
2 Chronicles 26:1

Inexperience of
1 Chronicles 22:5

Instructions for
Titus 2:6-8

The Biblical Counseling Reference Guide

Integrity in
2 Chronicles 34:1-5

In the Lord's service
Jeremiah 1:6-8
Acts 2:17

Joy of
Ecclesiastes 11:9

**Kingdom of
heaven and**
Matthew 19:13-14

Mistakes of
2 Kings 2:23-24
2 Chronicles 10:6-11
2 Chronicles 13:7

Obedience to parents
Ephesians 6:1-3

Rebellion of
Luke 15:11-32

**Relationship
to conceit**
1 Timothy 3:6

Respect in
Job 32:4
1 Peter 5:5

Sins of
Psalm 25:7
Isaiah 54:4
2 Timothy 2:22

Strength of
Proverbs 20:29

Wisdom in
Psalm 119:9
Psalm 119:100

Zeal

Definition:
Enthusiastic, earnest,
or passionate pursuit
or support; used espe-
cially of religions or
causes.

Key Verses:
Proverbs 23:17
Romans 12:11

See Also:
Boldness
Desire
Spiritual Abuse

**For ancestral
traditions**
Galatians 1:13-14

For Christ
Philippians 3:7-14

For God
Deuteronomy 6:4-5
Psalm 42:1-2
Acts 5:29
Romans 10:1-2

For God's house
Psalm 69:9
John 2:16-17

For righteousness
Numbers 25:11

In the Lord's work
1 Corinthians 15:58

Of God
Isaiah 9:7

**Of religious teachers
to make disciples**
Matthew 23:15

Spiritual fervor
Romans 12:11

**To help God's
servants**
Galatians 4:15

To preach
Acts 18:24-28

Part 2:

Key Bible Verses for Biblical Counseling

Abortion

Jeremiah 1:5: Before I formed you in the womb I knew you, before you were born I set you apart; I appointed you as a prophet to the nations.

Psalm 139:13-16: You created my inmost being; you knit me together in my mother's womb. I praise you because I am fearfully and wonderfully made; your works are wonderful, I know that full well. My frame was not hidden from you when I was made in the secret place, when I was woven together in the depths of the earth. Your eyes saw my unformed body; all the days ordained for me were written in your book before one of them came to be.

Adoption

Romans 8:15-18: The Spirit you received does not make you slaves, so that you live in fear again; rather, the Spirit you received brought about your adoption to sonship. And by him we cry, "Abba, Father." The Spirit himself testifies with our spirit that we are God's children. Now if we are children, then we are heirs—heirs of God and co-heirs with Christ, if indeed we share in his sufferings in order that we may also share in his glory.

Ephesians 1:5: He predestined us for adoption to sonship through Jesus Christ, in accordance with his pleasure and will...

Adultery

Matthew 5:27-28: You have heard that it was said, "You shall not commit adultery." But I tell you that anyone who looks at a woman lustfully has already committed adultery with her in his heart.

1 Corinthians 6:18: Flee from sexual immorality. All other sins a person commits are outside the body, but whoever sins sexually, sins against their own body.

Aging

Isaiah 46:4: Even to your old age and gray hairs I am he, I am he who will sustain you. I have made you and I will carry you; I will sustain you and I will rescue you.

2 Corinthians 4:16; 5:10: Therefore we do not lose heart. Though outwardly we are wasting away, yet inwardly we are being renewed day by day...For we must all appear before the judgment seat of Christ, so that each of us may receive what is due us for the things done while in the body, whether good or bad.

Alcohol and Drug Abuse

Isaiah 5:22-24: Woe to those who are heroes at drinking wine and champions at mixing drinks, who acquit the guilty for a bribe, but deny justice to the innocent. Therefore, as tongues of fire lick up straw and as dry grass sinks down in the flames, so their roots will decay and their flowers blow away like dust; for they have rejected the law of the LORD Almighty and spurned the word of the Holy One of Israel.

1 Corinthians 10:12-13: So, if you think you are standing firm, be careful that you don't fall! No temptation has overtaken you except what is common to mankind. And God is faithful; he will not let you be tempted beyond what you can bear. But when you are tempted, he will also provide a way out so that you can endure it.

Anger

Ephesians 4:26-27, 31: "In your anger do not sin": Do not let the sun go down while you are still angry, and do not give the devil a foothold…Get rid of all bitterness, rage and anger, brawling and slander, along with every form of malice.

James 1:19-20: My dear brothers and sisters, take note of this: Everyone should be quick to listen, slow to speak and slow to become angry, because human anger does not produce the righteousness that God desires.

Anorexia and Bulimia

1 Corinthians 6:19-20: Do you not know that your bodies are temples of the Holy Spirit, who is in you, whom you have received from God? You are not your own; you were bought at a price. Therefore honor God with your bodies.

1 Corinthians 10:31: So whether you eat or drink or whatever you do, do it all for the glory of God.

Assurance of Salvation

Romans 8:1: There is now no condemnation for those who are in Christ Jesus.

1 John 5:13: I write these things to you who believe in the name of the Son of God so that you may know that you have eternal life.

Atheism and Agnosticism

Psalm 14:1: The fool says in his heart, "There is no God." They are corrupt, their deeds are vile; there is no one who does good.

1 Corinthians 1:18: The message of the cross is foolishness to those who are perishing, but to us who are being saved it is the power of God.

Bible Reliability

Psalm 12:6: The words of the LORD are flawless, like silver purified in a crucible, like gold refined seven times.

2 Timothy 3:16: All Scripture is God-breathed and is useful for teaching, rebuking, correcting and training in righteousness.

Blended Family

Romans 14:19: Let us therefore make every effort to do what leads to peace and to mutual edification.

The Biblical Counseling Reference Guide

Colossians 3:12-15: As God's chosen people, holy and dearly loved, clothe yourselves with compassion, kindness, humility, gentleness and patience. Bear with each other and forgive one another if any of you has a grievance against someone. Forgive as the Lord forgave you. And over all these virtues put on love, which binds them all together in perfect unity. Let the peace of Christ rule in your hearts, since as members of one body you were called to peace. And be thankful.

Bullying

Proverbs 29:25: Fear of man will prove to be a snare, but whoever trusts in the LORD is kept safe.

Romans 12:18: If it is possible, as far as it depends on you, live at peace with everyone.

Caregiving

Matthew 25:35-36, 40: "I was hungry and you gave me something to eat, I was thirsty and you gave me something to drink, I was a stranger and you invited me in, I needed clothes and you clothed me, I was sick and you looked after me, I was in prison and you came to visit me."... The King will reply, "Truly I tell you, whatever you did for one of the least of these brothers and sisters of mine, you did for me."

Luke 10:34-35: He went to him and bandaged his wounds, pouring on oil and wine. Then he put the man on his own donkey, brought him to an inn and took care of him. The next day he took out two denarii and gave them to the innkeeper. "Look after him," he said, "and when I return, I will reimburse you for any extra expense you may have."

Child Evangelism

Psalm 78:4, 6-7: We will not hide them from their descendants; we will tell the next generation the praiseworthy deeds of the LORD, his power, and the wonders he has done...so the next generation would know them, even the children yet to be born, and they in turn would tell their children. Then they would put their trust in God and would not forget his deeds but would keep his commands.

Matthew 18:3: He said: "Truly I tell you, unless you change and become like little children, you will never enter the kingdom of heaven."

Childhood Sexual Abuse

Isaiah 12:2: Surely God is my salvation; I will trust and not be afraid. The LORD, the LORD himself, is my strength and my defense; he has become my salvation.

Psalm 82:3: Defend the weak and the fatherless; uphold the cause of the poor and the oppressed.

Chronic Illness

Romans 8:18: I consider that our present sufferings are not worth comparing with the glory that will be revealed in us.

2 Corinthians 12:9: He said to me, "My grace is sufficient for you, for my power is made perfect in weakness." Therefore I will boast all the more gladly about my weakness, so that Christ's power may rest on me.

Coaching

Proverbs 9:9: Instruct the wise and they will be wiser still; teach the righteous and they will add to their learning.

1 Corinthians 4:14-16: I am writing this not to shame you but to warn you as my dear children. Even if you had ten thousand guardians in Christ, you do not have many fathers, for in Christ Jesus I became your father through the gospel. Therefore I urge you to imitate me.

Codependency

Jeremiah 17:5-8: This is what the LORD says: "Cursed is the one who trusts in man, who draws strength from mere flesh and whose heart turns away from the LORD. That person will be like a bush in the wastelands; they will not see prosperity when it comes. They will dwell in the parched places of the desert, in a salt land where no one lives. But blessed is the one who trusts in the LORD, whose confidence is in him. They will be like a tree planted by the water that sends out its roots by the stream. It does not fear when heat comes; its leaves are always green. It has no worries in a year of drought and never fails to bear fruit."

Galatians 1:10: Am I now trying to win the approval of human beings, or of God? Or am I trying to please people? If I were still trying to please people, I would not be a servant of Christ.

Communication

Proverbs 15:23: A person finds joy in giving an apt reply—and how good is a timely word!

Ephesians 4:29: Do not let any unwholesome talk come out of your mouths, but only what is helpful for building others up according to their needs, that it may benefit those who listen.

Conflict Resolution

Proverbs 15:18: A hot-tempered person stirs up conflict, but the one who is patient calms a quarrel.

Romans 14:19: Let us therefore make every effort to do what leads to peace and to mutual edification.

Confrontation

Matthew 18:15-17: If your brother or sister sins, go and point out their fault, just between the two of you. If they listen to you, you have won them over.

But if they will not listen, take one or two others along, so that "every matter may be established by the testimony of two or three witnesses." If they still refuse to listen, tell it to the church; and if they refuse to listen even to the church, treat them as you would a pagan or a tax collector.

Galatians 6:1-2: Brothers and sisters, if someone is caught in a sin, you who live by the Spirit should restore that person gently. But watch yourselves, or you also may be tempted. Carry each other's burdens, and in this way you will fulfill the law of Christ.

Counseling

1 Kings 22:5: Jehoshaphat also said to the king of Israel, "First seek the counsel of the LORD."

Proverbs 2:1-2, 5: My son, if you accept my words and store up my commands within you, turning your ear to wisdom and applying your heart to understanding...then you will understand the fear of the LORD and find the knowledge of God.

Critical Spirit

Colossians 4:6: Let your conversation be always full of grace, seasoned with salt, so that you may know how to answer everyone.

James 3:9-10: With the tongue we praise our Lord and Father, and with it we curse human beings, who have been made in God's likeness. Out

of the same mouth come praise and cursing. My brothers and sisters, this should not be.

Cults

John 1:1: In the beginning was the Word, and the Word was with God, and the Word was God.

2 Timothy 2:15: Do your best to present yourself to God as one approved, a worker who does not need to be ashamed and who correctly handles the word of truth.

Dating

Psalm 119:9: How can a young person stay on the path of purity? By living according to your word.

2 Timothy 2:22: Flee the evil desires of youth and pursue righteousness, faith, love and peace, along with those who call on the Lord out of a pure heart.

Death

John 11:25-26: Jesus said to her, "I am the resurrection and the life. The one who believes in me will live, even though they die; and whoever lives by believing in me will never die. Do you believe this?"

1 Corinthians 15:42-44: So will it be with the resurrection of the dead. The body that is sown is perishable, it is raised imperishable; it is sown in dishonor, it is raised in glory; it is sown in weakness, it is raised in power; it is sown a natural body, it is raised a spiritual body. If there is a natural body, there is also a spiritual body.

Decision Making

Romans 12:1-2: I urge you, brothers and sisters, in view of God's mercy, to offer your bodies as a living sacrifice, holy and pleasing to God—this is your true and proper worship. Do not conform to the pattern of this world, but be transformed by the renewing of your mind. Then you will be able to test and approve what God's will is—his good, pleasing and perfect will.

Philippians 1:9-10: This is my prayer: that your love may abound more and more in knowledge and depth of insight, so that you may be able to discern what is best and may be pure and blameless for the day of Christ.

Depression

Psalm 27:13: I remain confident of this: I will see the goodness of the LORD in the land of the living.

1 Thessalonians 5:16-17: Rejoice always, pray continually...

Dissociative Identity Disorder

Lamentations 1:20: See, LORD, how distressed I am! I am in torment within, and in my heart I am disturbed, for I have been most rebellious. Outside, the sword bereaves; inside, there is only death.

John 8:31-32: To the Jews who had believed him, Jesus said, "If you hold to my teaching, you are really my disciples. Then you will know the truth, and the truth will set you free."

Divorce

Malachi 2:16: "The man who hates and divorces his wife," says the LORD, the God of Israel, "does violence to the one he should protect," says the LORD Almighty. So be on your guard, and do not be unfaithful.

1 Corinthians 7:15-17: If the unbeliever leaves, let it be so. The brother or the sister is not bound in such circumstances; God has called us to live in peace. How do you know, wife, whether you will save your husband? Or, how do you know, husband, whether you will save your wife? Nevertheless, each person should live as a believer in whatever situation the Lord has assigned to them, just as God has called them. This is the rule I lay down in all the churches.

Dysfunctional Family

Genesis 37:3-4: Now Israel loved Joseph more than any of his other sons, because he had been born to him in his old age; and he made an ornate robe for him. When his brothers saw that their father loved him more than any of them, they hated him and could not speak a kind word to him.

The Biblical Counseling Reference Guide

Romans 15:5: May the God who gives endurance and encouragement give you the same attitude of mind toward each other that Christ Jesus had...

Employment

Colossians 3:23: Whatever you do, work at it with all your heart, as working for the Lord, not for human masters.

2 Thessalonians 3:7-8: You yourselves know how you ought to follow our example. We were not idle when we were with you, nor did we eat anyone's food without paying for it. On the contrary, we worked night and day, laboring and toiling so that we would not be a burden to any of you.

Envy and Jealousy

Matthew 6:33: Seek first his kingdom and his righteousness, and all these things will be given to you as well.

James 3:16: Where you have envy and selfish ambition, there you find disorder and every evil practice.

Ethics and Integrity

Micah 6:8: He has shown you, O mortal, what is good. And what does the LORD require of you? To act justly and to love mercy and to walk humbly with your God.

2 Corinthians 1:12: Now this is our boast: Our conscience testifies that we have conducted ourselves in the world, and especially in our relations with you, with integrity and godly sincerity. We have done so, relying not on worldly wisdom but on God's grace.

Euthanasia

Leviticus 24:17: Anyone who takes the life of a human being is to be put to death.

Deuteronomy 32:39: See now that I myself am he! There is no god besides me. I put to death and I bring to life, I have wounded and I will heal, and no one can deliver out of my hand.

Evil and Suffering

Romans 8:28: We know that in all things God works for the good of those who love him, who have been called according to his purpose.

1 Peter 4:19: Those who suffer according to God's will should commit themselves to their faithful Creator and continue to do good.

Fear

Isaiah 41:10: Do not fear, for I am with you; do not be dismayed, for I am your God. I will strengthen you and help you; I will uphold you with my righteous right hand.

Psalm 56:3: When I am afraid, I put my trust in you.

Finances

Luke 14:28: Suppose one of you wants to build a tower. Won't you first sit down and estimate the cost to see if you have enough money to complete it?

2 Corinthians 9:7: Each of you should give what you have decided in your heart to give, not reluctantly or under compulsion, for God loves a cheerful giver.

Forgiveness

Colossians 3:13: Bear with each other and forgive one another if any of you has a grievance against someone. Forgive as the Lord forgave you.

Hebrews 9:22: The law requires that nearly everything be cleansed with blood, and without the shedding of blood there is no forgiveness.

Friendship

Proverbs 17:17: A friend loves at all times, and a brother is born for a time of adversity.

John 15:13: Greater love has no one than this: to lay down one's life for one's friends.

Gambling

Ecclesiastes 5:10: Whoever loves money never has enough; whoever loves wealth is never satisfied with their income. This too is meaningless.

Proverbs 16:33: The lot is cast into the lap, but its every decision is from the LORD.

God

Deuteronomy 4:39: Acknowledge and take to heart this day that the LORD is God in heaven above and on the earth below. There is no other.

Matthew 22:37-38: Jesus replied: "'Love the Lord your God with all your heart and with all your soul and with all your mind.' This is the first and greatest commandment."

Grief

Psalm 57:1: Have mercy on me, my God, have mercy on me, for in you I take refuge. I will take refuge in the shadow of your wings until the disaster has passed.

1 Thessalonians 4:13-14: Brothers and sisters, we do not want you to be uninformed about those who sleep in death, so that you do not grieve like the rest of mankind, who have no hope. For we believe that Jesus died and rose again, and so we believe that God will bring with Jesus those who have fallen asleep in him.

Guilt

Psalm 32:5: Then I acknowledged my sin to you and did not cover up my iniquity. I said, "I will confess my transgressions to the LORD." And you forgave the guilt of my sin.

James 2:10: Whoever keeps the whole law and yet stumbles at just one point is guilty of breaking all of it.

Habits

Matthew 7:26-27: Everyone who hears these words of mine and does not put them into practice is like a foolish man who built his house on sand. The rain came down, the streams rose, and the winds blew and beat against that house, and it fell with a great crash.

Romans 8:9: You, however, are not in the realm of the flesh but are in the realm of the Spirit, if indeed the Spirit of God lives in you. And if anyone does not have the Spirit of Christ, they do not belong to Christ.

Holy Spirit

John 14:16-18: I will ask the Father, and he will give you another advocate to help you and be with you forever— the Spirit of truth. The world cannot accept him, because it neither sees him nor knows him. But you know him, for he lives with you and will be in you. I will not leave you as orphans; I will come to you.

Ephesians 1:13: You also were included in Christ when you heard the message of truth, the gospel of your salvation. When you believed, you were marked in him with a seal, the promised Holy Spirit.

Homosexuality

Romans 1:26-27: Because of this, God gave them over to shameful lusts. Even their women exchanged natural sexual relations for unnatural ones. In the same way the men also abandoned natural relations with women and were inflamed with lust for one another. Men committed shameful acts with other men, and received in themselves the due penalty for their error.

1 Corinthians 6:9-11: Do you not know that wrongdoers will not inherit the kingdom of God? Do not be deceived: Neither the sexually immoral nor idolaters nor adulterers nor men who have sex with men nor thieves nor the greedy nor drunkards nor slanderers nor swindlers will inherit the kingdom of God. And that is what some of you were. But you were washed, you were sanctified, you were justified in the name of the Lord Jesus Christ and by the Spirit of our God.

Hope

Jeremiah 29:11: "I know the plans I have for you," declares the LORD, "plans to prosper you and not to harm you, plans to give you hope and a future."

Hebrews 6:19-20: We have this hope as an anchor for the soul, firm and secure. It enters the inner sanctuary behind the curtain, where our forerunner, Jesus, has entered on our behalf. He has become a high priest forever, in the order of Melchizedek.

Identity

2 Corinthians 5:17: If anyone is in Christ, the new creation has come: The old has gone, the new is here!

Galatians 2:20: I have been crucified with Christ and I no longer live, but Christ lives in me. The life I now live in the body, I live by faith in the Son of God, who loved me and gave himself for me.

Infertility

Isaiah 54:1: "Sing, barren woman, you who never bore a child; burst into song, shout for joy, you who were never in labor; because more are the children of the desolate woman than of her who has a husband," says the LORD.

Proverbs 13:12: Hope deferred makes the heart sick, but a longing fulfilled is a tree of life.

Intimacy

Ephesians 1:17: I keep asking that the God of our Lord Jesus Christ, the glorious Father, may give you the Spirit of wisdom and revelation, so that you may know him better.

Philippians 2:1-2: If you have any encouragement from being united with Christ, if any comfort from his love, if any common sharing in the Spirit, if any tenderness and compassion, then make my joy complete by being like-minded, having the same love, being one in spirit and of one mind.

Islam

Romans 5:8: God demonstrates his own love for us in this: While we were still sinners, Christ died for us.

Philippians 2:6-8: [Christ Jesus], who, being in very nature God, did not consider equality with God something to be used to his own advantage; rather, he made himself nothing by taking the very nature of a servant, being made in human likeness. And being found in appearance as a man, he humbled himself by becoming obedient to death—even death on a cross!

Jehovah's Witness

John 1:1-3: In the beginning was the Word, and the Word was with God, and the Word was God. He was with God in the beginning. Through him all things were made; without him nothing was made that has been made.

1 John 5:13: I write these things to you who believe in the name of the Son of God so that you may know that you have eternal life.

Jesus Christ

John 1:1: In the beginning was the Word, and the Word was with God, and the Word was God.

1 John 5:1: Everyone who believes that Jesus is the Christ is born of God, and everyone who loves the father loves his child as well.

The Biblical Counseling Reference Guide

Jewish Fulfillment

Romans 8:3-4: What the law was powerless to do because it was weakened by the flesh, God did by sending his own Son in the likeness of sinful flesh to be a sin offering. And so he condemned sin in the flesh, in order that the righteous requirement of the law might be fully met in us, who do not live according to the flesh but according to the Spirit.

Hebrews 3:3: Jesus has been found worthy of greater honor than Moses, just as the builder of a house has greater honor than the house itself.

Loneliness

Psalm 139:7-8: Where can I go from your Spirit? Where can I flee from your presence? If I go up to the heavens, you are there; if I make my bed in the depths, you are there.

James 2:23: The scripture was fulfilled that says, "Abraham believed God, and it was credited to him as righteousness," and he was called God's friend.

Lying

Job 27:4: My lips will not say anything wicked, and my tongue will not utter lies.

Psalm 141:3: Set a guard over my mouth, LORD; keep watch over the door of my lips.

Manipulation

Psalm 101:7: No one who practices deceit will dwell in my house; no one who speaks falsely will stand in my presence.

Galatians 1:10: Am I now trying to win the approval of human beings, or of God? Or am I trying to please people? If I were still trying to please people, I would not be a servant of Christ.

Marriage

Matthew 19:4-5: "Haven't you read," he replied, "that at the beginning the Creator 'made them male and female,' and said, 'For this reason a man will leave his father and mother and be united to his wife, and the two will become one flesh'?"

1 Corinthians 7:8-9: Now to the unmarried and the widows I say: It is good for them to stay unmarried, as I do. But if they cannot control themselves, they should marry, for it is better to marry than to burn with passion.

Mentoring

2 Timothy 1:13-14: What you heard from me, keep as the pattern of sound teaching, with faith and love in Christ Jesus. Guard the good deposit that was entrusted to you—guard it with the help of the Holy Spirit who lives in us.

Titus 2:3-5: Likewise, teach the older women to be reverent in the way they live, not to be slanderers or addicted to much wine, but to teach what is good. Then they can urge the younger women to love their husbands and children, to be self-controlled and pure, to be busy at home, to be kind, and to be subject to their husbands, so that no one will malign the word of God.

Midlife Crisis

Psalm 90:12: Teach us to number our days, that we may gain a heart of wisdom.

Ecclesiastes 5:18-20: This is what I have observed to be good: that it is appropriate for a person to eat, to drink and to find satisfaction in their toilsome labor under the sun during the few days of life God has given them—for this is their lot. Moreover, when God gives someone wealth and possessions, and the ability to enjoy them, to accept their lot and be happy in their toil—this is a gift of God. They seldom reflect on the days of their life, because God keeps them occupied with gladness of heart.

Mormonism

Isaiah 43:10-11: "You are my witnesses," declares the Lord, "and my servant whom I have chosen, so that you may know and believe me and understand that I am he. Before me no god was formed, nor will there be one after me. I, even I, am the Lord, and apart from me there is no savior."

Revelation 22:18: I warn everyone who hears the words of the prophecy of this scroll: If anyone adds anything to them, God will add to that person the plagues described in this scroll.

New Age Spirituality

Colossians 2:8: See to it that no one takes you captive through hollow and deceptive philosophy, which depends on human tradition and the elemental spiritual forces of this world rather than on Christ.

1 John 4:1: Dear friends, do not believe every spirit, but test the spirits to see whether they are from God, because many false prophets have gone out into the world.

Occult

Isaiah 5:20: Woe to those who call evil good and good evil, who put darkness for light and light for darkness, who put bitter for sweet and sweet for bitter.

Luke 10:18-20: He replied, "I saw Satan fall like lightning from heaven. I have given you authority to trample on snakes and scorpions and to overcome all the power of the enemy; nothing will harm you. However, do not rejoice that the spirits submit to you, but rejoice that your names are written in heaven."

Overeating

1 Corinthians 10:31: Whether you eat or drink or whatever you do, do it all for the glory of God.

Proverbs 23:1-2: When you sit to dine with a ruler, note well what is before you, and put a knife to your throat if you are given to gluttony.

Parenting

Proverbs 23:13: Do not withhold discipline from a child; if you punish them with the rod, they will not die.

Ephesians 6:4: Fathers, do not exasperate your children; instead, bring them up in the training and instruction of the Lord.

Perfectionism

Philippians 3:12: Not that I have already obtained all this, or have already arrived at my goal, but I press on to take hold of that for which Christ Jesus took hold of me.

Colossians 1:28: He is the one we proclaim, admonishing and teaching everyone with all wisdom, so that we may present everyone fully mature in Christ.

Pregnancy...Unplanned

Ecclesiastes 11:5: As you do not know the path of the wind, or how the body is formed in a mother's womb, so you cannot understand the work of God, the Maker of all things.

Psalm 139:13-14: You created my inmost being; you knit me together in my mother's womb. I praise you because I am fearfully and wonderfully made; your works are wonderful, I know that full well.

Prejudice

1 Timothy 5:21: I charge you, in the sight of God and Christ Jesus and the elect angels, to keep these instructions without partiality, and to do nothing out of favoritism.

James 2:1: My brothers and sisters, believers in our glorious Lord Jesus Christ must not show favoritism.

Premarital Counseling

Proverbs 15:22: Plans fail for lack of counsel, but with many advisers they succeed.

2 Corinthians 6:14: Do not be yoked together with unbelievers. For what do righteousness and wickedness have in common? Or what fellowship can light have with darkness?

Pride and Humility

Proverbs 16:18: Pride goes before destruction, a haughty spirit before a fall.

James 4:6: But he gives us more grace. That is why Scripture says: "God opposes the proud but shows favor to the humble."

Procrastination

Ephesians 5:15-16: Be very careful, then, how you live—not as unwise but as wise, making the most of every opportunity, because the days are evil.

Proverbs 10:4: Lazy hands make for poverty, but diligent hands bring wealth.

Prosperity Gospel

Matthew 7:15: Watch out for false prophets. They come to you in sheep's clothing, but inwardly they are ferocious wolves.

Philippians 4:12: I know what it is to be in need, and I know what it is to have plenty. I have learned the secret of being content in any and every situation, whether well fed or hungry, whether living in plenty or in want.

Purpose in Life

Ecclesiastes 4:8: There was a man all alone; he had neither son nor brother. There was no end to his toil, yet his eyes were not content with his wealth. "For whom am I toiling," he asked, "and why am I depriving myself of enjoyment?" This too is meaningless—a miserable business!

Ephesians 1:4-6: He chose us in him before the creation of the world to be holy and blameless in his sight. In love he predestined us for adoption to sonship through Jesus Christ, in accordance with his pleasure and will—to

the praise of his glorious grace, which he has freely given us in the One he loves.

Rape

Psalm 34:18: The LORD is close to the brokenhearted and saves those who are crushed in spirit.

Psalm 103:6: The LORD works righteousness and justice for all the oppressed.

Rebellion

Psalm 25:7: Do not remember the sins of my youth and my rebellious ways; according to your love remember me, for you, LORD, are good.

Proverbs 17:11: Evildoers foster rebellion against God; the messenger of death will be sent against them.

Reconciliation

Romans 5:10: If, while we were God's enemies, we were reconciled to him through the death of his Son, how much more, having been reconciled, shall we be saved through his life!

2 Corinthians 5:19: God was reconciling the world to himself in Christ, not counting people's sins against them. And he has committed to us the message of reconciliation.

Rejection

Deuteronomy 31:8: The LORD himself goes before you and will be with you; he will never leave you nor forsake you. Do not be afraid; do not be discouraged.

Luke 6:22-23: Blessed are you when people hate you, when they exclude you and insult you and reject your name as evil, because of the Son of Man. Rejoice in that day and leap for joy, because great is your reward in heaven. For that is how their ancestors treated the prophets.

Salvation

John 3:16-17: God so loved the world that he gave his one and only Son, that whoever believes in him shall not perish but have eternal life. For God did not send his Son into the world to condemn the world, but to save the world through him.

Romans 5:9: Since we have now been justified by his blood, how much more shall we be saved from God's wrath through him!

Satan, Demons, and Satanism

2 Corinthians 2:10-11: Anyone you forgive, I also forgive. And what I have forgiven—if there was anything to forgive—I have forgiven in the sight of Christ for your sake, in order that Satan might not outwit us. For we are not unaware of his schemes.

1 Peter 5:8: Be alert and of sober mind. Your enemy the devil prowls around like a roaring lion looking for someone to devour.

Self-Worth

Matthew 6:26: Look at the birds of the air; they do not sow or reap or store away in barns, and yet your heavenly Father feeds them. Are you not much more valuable than they?

Psalm 8:4-5: What is mankind that you are mindful of them, human beings that you care for them? You have made them a little lower than the angels and crowned them with glory and honor.

Sexual Addiction

Galatians 5:16: So I say, walk by the Spirit, and you will not gratify the desires of the flesh.

1 Thessalonians 5:8: Since we belong to the day, let us be sober, putting on faith and love as a breastplate, and the hope of salvation as a helmet.

Sexual Integrity

Proverbs 10:9: Whoever walks in integrity walks securely, but whoever takes crooked paths will be found out.

Ephesians 5:3: Among you there must not be even a hint of sexual immorality, or of any kind of impurity, or of greed, because these are improper for God's holy people.

Singleness

1 Corinthians 7:7: I wish that all of you were as I am. But each of you has your own gift from God; one has this gift, another has that.

2 Peter 1:3: His divine power has given us everything we need for a godly life through our knowledge of him who called us by his own glory and goodness.

Spiritual Abuse

Galatians 5:1: It is for freedom that Christ has set us free. Stand firm, then, and do not let yourselves be burdened again by a yoke of slavery.

Titus 1:10-11: There are many rebellious people, full of meaningless talk and deception, especially those of the circumcision group. They must be silenced, because they are disrupting whole households by teaching things they ought not to teach—and that for the sake of dishonest gain.

Spiritual Warfare

Ephesians 6:13-18: Put on the full armor of God, so that when the day of evil comes, you may be able to stand your ground, and after you have done everything, to stand. Stand firm then, with the belt of truth buckled around your waist, with the breastplate of righteousness in place, and with your feet fitted with the readiness that comes from the gospel of peace. In addition to all this, take up the shield of faith, with which you can extinguish all the flaming arrows of the evil one. Take the helmet of salvation and the sword of the Spirit, which is the word of God. And pray in the Spirit on all occasions with all kinds of prayers and requests. With this in mind, be alert and always keep on praying for all the Lord's people.

1 John 4:4: You, dear children, are from God and have overcome them, because the one who is in you is greater than the one who is in the world.

Stealing

Deuteronomy 5:19: You shall not steal.

Ephesians 4:28: Anyone who has been stealing must steal no longer, but must work, doing something useful with their own hands, that they may have something to share with those in need.

Stress

Psalm 116:7: Return to your rest, my soul, for the LORD has been good to you.

Philippians 4:6-7: Do not be anxious about anything, but in every situation, by prayer and petition, with thanksgiving, present your requests to God. And the peace of God, which transcends all understanding, will guard your hearts and your minds in Christ Jesus.

The Biblical Counseling Reference Guide

Submission

James 3:17: The wisdom that comes from heaven is first of all pure; then peace-loving, considerate, submissive, full of mercy and good fruit, impartial and sincere.

James 4:7: Submit yourselves, then, to God. Resist the devil, and he will flee from you.

Success

Genesis 39:23: The warden paid no attention to anything under Joseph's care, because the LORD was with Joseph and gave him success in whatever he did.

Philippians 3:7: Whatever were gains to me I now consider loss for the sake of Christ.

Suicide Prevention

Psalm 62:5-6: Yes, my soul, find rest in God; my hope comes from him. Truly he is my rock and my salvation; he is my fortress, I will not be shaken.

John 10:10: The thief comes only to steal and kill and destroy; I have come that they may have life, and have it to the full.

Teenagers

Proverbs 3:11-12: My son, do not despise the LORD's discipline, and do not resent his rebuke, because the LORD disciplines those he loves, as a father the son he delights in.

2 Timothy 2:22: Flee the evil desires of youth and pursue righteousness, faith, love and peace, along with those who call on the Lord out of a pure heart.

Temptation

1 Corinthians 10:13: No temptation has overtaken you except what is common to mankind. And God is faithful; he will not let you be tempted beyond what you can bear. But when you are tempted, he will also provide a way out so that you can endure it.

Hebrews 2:18: Because he himself suffered when he was tempted, he is able to help those who are being tempted.

Terminal Illness

Psalm 23:4: Even though I walk through the darkest valley, I will fear no evil, for you are with me; your rod and your staff, they comfort me.

Psalm 139:16: Your eyes saw my unformed body; all the days ordained for me were written in your book before one of them came to be.

Time Management

Ecclesiastes 11:6: Sow your seed in the morning, and at evening let your hands not be idle, for you do not know which will succeed, whether this or that, or whether both will do equally well.

Ephesians 5:15-16: Be very careful, then, how you live—not as unwise but as wise, making the most of every opportunity, because the days are evil.

Trials

Isaiah 43:2: When you pass through the waters, I will be with you; and when you pass through the rivers, they will not sweep over you. When you walk through the fire, you will not be burned; the flames will not set you ablaze.

James 1:2-3: Consider it pure joy, my brothers and sisters, whenever you face trials of many kinds, because you know that the testing of your faith produces perseverance.

Unbelieving Mate

2 Corinthians 6:14-15: Do not be yoked together with unbelievers. For what do righteousness and wickedness have in common? Or what fellowship can light have with darkness? What harmony is there between Christ and Belial? Or what does a believer have in common with an unbeliever?

1 Peter 3:1-2: Wives, in the same way submit yourselves to your own husbands so that, if any of them do not believe the word, they may be won over without words by the behavior of their wives, when they see the purity and reverence of your lives.

Verbal and Emotional Abuse

Luke 4:18-19: The Spirit of the Lord is on me, because he has anointed me to proclaim good news to the poor. He has sent me to proclaim freedom for the prisoners and recovery of sight for the blind, to set the oppressed free, to proclaim the year of the Lord's favor.

Romans 13:10: Love does no harm to a neighbor. Therefore love is the fulfillment of the law.

Victimization

Psalm 22:24: He has not despised or scorned the suffering of the afflicted one; he has not hidden his face from him but has listened to his cry for help.

Jeremiah 31:13: Then young women will dance and be glad, young men and old as well. I will turn their mourning into gladness; I will give them comfort and joy instead of sorrow.

Violence

Isaiah 60:18: No longer will violence be heard in your land, nor ruin or destruction within your borders, but you will call your walls Salvation and your gates Praise.

Jeremiah 22:3: This is what the Lord says: Do what is just and right. Rescue from the hand of the oppressor the one who has been robbed. Do no wrong or violence to the foreigner, the fatherless or the widow, and do not shed innocent blood in this place.

The Biblical Counseling Reference Guide

Widowhood

Isaiah 66:13: As a mother comforts her child, so will I comfort you; and you will be comforted over Jerusalem.

James 1:27: Religion that God our Father accepts as pure and faultless is this: to look after orphans and widows in their distress and to keep oneself from being polluted by the world.

Wife Abuse

Psalm 140:1: Rescue me, LORD, from evildoers; protect me from the violent.

Colossians 3:19: Husbands, love your wives and do not be harsh with them.

Workaholism

Ecclesiastes 2:21-22: A person may labor with wisdom, knowledge and skill, and then they must leave all they own to another who has not toiled for it. This too is meaningless and a great misfortune. What do people get for all the toil and anxious striving with which they labor under the sun?

Ecclesiastes 8:15: I commend the enjoyment of life, because there is nothing better for a person under the sun than to eat and drink and be glad. Then joy will accompany them in their toil all the days of the life God has given them under the sun.

Worry

Matthew 6:27-30: Can any one of you by worrying add a single hour to your life? And why do you worry about clothes? See how the flowers of the field grow. They do not labor or spin. Yet I tell you that not even Solomon in all his splendor was dressed like one of these. If that is how God clothes the grass of the field, which is here today and tomorrow is thrown into the fire, will he not much more clothe you— you of little faith?

1 Peter 5:7: Cast all your anxiety on him because he cares for you.

Other Harvest House
Books by June Hunt

Counseling Through Your Bible Handbook

The Bible is richly relevant when it comes to the difficult dilemmas of life. Here are 50 chapters of spiritual wisdom and compassionate counsel on issues such as anger, adultery, depression, fear, guilt, grief, rejection, and self-worth.

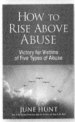

How to Rise Above Abuse

Compassionate, practical, hands-on guidance for the toughest issues to talk about—childhood sexual abuse, spiritual abuse, verbal and emotional abuse, victimization, and wife abuse. Filled with the hope and healing only Christ can give.

How to Handle Your Emotions

In Scripture, God gives counsel that helps us process our full range of emotions in a healthy way. Learn how to better navigate your emotions by understanding their definitions, characteristics, and causes, as well as the solutions that lead to emotional growth.

How to Defeat Harmful Habits

Addictions are powerful—and persuasive. So how can you help a friend, loved one, or even yourself overcome an entrenched addiction? Discover the underlying causes of addictions and the keys to experiencing complete freedom—permanently.

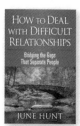

How to Deal with Difficult Relationships

God wants us to enjoy relationships filled with trust, purpose, and peace. In the Bible, He provides guidance on how to bridge broken relationships in order to build healthy ones. You'll learn about conflict resolution, building trust, and the importance of forgiveness.

How to Forgive…When You Don't Feel Like It

Though we know God has called us to forgive, we find ourselves asking hard questions: What if it hurts too much to forgive? What if the other person isn't sorry? How can I let the other person off the hook for doing something so wrong? June Hunt speaks from experience as she offers biblical answers, hope, and true freedom through forgiveness.

The Answer to Anger

This book explores the causes and kinds of anger and the biblical steps toward resolution. You will learn how to identify the triggers of anger, ways of dealing with past angers, what the Bible says about righteous and unrighteous anger, and how to bring about real and lasting change.

About the Author

June Hunt is founder and CEO of Hope For The Heart (www.Hope ForTheHeart.org) and is a dynamic Christian leader who has yielded landmark contributions to the field of Christian counseling. Hope For The Heart provides biblically based counsel in 24 languages and has worked in 60 countries on six continents. June, who celebrated 25 years of ministry in 2011, is also an author, speaker, and musician, and has served as guest professor to a variety of colleges and seminaries.

Early family pain shaped June's heart of compassion. Her bizarre family background left her feeling hopeless and caused June to contemplate "drastic solutions." But when she entered into a life-changing relationship with Jesus Christ, the trajectory of her life was forever altered. As a result, she grew passionate about helping people face life's tough circumstances.

As a youth director, June became aware of the need for real answers to real questions. Her personal experiences with pain and her practical experience with youth and parents led June into a lifelong commitment to *Providing God's Truth for Today's Problems*. She earned a master's in counseling at Criswell College in 2007 and has been presented with two honorary doctorates.

Between 1989 and 1992, June Hunt developed and taught *Counseling Through The Bible*, a scripturally based counseling course addressing 100 topics in categories such as marriage and family, emotional entrapments and cults, as well as addictions, abuse, and apologetics. Since then, the coursework has continuously been augmented and refined, forming the basis for the *Biblical Counseling Library*. Her *Biblical Counseling Keys* became the foundation of the ministry's expansion, including the 2002 creation of the *Biblical Counseling Institute* (BCI) initiated by Criswell College to equip spiritual leaders, counselors, and people with hearts to help others with practical solutions for life's most pressing problems.

The *Biblical Counseling Keys* provide a foundation for the ministry's two daily radio programs, *Hope For The Heart* and *Hope In The Night*, both hosted by June. *Hope For The Heart* is a half-hour of interactive teaching heard on over 100 radio outlets across America, and *Hope In The Night* is June's live two-hour call-in counseling program. Together, both programs air domestically and internationally on more than 1000 stations. In 1986, the National Religious Broadcasters (NRB) honored *Hope For The Heart* as "Best New Radio Program" and awarded it Radio Program of the Year in 1989. Women in Christian Media presented June Hunt with an Excellence in Communications award in 2008. The ministry received NRB's Media Award for International Strategic Partnerships in 2010.

As an accomplished musician, June has been a guest on numerous national TV and radio programs, including NBC's *Today*. She has toured overseas with the USO and has been a guest soloist at Billy Graham Crusades. June communicates her message of hope on five music recordings: *The Whisper of My Heart, Hymns of Hope, Songs of Surrender, Shelter Under His Wings*, and *The Hope of Christmas*.

June Hunt's numerous books include *Seeing Yourself Through God's Eyes, How to Forgive…When You Don't Feel Like It, Counseling Through Your Bible Handbook, How to Handle Your Emotions, How to Rise Above Abuse, How to Deal with Difficult Relationships, Binding with Your Teen through Boundaries, The Answer to Anger, Caring for a Loved One with Cancer* (June is a cancer survivor), and *Hope for Your Heart: Finding Strength in Life's Storms*. She is also a contributor to the *Soul Care Bible* and the *Women's Devotional Bible*.

June Hunt resides in Dallas, Texas, home of the international headquarters of Hope For The Heart.